THE NEXUS OF LAW AND BIOLOGY

This book is dedicated to the memory of Geoffrey Arthur Bentley, former Associate-Professor of Pharmacology at Monash University, Melbourne, who died in 2008 but will be long remembered

The Nexus of Law and Biology

New Ethical Challenges

Edited by

BARBARA ANN HOCKING
Queensland University of Technology, Australia

ASHGATE

Published by
Ashgate Publishing Limited
Wey Court East
Union Road
Farnham
Surrey, GU9 7PT
England

Ashgate Publishing Company
Suite 420
101 Cherry Street
Burlington
VT 05401-4405
USA

www.ashgate.com

British Library Cataloguing in Publication Data
The nexus of law and biology : new ethical challenges. -
(Law, justice and power series)
1. Medical laws and legislation 2. Bioethics
I. Hocking, Barbara Ann
344'.0419

Library of Congress Cataloging-in-Publication Data
The nexus of law and biology : new ethical challenges / by Barbara Ann Hocking.
p. cm. -- (Law, justice and power)
Includes bibliographical references and index.
ISBN 978-0-7546-2380-9
1. Law and biology. 2. Biotechnology--Law and legislation. 3. Indigenous peoples--Legal status, laws, etc. 4. Bioethics. I. Hocking, Barbara Ann.

K328.N494 2008
343'.0786606--dc22

2008030029

ISBN 978-0-7546-2380-9
e-ISBN 978-0-7546-9495-3

Mixed Sources
Product group from well-managed forests and other controlled sources
www.fsc.org Cert no. SA-COC-1565
© 1996 Forest Stewardship Council
FSC

Printed and bound in Great Britain by
MPG Books Ltd, Bodmin, Cornwall.

Contents

List of Contributors

Christian Byk University of Paris 8, France.

Piero P. Giorgi Adjunct Professor, Australian Centre for Peace and Conflict Studies, University of Queensland, Faculty of Social and Behavioural Sciences, University of Queensland, Brisbane, Australia.

Scott Guy Lecturer, School of Business, Griffith University, Brisbane, Australia.

Richard Hindmarsh Associate-Professor, Griffith University, Brisbane, Australia.

Barbara Ann Hocking Associate-Professor, Faculty of Law, Queensland University of Technology, Brisbane, and University of Tasmania, Hobart, Australia.

Edwin Hui Professor, University of Hong Kong.

Helena Kajlich PhD candidate, University of Tasmania, Hobart, Australia.

Justice Michael Kirby High Court of Australia, Level 19, Law Courts Building, 184 Phillip Street, Sydney NSW 2000, Australia. Janet Saleh is the judge's Personal Assistant. Telephone: +61 2 9230 8203, Fax: +61 2 9230 8626, email: JSaleh@hcourt.gov.au.

Charles Lawson Senior Lecturer, Griffith University, Gold Coast, Australia.

Hamish McCallum Professor, University of Tasmania, Hobart, Australia.

Christopher Rodgers Professor, University of Newcastle, UK.

Eva Ryrstedt Professor, University of Lund, Sweden.

Joseph Henry Vogel Professor, University of Puerto Rico, USA.

Foreword

The Hon Justice Michael Kirby AC CMG*

One of the most precious books I ever received was presented to me soon after I arrived at High School. It was an anthology of English verse. I did not appreciate the requirement that accompanied the gift, that I should learn many of the poems by heart. Up and down the driveway of our family home I walked, reciting verses set for memorization by my teachers – examples of civilization from five centuries of English poetic composition.

Now, these treasures of memory accompany me wherever I go. Like Rumpole of the Bailey, I am never entirely alone. These compositions go on rattling around in my brain. Their creative power augments my own puny endeavours. Sometimes, when least expecting them to do so, they revisit me. They are ancient and modern. From England, Ireland, Australia and other lands of Anglophonia. Occasionally an English translation of a poem written in Ancient Greece or Rome turns up. Quite often I get an insight into the slightly different way of seeing familiar things expressed in French or German. There are realists and romantics. Sonnets and iambic pentameters. Rhyming couplets and prose. All thrown together in the one anthology. It is the differences within the collection that heighten its interest. Contrast and comparison stimulate creativity in thought.

So it is with this anthology. There are, of course, links that bind together the chapters and thus present common themes. The essential link is the mysterious phenomenon of biological life, made even more puzzling when consciousness, intelligence and the moral sense emerge in the higher life forms.

Like my book of poems, we have a cornucopia here. It mixes together an amazing variety of subjects. The quandary of the so-called 'saviour sibling'. The puzzle of bacteriological and biological warfare. The dilemma of genetic population research. The tragedy of the dwindling global commons. The specific challenges of the SARS and HIV epidemics, wildlife disease and genetically modified organisms. The story of responses to problems of this kind both at a national and at an international level. A chapter on the development of the Australian *Gene Technology Act 2000* (Cth) and the global development, within UNESCO, of the *Universal Declaration on Bioethics and Human Rights* 2005.

The human mind seeks out linkages that will imprint an intellectual unity upon such diverse topics. Yet we should not be surprised that the unity is not always immediately apparent. It is so in an anthology of verse. The only unity that it

* Justice of the High Court of Australia.

affords lies in its demonstration of the variety of the special discourse that we call poetry. In this anthology we are presented with a disparate collection of ideas by writers who are experts in their sub-topics involving the meeting ground of biology and law. As with the anthology of verse, it cannot be expected that the reader will enjoy each contribution equally. Some we may even dislike, seriously question and disagree with. Others we may embrace because they appear closer to our own experience and more welcome because they are more familiar and seem more acceptable.

The editor reminds us, at the end, that even this diverse collection by no means exhausts the challenges that biology now presents to the discipline of law. Nanotechnology is a new development that opens up many questions, some of them closely related to the likely future of the human species. As well, we could multiply the chapters of this book many times over with old and new problems that exist at the point where law meets biology. The problems of intellectual property protection and biological inventions. The problems of the human diseases of malaria and HIV that have so far eluded the search for a vaccine or a cure. The equine influenza epidemic with its global and national ramifications. The controversies over hybridization of human and other animal life forms.

If there is a common theme revealed by this anthology (apart from the variety and complexity of the problem) it is the puzzle of how the human construct of law should respond to the issues presented by this book. Like Rosencrantz and Guildenstern in Shakespeare's *Hamlet*, I feel that I have wandered across the face of this anthology, in search of a useful path for myself and my discipline; but never sure that I will find one.

The opening chapter by Barbara Ann Hocking and Eva Ryrstedt, which addresses the 'saviour sibling' dilemma is useful, not only for the legal and ethical puzzles that it presents but also for the basic lesson that it teaches. In common law countries there is never ultimately a legal vacuum. If Parliament or the Executive Government have not made binding rules to cover a problem presented by new technology, our system of law is never silent. In such a case, it is left to other officials, namely judges, to develop and express the governing law. They do this by calling upon earlier broad statements of the common law and developing those statements, by analogical reasoning, so as to be applicable to the new case.

This was the challenge presented to the English courts by the *Quintavalle* litigation [2005] 1 WLR 1061 which provides the challenging focus of the first chapter. Also mentioned there is a pair of cases that fell to be decided by the High Court of Australia concerning instances of so-called 'wrongful birth' and 'wrongful life': *Cattanach v Melchoir* (2003) 215 CLR 1 and *Harriton v Stephens* (2006) 226 CLR 52.

The divisions between the judges over these cases and the solutions that should be offered for the puzzles presented there demonstrate, at once, the utility of having a decisional safeguard but also the desirability of generally keeping it in reserve. Normally, in expressing legal solutions for the kinds of problems presented in this anthology, it is preferable that they be produced in close consultation with the affected actors and also with the general community.

This is the endeavour described by Charles Lawson and Richard Hindmarsh in their chapter that explains the development of the *Gene Technology Act*. The product may have been, as they believe, imperfect. But the methodology is preferable because of the wider range of data upon which such lawmakers can draw. Relying on parties to litigation, often with restrictive and wholly selfish objectives, may not afford the decision-maker the best sources of scientific, economic, social and other data that should be taken into account to arrive at a fully informed conclusion.

In his chapter on the *Universal Declaration on Bioethics and Human Rights*, Christian Byk explains both the necessity and the problem of developing general principles that will guide the international community in tackling contemporary bioethical dilemmas. When, on the instigation of the French President Jacques Chirac, UNESCO embarked upon an urgent project to develop the new Universal Declaration, I was a member of that Organisation's International Bioethics Committee. I had served in that capacity in the concluding stages of the adoption of the earlier *Universal Declaration on the Human Genome and Human Rights*. That document had been regarded as a successful first step in expressing the universal principles that should govern humanity's response to the discovery, adaptation and use of the human genome. Thirsting for more progress, UNESCO set itself a severe discipline, effectively of two years, within which to prepare the far more comprehensive *Universal Declaration on Bioethics and Human Rights*. I was elected to chair the drafting group for that project. Eventually, a draft was adopted by the Group and endorsed by the International Bioethics Committee. With a number of changes, that document was accepted by the General Conference of UNESCO in 2005. It has now been placed before the international community.

In his chapter, Christian Byk describes the difficulties that lie in the way of securing agreement on broad principles such as are needed to provide a foundation for legal responses to contemporary bioethical dilemmas. The difficulties include:

- How to bring together the ancient principles of medical ethics with the more modern legal principles of fundamental human rights so as to secure common solutions from them both for new biological dilemmas;
- How to reconcile the differing stages of social and scientific developments and different economic interests when countries address biological dilemmas and solutions that are seen as ethically sound but also nationally advantageous; and
- How to accommodate the force of globalism that is generally at work in scientific developments with the diversity of cultures and interests of nation states and the divergent ethical principles that such diversity brings in its wake.

The work of UNESCO on the two *Universal Declarations* demonstrate that progress can be made towards framing broad principles that seek to attract a large measure of consensus in international organizations. Nevertheless, such broad principles frequently break down when lawmakers face the difficult task of drafting binding rules that will impact, in the workplace and laboratory, upon the conduct of individuals, corporations and nation states. This is where the going will often get tough.

The variety, diversity and importance of the challenges that are presented to law-making by advances in biotechnology are well illustrated in this book. Indeed, this is the chief value of this anthology. It demonstrates the complexity of securing effective legal responses to biotechnology when international cooperation is essential to effectiveness. Particularly so when international cooperation is hard to achieve because of the dialectical, economic, religious and cultural impediments that stand in the way.

In 2007, the King's College School of Law in London launched a new Centre for the Study of Technology, Ethics and Law in Society (TELOS). At a conference called to mark the creation of TELOS, I was asked to identify some of the main challenges, paradoxes and pathways for the future. The collection of papers of the conference is published at the same time as this anthology (Roger Brownsword and Karen Yeung (eds) (2008) *Regulating Technologies* (Oxford: Hart). In effect, the chapters of this book supplement and illustrate the themes of the TELOS meeting.

Among the chief lessons that I derived from the TELOS conference, several of them have significance for the subject matters of this book:

1. The regulation of technology presents a new dilemma hitherto uncommon in the law. Technology, of its character, is normally global. Law being the command of an organized community is traditionally tied to a particular geographical jurisdiction. It is into this context that direct enforcement of rules by 'Code', embedded into the technology itself, sometimes imposes a novel and distinctive dimension of law-making. Occasionally, that dimension presents itself to law courts as happened in Australia in the PlayStation case: *Stevens v Kabushi Kaisha Sony Computer Entertainment* (2005) 225 CLR 193;
2. Unless limits on the development and use of biotechnology are clearly expressed and upheld in an effective way, the absence of regulation will normally mean that the society in question has effectively made a decision to permit the technological development to occur without impediment. Thus, in a practical sense, legal inaction in this field can effectively amount to a decision;
3. The normal organs of legal regulation often appear powerless in the face of a new global technology. An attempt by one nation's laws to prohibit or regulate transnational technology will often face difficulties of acceptance

and enforcement. Yet this demonstrates that regulation must often be global if it is truly to be effective;

4. In responding to biotechnology it is important to appreciate that one response does not necessarily fit all problems. Self-evidently, some forms of technology addressed in this book, are highly sensitive and urgently in need of regulation. Unless nuclear, bacteriological and toxin weapons, as described in Chapter 2, are effectively controlled by the global community, their destructive power has the potential to render all other topics in this anthology theoretical. The realization that this is so adds a sense of urgency to addressing some of the subjects of this book;
5. A particular challenge in the current age is the growth of religious and moral fundamentalism. This development presents practical difficulties of actually securing common ground that is essential to the development of the mutuality and compromise necessary for effective legal regulation;
6. All regulation of technology, including biotechnology, information technology and neuroscience, must, in order to be effective, be based upon a sound understanding of the technology concerned. Most of the subjects recounted in this book portray significant controversies about the state of the art. Those who set out to design regulation must first master the technology that they hope to regulate. Often this is difficult or impossible because of the different training and mindsets of the scientist/technologist and the lawyer; and
7. Finally, it is necessary always to be aware of the potential democratic deficit that exists in the regulation of technology. Confronting questions of the kind described in the chapters of this book is rarely politically popular. Elected lawmakers are prone to leave such dilemmas unattended because of the controversies which they present. Alternatively, noisy lobby groups with uncompromising standpoints may seize the initiative. They may impose dogmatic positions on the law that then take time to be reconsidered and amended. Reconciling the complex, fast moving, often emotive subjects of biotechnology reviewed here with the general democratic character of a nation state such as Australia is an important puzzle. Addressing the democratic deficit at the level of international organizations, such as UNESCO, presents an even greater puzzle, perhaps insoluble. Ensuring that law keeps pace with fast moving technology, and with the challenges that technology presents, constitutes one of the major social and political puzzles of the current age. The puzzle does not go away because it is so complicated nor because we would prefer not to have to consider it.

So this is the ultimate value of this anthology. Authors with knowledge and expertise in particular spheres have written chapters on nine distinct controversies linked only by the thread that each chapter, somehow, concerns the interface of law with living matter. Most of the chapters are concerned with highly particular but concrete and practical problems. Those problems are not resolved by ignoring them and doing nothing. Yet to do something, and to do it wisely, is not always easy.

In part, this is so because of the complexity and controversy of the science, and in part, it is because of the complexity and controversy of the social assessments.

The great value of this book is that it gathers together a collection of contemporary biotechnological questions that we may know about generally from the media. It presents them to us in detail and from informed perspectives that we may accept or reject. We cannot reject the challenge which demands that we respond. Once again, the lesson is taught. To do nothing is to make a decision. And that is why this book is important because it stimulates us to consider the responses to difficult dilemmas that will be, at once, both just and effective.

Michael Kirby
High Court of Australia
Canberra
2009

Preface

Barbara Ann Hocking and Joseph Henry Vogel

In the course of the 2007 Australian federal election campaign, Kevin Rudd, then Opposition leader and now Prime Minister of Australia, declared that as a nation, 'fairness is in our DNA'. The comment is interesting as it reveals how the biological revolution has penetrated the social sphere while also hinting at the complexity of the interface of biology and law. Did fairness evolve? And if so, how does it translate from genes to mind to culture? Why do understandings of fairness differ so greatly, even within families, let alone within and across societies? Although this book looks at the many and varied issues arising from the biological revolution, it is essentially about the ways in which we grapple with ethical issues via law. To what extent should we regulate novel situations and express the fairness that arose in our own biological evolution?

'Everything you think about law might be wrong' is the opening salvo of Bryan Horrigan's *Adventures in Law and Justice* (Horrigan 2003, 31). We can now do him one better and say 'Everything you think you know about law may not *even* be wrong'. By that we mean that the analogical reasoning that underpins legal argumentation is now stretched to the point of snapping. Through biotechnological innovations, situations have arisen which frustrate apparent analogies. Precedents are increasingly suspect as underpinning values shift in the light of new technologies. What we think we know may not even be wrong as we enter an age of 'situation ethics'.[1]

Our salvo coheres with Horrigan's as he explains the ways by which modern biology is challenging the law on multiple fronts. 'Law is a lot less certain and objective than most people think, but it is also a lot less random and subjective than many critics suggest' (Horrigan 2003, 31). Although the emerging regulation that addresses the implications of biotechnology is not predictable, it is also not random. Although it seeks to be objective, it nevertheless absorbs the values of the stakeholders. Because the responses to the legal challenges are varied, we also address the core question posed by Horrigan: 'What are the elements of a good justice system and how do we identify what counts as law in any justice system?' (Horrigan 2003, 31).

Many of the ever expanding dilemmas confronting the law have become 'standard topics' in medical bioethics, viz., abortion, cloning, euthanasia, prenatal

1 The term was coined by J. Fletcher in his book by the same title.

screening and stem cell research.[2] The field is dominated by situations which arise from choices which were, until recently, thought illusory or even something of science fiction. Eclipsed in the discussion are the bioethics typical of poverty and our own evolutionary past, viz., the mother who must choose between buying medicine for a sick child and risking the food security of her other ten children (Scheper-Hughes 1992). Similarly eclipsed is the bioethics of indifference between the first world and the third, fourth and fifth worlds where a redistribution of economic resources could save hundreds of millions who need relatively cheap things like potable water and vaccinations (Singer 2006).

Michael Selgelid observes that both interest and research funding in bioethics tends to focus on the major first world preoccupations, for instance, abortion, etc. (Selgelid 2005, 272). Although *The Nexus of Law and Biology: New Ethical Challenges* focuses on the standard topics of medical bioethics, it also broaches a burning issue of conservation bioethics vital to the peoples of the third, fourth and fifth worlds: access to genetic resources and the fair and equitable sharing of benefits as established in The Convention on Biological Diversity (CBD). The connection between medical and conservation bioethics lies in the fact that research and development often draws on genomes accessed from jurisdictions where the poor and the desperately poor live. If access to genetic resources and the fair and equitable sharing of benefits can be resolved, the economic potential exists to reduce the frequency of the cruel dilemmas of the bioethics typical of poverty.

Garrett Hardin made 'situation ethics' foundational in his famous *Tragedy of the Commons* (1968): 'the morality of an act is a function of the state of the system at the time it is performed.' Situation ethics is not only foundational to our argument, but also quite humbling. Situations change and today they change extremely rapidly. What we think is right now may soon be found to be not even wrong. Jared Diamond emphasizes a similar point in the conclusion to his best-selling *Collapse: How Societies Choose to Fail or Succeed:*

> The modern world provides us with abundant secular examples of admirable values to which we cling under conditions where those values no longer make sense...[p]erhaps a crux of success or failure as a society is to know which core values to hold on to, and which ones to discard and replace with new values, when times change (Diamond 2005, 432–3).

Like the metaphor about wine and bottles, new values can be put into old rubrics. Nowhere is this more evident than in the conceptual category of 'family

2 See Selgelid et al. (2006) 111. The authors note the neglect, by way of comparison with these other widely publicized areas, of infectious diseases. That there has been little judicial attention on the exercise of public health powers in the context of infectious disease has also been noted by Robyn Martin in a comment on *Enhorn v Sweden* [2005] E.C.H.R. 56529/00 'The exercise of public health powers in cases of infectious disease: human rights implications' *Medical Law Review*, 14, Spring 2006, 132–43.

values' that organizes whole branches of the law. Coined in the late 1960s to signify adherence to century-old traditions, 'family values' can now also signify inclusion. The lyrics from the 1979 song 'We Are Family' recorded by Sister Sledge (www.wearefamilyfoundation.org) are a good example of discarding values that no longer make sense while clinging to the rubric.[3]

Having edited and re-edited the contributions of this anthology over the last five years, we are struck by just how *courant* is 'situation ethics'. As we write, developing countries are citing the sovereignty over genetic resources, as established in the Convention on Biological Diversity (CBD), as grounds for withholding strains of avian flu virus (*New Scientist* 2007, 5; *Intellectual Property Watch* 2007). The issues of access to patent medicines are of paramount importance. To grant access, what will be the fair and equitable sharing of benefits? The poor must not be priced out of a patented vaccine. Is the Indonesian claim blackmail? Or is it just? The ethics of such a situation must be vetted. To return again to Prime Minister Rudd's DNA analogy, how can we achieve universal values in the biomedical sphere, and are universal declarations of ethics the answer?

Even human rights can be viewed through the DNA lens, as Gearty notes in his question about the United Kingdom's anxiety about terrorism:

> How have such draconian attacks on the basic DNA of human rights – dignity, legality and democracy – been able to take place in a society presided over by a human-rights-respecting administration, one which requires of its public authorities that they adhere to the extensive range of political, civil and some social and economic rights that are to be found in the European Convention on Human Rights and Fundamental Freedoms? (Gearty 2006, 107).

Each contributor to this anthology explores some implications of modern biology on law and justice and conversely some implications of modern law and justice on biology. Each fleshes out a key issue from a specific situation or set

---

3 'We are family
I got all my sisters with me
We are family
Get up ev'rybody and sing
Ev'ryone can see we're together
As we walk on by
(FLY!) and we fly just like birds of a feather
I won't tell no lie
(ALL!) all of the people around us they say
Can they be that close
Just let me state for the record
We're giving love in a family dose'(www.wearefamilyfoundation.org).

of situations in order to illuminate the complexities of the nexus between law and biology. By its nature, this anthology cannot be comprehensive. A myriad of situations have arisen and will continue to arise that defy the confining analogical reasoning of textbook law. The contributors hope that the chapters will form a mosaic that impresses on the reader the need for legal reform in light of specific situations that are rich in detail. The accelerating rate of biological discovery will require an accelerating rate of legal reform based on understanding those details and their full ethical implications. As Justice Michael Kirby emphasizes in his foreword, the challenges are breathtaking as law confronts a new age of biological situation ethics.

Chapter 1

The Perils of Terminology and the 'Saviour Sibling' Dilemma
Barbara Ann Hocking and Eva Ryrstedt

Is family love unconditional or does it come with strings attached? What is the basis of love between siblings, and to what extent are they responsible for each other? This chapter examines the recent emergence of 'saviour siblings' which label we suggest implies that strings are attached in circumstances where one sibling is sought to provide tissue for another. We focus upon the most well-known decision by the House of Lords on this issue, *Quintavalle (on behalf of Comment on Reproductive Ethics (Appellant) v Human Fertilisation and Embryology Authority (Respondents)* [2005] UKHL 28. In the case, the ethical dilemma pivots around the extent to which one (as yet unborn) family member can be called upon to assist the quality of life of another, in the interests of the stability and health of those collective family relationships. The decision is rich in legal and ethical implications. We explore also some Australian and Swedish approaches to 'saviour siblings' and child donor situations, and argue that the key distinction between these approaches is that the English and Australian approach relies upon regulation through the judicial system whereas the Swedish model relies primarily upon its hospital or medical-based system.

In the United Kingdom, the Human Fertilisation and Embryology Authority (HFEA) is responsible for the issuing of any licence in a 'savour sibling' context, which has occasionally been challenged by a third party, even though that third party may have no relationship to the family. Bioethical dilemmas are writ large in such situations. Reflecting a trend towards intervention by religious lobby groups to resolutions of those dilemmas, the licence approved by HFEA for the Hashmi family was objected to by Ms Josephine Quintavalle, director and founder of a group believing in absolute respect for the human embryo named Comment on Reproductive Ethics or CORE. Besides the key ethical dilemma as to the selection of an embryo primarily for the purpose of 'saving' the ailing sibling, related bioethical issues raised by this case include the extent to which a third party is able to invade the privacy of a family in order to object to their proposed uses of reproductive technology, bringing the dilemma into the public domain. The ailing child's name is directly upfront in the House of Lords judgments, in articles and on the internet. There are also issues of the inconsistency in outcome of licensing applications, given that the Whittaker family had to move to the USA to obtain tissue for their son Charlie in relatively similar circumstances. In justifying the granting of the licence in the Hashmi case, the House of Lords pursued a narrow line of reasoning, honing in on the licensing powers of the HFEA as they were then articulated. Thus they prompted Sheldon's lament that human rights are 'notable by their complete absence in this judgment' (Sheldon 2005, 403). We suggest that a way to ensure we hear those voices is to avoid the label 'saviour sibling' which may imply that the giving of tissue has strings attached. We point by way of comparison to cases decided in Australia, concerning older child donors, where judges have been able to draw on the Convention on the Rights of the Child in order to ascertain an understanding of the family dynamics that may or may not be consequent upon approval of a donation. In the background, we hear however the (fictional yet powerful) voice of Jodi Picoult in her book *My Sister's Keeper*, which presages unknown and unknowable demands upon the 'saviour' infant even though they receive the gift of life itself. A key conclusion in this first chapter is recognition, therefore, that language very much matters in the law–biology nexus. As Bartha Maria Knoppers has observed in the context of samples deposited in biobanks; 'there is considerable confusion in the terminology used to describe the identifiability of the samples deposited in biobanks' (Knoppers 2005, 7). There is disquiet with the deployment of commercial-type language (words like 'bank', 'donor' and 'deposit', and relatedly, we suggest there ought be disquiet with the language of the 'saviour sibling'. Because the search for suitable language is even more problematic in the context of the 'saviour sibling', the chapter argues for heightened sensitivity and avoidance of emotionally charged labels such as 'saviour' that resonate with religious implications.

Chapter 2

I Sing of Arms and the Doctor: What Role for Law When Biology is Called to War?
Piero P. Giorgi, Scott Guy and Barbara Ann Hocking

This chapter deals with two key areas that are uniting policymakers in their concern for national and international security: the 'war on terror' and the fears of bio-terrorism and biological warfare. In the midst of the 'war on terror', people in the countries of 'The Alliance of the Willing' were alerted to the possibility of biological warfare attacks which have 'often been dismissed as science fiction or as too immoral as to be beyond imagination' (Fraser and Dando 2001, 253–6). Yet as the 'war on terror' has dragged on even to the 2008 US Presidential election, we have become more reluctant to dismiss biological warfare as the stuff of Hollywood fantasy. Indeed, we have begun to acknowledge the view that 'biological weapons pose by far the greatest threat' of the proliferation of nuclear, chemical and biological weapons of mass destruction. The fear is now that: '... the revolution in biology could be misused in offensive biological weapons programs directed against human beings and their staple crops or livestock' (Fraser and Dando 2001, 253).

The problem is compounded by the fact that when the Convention on the Prohibition of the Development, Production and Stockpiling of Bacteriological (Biological) and Toxin Weapons and on their Destruction (BTWC) or BWC was opened for signature in 1972, the military significance of biological weapons was considered less than that of conventional nuclear and chemical weapons. The BWC sought to ban a whole host of weapons, and restrict the purposes of biological and toxin agents but it still lacks adequate compliance mechanisms and with its fifth review conference occurring in 2001, the US took fright at its potential interference with bio-defense activity, particularly due to its potential application to private parties and the near reminders of September 11 and the anthrax scare, drawing upon this imperative, that new and international legally binding measures to enhance biosafety and bio-security are urgently needed. The effectiveness of the BWC is therefore highly questionable and this chapter argues for a renewed commitment to strengthening it. The experiences in the Vietnam War and uses of Agent Orange are discussed to provide a close reminder of why that strengthening is so important. The second major topic of this chapter is the necessity of ensuring that our medical profession is engaged in the public good, and not diverted into caring for military and civilian casualties of avoidable and unnecessary wars or drawn into the security web of the 'war on terror' that has changed the landscape since 9/11.

Chapter 3

Indigenous Peoples and Genetic Population Research: Reflections on a Culturally Appropriate Model of Indigenous Participant Consent
Helena Kajlich

Genetic population studies, such as the Human Genome Diversity Project (HGDP), have captured the imagination of the wider public, promising to reveal the shared origins of humanity by tracing humanity's global migration patterns. In pursuing this objective, the HGDP identified isolated indigenous populations as holding unique and irreplaceable genetic information that is vital to unlocking the history of humanity's genetic origins.

The aim of this chapter is twofold: first, to trace the use of language in genetic population studies, specifically tracing the language used in the HGDP in relation to its targeting of indigenous *populations* and second, to examine the methodology relating to indigenous participant consent. Drawing upon the arguments of Joanne Barker, the implications of the use of the term indigenous *populations* as distinct from *peoples* is first considered. Barker argues that there is an inherent tension between these two concepts as the term indigenous *populations* does not recognize the political and cultural autonomy of indigenous peoples (2004, 578–80). In adopting the language of populations, the HGDP risks re-inscribing the inequalities that proponents of the project argue will be eradicated by genetic population studies. Proponents of the HGDP claim that the project will bring an end to racism by exposing our shared genetic ancestry (Wald 2006, 321).

The chapter then turns to the issue of indigenous participant consent. The protocol adopted in the HGDP relating to methodology for obtaining indigenous participant consent is examined as well as current international protocols and domestic protocols in Australia that relate to genetic research involving indigenous peoples. The chapter concludes by considering a recent genetic population sampling carried out in Tasmania involving Aboriginal Tasmanians. This experience reveals a significant disconnect between protocol and practice. Despite there being quite rigorous international and domestic protocols that require researchers take account of the cultural situatedness of indigenous peoples when framing their consent methodology, the Tasmanian example demonstrates a basic failure to meet these standards. The chapter concludes that genetic research must be conducted in a manner that is consistent with indigenous peoples rights under the *United Nations Declaration on the Rights of Indigenous Peoples* both in terms of the language used and methodologies employed if genetic research is to renegotiate the inequalities that frame indigenous/western scientific relations.

Chapter 4

The SARS Epidemic in Hong Kong 2003: Interplay of Law, Medicine and Ethics
Edwin Hui

This chapter takes a comparative look at the experiences of Hong Kong and Canada in dealing with SARS, a disease that crossed global borders and demonstrated the need for global legal responses underpinned by globally recognized ethical values. For both countries, the SARS outbreak 'posed a challenge to traditional disease-control mechanisms, as information about the emerging infection was scant and public concern was high' (Samaan et al. 2004, 220). Several significant issues emerged including the capacity of the public health system, the capacity of the state and public health officials to mandatorily quarantine, and in what circumstances, and the rights of individuals to resist quarantine orders. With the outbreak of SARS, Canada had to confront and respond to the very real threat posed by its own political and administrative neglect of important public health issues – and confront them as a developed nation with the capacity to effectively deal with such threats according to the principle of the rule of law. In Canada, SARS, in fact, 'transpired to be controllable through careful containment of cases' and it did not have the consequence of resulting in extensive resort to mandatory quarantine (Weiss and McLean 2004, 113). The SARS outbreaks provide salutary lessons for future pandemic planning, even though responses in the future may need to be more severe, for with SARS, as Weiss and McLean observe: 'Although the *Health Protection and Promotion Act* gives officials the power to force non-compliant individuals into quarantine, this was used only once during the outbreak.' Even if used only once in Canada, that, coupled with Hong Kong's mandated post-mortem of bodies (Hong Kong Museum of Medical Sciences Society (2006) 72), is enough to prompt consideration of the many ethical issues awaiting in the future as we confront the challenges of emerging infectious diseases.

Chapter 5

A Proposal Based on 'The Tragedy of the Commons': A Museum of Bioprospecting, Intellectual Property Rights and the Public Domain
Joseph Henry Vogel

'The Tragedy of the Commons' by Garrett Hardin provides counter-intuitive lessons. The most salient is that a class of problems exists for which there is no technical solution. Hardin's advice, often overlooked by economists, is that the enclosure of the commons must be accompanied by continuing education. Genetic resources provide an excellent example. Although the Convention on Biological Diversity was ratified in 1993 and revoked 'open access' over genetic resources, enclosure did not resolve the problem of access and fair and equitable benefit-sharing. Each nation, now sovereign over its genetic resources, entered into a bidding war. 'Open access' was re-established *de facto* as the competitive price fell to marginal cost. To attain access and fair and equitable benefit-sharng, the public must understand how governments, acting in unison, can avert the tragedy. Education is a necessary condition. A network of museums is proposed, with the node in San Juan, Puerto Rico, dedicated to bioprospecting, intellectual property rights and the public domain.

Chapter 6

Law, Ethics and Wildlife Disease: An Australian Perspective
Hamish McCallum

Over the last few years, interest in wildlife disease has burgeoned. The major role that infectious diseases have played in the history of human civilization and in livestock husbandry is well known. Until recently, diseases were not considered to be important in the ecology of wild populations. Diseases are now being recognized as important drivers of the population dynamics of wild populations. They also have direct and indirect impacts on human well-being, which can be divided into four categories. First, the majority of emerging infectious diseases of humans arise from wildlife reservoirs. Second, diseases of livestock can be extraordinarily significant economically. Third, diseases of wildlife may be critically important for biodiversity conservation. Fourth, wildlife diseases are being used and are proposed as control agents for over abundant pest species. This chapter explores the legal and ethical issues arising from each of these impacts, using Australian examples as case studies. As an island continent that has been isolated over evolutionary time and can feasibly be isolated from many diseases by quarantine, Australia is an ideal context with which to examine general issues associated with emerging and invasive diseases.

Chapter 7

Environmental Risk, Environmental Liability and the Regulation of Biotechnology: Mediating Law and Biology?
Christopher Rodgers

The widespread use of Genetically Modified Organisms (GMOs) in agriculture raises challenging problems as to the allocation of risk and liability for alleged environmental 'damage' caused by colonization (genetic drift). This raises issues of possible biodiversity loss, risk assessment and risk management, and the approach the law should adopt given the inherent uncertainty of the interaction of GMOs with ecosystems. These issues raise interesting governance problems in international law, for example, within the context of both the Sanitary and Phytosanitary Agreement of the World Trade Organisation, and the Cartagena Protocol on Biosafety. They have also been addressed in European Commission (EC) law, where attention has focused on the need to develop a liability regime to address potential claims from organic and other non-Genetically Modified (GM) producers whose businesses may be affected by alleged 'contamination' from GM crops, and to identify and address 'environmental' damage alleged to arise from GMO releases to the environment. This chapter discusses the prospects for the development of International mechanisms under the aegis of the Cartagena Protocol on Biosafety, and the development of a liability mechanism for GMOs under the 2004 Environmental Liability Directive of the European Community. The chapter will give an assessment of the EC Directive as a possible model for the wider adoption of environmental liability regimes, including that posited under the aegis of the Cartagena Protocol.

Chapter 8

Legitimizing Regulatory Decision-Making about Genetically Modified Organisms under the *Gene Technology Act 2000* (Cth)
Charles Lawson and Richard Hindmarsh

The Australian *Gene Technology Act 2000* (Cth) (the GT Act) sets out a licensing scheme for dealings with genetically modified organisms (GMOs) and Genetically

Modified (GM) products. Central to the scheme's operation is that the government sanctioned license provides the kinds of assurances necessary to reassure consumers about human health and safety, and environmental harms likely to result from dealing with GMOs and GM products (addressing the asymmetric information in the markets for GMOs and GM products). The chapter presents an analysis of first, the liability regime, and second, the rigor of the regulatory decision-making, both in the context of information asymmetry. The chapter concludes that by failing to address these sorts of concerns the GT Act and its implementation will fail to provide the kinds of assurances necessary to address the asymmetric information in the markets for GMOs (and GM products). The consequences will be ever decreasing market price, market quality and market size.

Chapter 9

The Universal Declaration on Bioethics and Human Rights: Bioethics, a Civilizing Utopia in the Age of Globalization?
Christian Byk

For a long time, 'the majestic and rather distant figure' of people's law did not appear to be in contradiction with the positive laws of states because, as it inspired them all, it did not, therefore, create any constraints for them. The writers of the Civil Code were able to proclaim: 'There is a universal, immutable law, source of all positive laws: it is only natural reason insofar as it governs all men.'

This is the paradox today of the debate between universality and particularism in law. The acceleration that has been evident since the late 1990s in the process of international standardization in the field of life sciences does not allow us to evade a concrete question. What is the point of drawing up an international code of bioethics if we remain convinced that the diversity of cultures gives a different and even divergent meaning and scope to ethical principles?

Legal and detailed, universalism in bioethics is opposed neither really to globalization nor to cultures. It complements them and offers them anchor points, the famous universal principles, but above all methods for rebalancing the pernicious effects of the absolutism of economic neoliberalism and cultural communitarianism. Human rights confronted with the progress of life sciences should not be taken as the 'rolling mill of culture'. Those with a taste for Manichean visions are sure to see in the situation of these two phenomena, bioethics and globalization, the certainty of a confrontation promised to mankind. On the one hand, bioethics, the refuge of values and human identity, might be our only hope to save our civilization's humanism, even its 'humanitude'. On the other hand, globalization, like a devastating comet, might attack both cultural diversity, by promoting standardization and science, by slotting science into a market logic which has become the sole driving force of the world. Faced with this vision of the world, does not the importance of the stakes raised by the relationship between life sciences and social organization deserve, on the contrary, our giving some consideration to the meaning and scope of the links between universalism and globalization?

Indeed, it is not just a question of fixing social and legal limits for techniques that have applications which are (judged to be) excessive. It is also necessary to draw the consequences of the appearance of new spheres of power which have a hold on the running and the structures of society and its institutions. It is also an opportunity to perceive the conflicts and convergences that model our era and open the way to new balances, dooming it temporarily to imbalances which are so liable to trigger social unrest.

The world, as we experience it and make it, cannot be thought of as an end of history; and bioethics, because it applies to one of these new spheres offered to man to conquer in society, could then be the prism that reveals the transformations, destructions and reconstructions which give globalization its true face: the reconfiguration of the international political order. It seems little wonder, drawing on the previous chapters, that Conor Gearty alerted us to the 'real human rights dilemmas about genetic technology' (Gearty 2006, 148) in asking whether human rights can survive. Gearty's concern is that with 'gene technology if uncontrolled' we may risk transforming 'our vision of ourselves as a gift of nature' into a product made by us, which flies in the face of 'our shared humanity' (Gearty 2006, 149). This is where human rights thinking fits, for as we work towards universal declarations, '… human rights thinking can help us draw the line' (Gearty 2006, 148). It can presage ways forward given cultural variation in our responses to gene technology and biological developments and reproductive possibilities, to seek universally acknowledged principles: bioethical incarnations of 'natural' law. By adopting in October 2005, the Universal Declaration on Bioethics and Human Rights, UNESCO has demonstrated its full capacity as a UN organization to elaborate within two years a universal instrument which takes into account both cultural diversity and pluralism. This chapter will, by way of conclusion to the book, attempt a detailed and critical approach to the UNESCO declaration.

Conclusion

Each case study or chapter in this book demonstrates how closing the gap between law and biology remains elusive and requires continuous re-examination of each discipline and the nexus between them. This is an area of accelerating change. The topics we chose for our project, five years ago, may not necessarily seem the most pressing today; unceasingly, new ones have arisen that might merit not only a chapter but perhaps a complementary anthology. Nanotechnology, for example, is now an area persistently pressing at the law for regulation. In the area of medical negligence, *in vitro* fertilization litigation is emerging, with an Australian case concerning the birth of two healthy babies when only one was 'ordered'. The emergence of equine influenza, or horse flu, has pressed the boundaries of quarantine and vaccine laws beyond the boundaries of current pandemic planning and reawakened our fears of an avian influenza or bird flu pandemic. Furthermore, there is much to be gained from adopting Rendtorff's argument:

> The extension of the sphere of legal and ethical concern to apply to the whole biosphere, nature and animals is necessary in an age of increased human intervention in the living nature (Rendtorff 2002, 236).

If there is a theme to our contributions here it is that as the biotechnological and biological revolution unfolds, human rights law has the potential to reflect the core values which we wish to hold on to, reflecting those which we have discarded and the new values which have replaced them. Through this book, we hope to show that human rights law is not only 'one of the great civilizing achievements of the modern era' (Gearty 2006, 1) but also prerequisite for the development of modern biotechnology and biology. As Justice Michael Kirby indicates in his Foreword, our purpose was never to be definitive and our contribution is inevitably disparate. This anthology integrates with a broad movement where scholars from any given discipline can draw from the way of thinking in another discipline and prompt evolving issues that defy traditional boundaries.

References

Barker, J. (2004) 'The Human Genome Diversity Project', *Cultural Studies* 18: 4, 571–606.

Diamond, J. (2005) *Collapse: How Societies Choose to Fail or Succeed* (New York: Viking).

Fletcher, J. (1966) *Situation Ethics* (Philadelphia: Westminster Press).

Gearty, C. (2006) *Can Human Rights Survive?* (Cambridge: Cambridge University Press).

Hardin, G. (1968) 'The Tragedy of the Commons', *Science*, 13 December 1968, 162: 3859, 1243–8.

Hong Kong Museum of Medical Sciences Society (2006) *Plague, SARS and the Story of Medicine in Hong Kong*.

Horrigan, B. (2003) *Adventures in Law and Justice* (Sydney, NSW: UNSW Press).

Intellectual Property Watch (2007) 'Indonesian Avian Flu Stance Reveals Potential Weakness In Global System', *Intellectual Property Watch* 8/3/2007 (www.ip-watch.org/weblog/index.php?p=562&res=1280&print=0).

Knoppers, B.M. (2005) 'Biobanking: International Norms', *Journal of Law, Medicine & Ethics*, Symposium, Regulation of Biobanks, Spring, 7–14.

New Scientist (2007) 'A Game We All Lose', *New Scientist*, 26 May 2007, 5.

Picoult, J. (2005) *My Sister's Keeper* (Sydney: Allen & Unwin).

Rendtorff, J.D. (2002) 'Basic Ethical Principles I in European Bioethics and Biolaw: Autonomy, Dignity, Integrity and Vulnerability – Towards a Foundation of Bioethics and Biolaw', *Medicine, Health Care and Philosophy* 5: 235–44.

Rimmer, M. (2004) 'The Race to Patent the SARS Virus: The TRIPS Agreement and Access to Essential Medicines', *Melbourne Journal of International Law*, 14.

Samaan, G., Patel, M., Spencer, J. and Roberts, L. (2004) 'Border Screening for SARS in Australia: What Has Been Learnt?', *Medical Journal of Australia*, 220–23.

Scheper-Hughes, N. (1992) *Death Without Weeping: the Violence of Everyday Life in Brazil* (Berkeley: University of California Press).

Selgelid, M.J., Battin, M.P. and Smith, C.B. (eds) (2006) *Ethics and Infectious Disease* (Malden, MA: Blackwell Publishing).

Sheldon, S. (2005) 'Saviour Siblings and the Discretionary Power of the Human Fertilisation and Embryology Authority', *Medical Law Review*, 403–11.

Singer, P. (2006) 'What Should a Billionaire Give – and What Should You?', *The New York Times Magazine*, 17 December.

Wald, P. (2006) 'Blood Stories: How Genomics is Rewriting Race, Medicine and Human History', *Patterns of Prejudice*, 40: 4, 303–33.

Weiss, R.A. and McLean, A.R. (2004) 'What Have We Learnt from SARS?' *Phil. Trans. Of the Royal Society, Biological Sciences* (London) 1137–40.

Acknowledgments

We thank first the Australian Research Council (ARC) for the award of an International Linkage Project on the topic of 'Towards a Nexus of Law and Biology' in 2003. Buoyed by the funding, over the three years of this project, an international and multidisciplinary research team wrestled with modern biology and the law, and realized just how vast the possibilities for analysis and synthesis are. Yet we were able to explore only a small fraction of those possibilities and we are all aware of how much more remains to be explored. Just how much remains is highlighted in the excellent Foreword to the anthology, for which we thank The Honourable Justice Michael Kirby very much. A further vote of thanks is owed to Justice Kirby for his initial support for this project, provided in a supporting letter for our nomination for one of the Eureka Prizes of the Australia Museum, for which nomination we thank Julia Playford of Queensland Parks and Wildlife Service. Besides the contributing team, three other original team members are also owed thanks: they are Professor Roxanne Mykitiuk, Dr Michele Harvey-Blankenship and particularly Professor Dick Cotton for their engagement on this and an earlier related (unfunded) project. We thank also the many colleagues who assisted us with comments along the way, particularly Sally Sheldon, Gudmundur Alfredsson, Camilo Gomides, Rosa Vasconcelos and Thilo Marauhn. We have been fortunate with our appointment of two excellent research assistants, who have assisted a great deal with the final stages of this manuscript. We express our gratitude to John Meyer and Helena Kajlich for that invaluable assistance, and to Ashgate for their patience in awaiting the final manuscript and their understanding of the many distractions of modern academic and family life. As to which, it may seem unusual that two chapters in this book deal with an issue that arose in the rather remote Australian island State of Tasmania, but the project commenced in 2003 when I was based at Queensland University of Technology (QUT) and concluded in 2008 when I was based at the University of Tasmania. This leads me to thank the former Head of the School of Justice at Queensland University of Technology, Professor Rod Broadhurst, as well as the Dean of Law at University of Tasmania, Professor Don Chalmers, for both Faculties' support of this project. On a more personal note, thanks to Hamish McCallum, who has provided long-standing emotional (and financial) support for a project that has been of great value but inevitably of considerable cost, and in particular, thanks to our children Alasdair and Maddy for enjoying the ride.

Chapter 1
The Perils of Terminology and the 'Saviour Sibling' Dilemma

Barbara Ann Hocking and Eva Ryrstedt

Introduction

Bioethical dilemmas concerning children and babies are perhaps the most poignant and the most appropriate with which to commence our anthology. Such is the 'saviour sibling' dilemma, which arises where one, usually infant, family member is ill and in need of specifically matching biological tissue in order to survive or alleviate suffering. Nature being the way it is, the most likely suitable donor will be a member of the biologically close family – probably a sibling – but this may be a child or a baby not yet even born. Modern reproductive technology accommodates procuring a baby with 'matching' tissue. So it is that the reproductive choice takes on distinctly ethical dimensions when parents seek to exercise that choice in order to produce a sibling with the necessary matching tissue. In such cases the 'saviour' epithet seems apt inasmuch as the child is brought into being partly, although by no means necessarily exclusively, to benefit and even 'heal' the ill sibling. But if modern reproductive technology offers the possibility of specifically screening for a baby with matching tissue, the law in response has prevaricated, with incremental caution and approval, negotiating hesitantly between competing interests, wary in a situation where a quasi-religious label has been attached to what is essentially a basic choice about reproduction and family: a choice that parents make every day on a myriad of major and minor matters. While this chapter is mostly concerned with the high-profile House of Lords decision in the case of *Quintavalle v HFEA* (a classic 'saviour sibling' scenario) we consider by way of comparison two 'saviour' scenarios that arose in Australia: one where the recipient was a family aunt and the donor a ten-year-old boy; the other where the donor was a thirteen-month-old child and the recipient her seven-month-old cousin. The issues of children's rights overarch the two Australian scenarios, but those rights are considered within the familial context, and a broad one. We look also at the means by which this area of reproductive decision-making – the classic 'saviour sibling' scenario – proceeds in Sweden by way of comparison. There, far less public attention is paid to such reproductive decisions, guidelines are provided and donors anonymous. We conclude that because there are many other incarnations of this reproductive dilemma – many other instances of inter-familial tissue donation – there ought be less resort to the charged 'saviour sibling' label even with infant sibling donors;

hence a more dispassionate consideration of the circumstances of the family may incarnate in each individual case.

What Does the Label Mean?

A 'saviour sibling' is '… a child selected as a result of genetic screening to have some innate characteristic that will help save the life of an existing brother or sister' (Quinion 2007). According to Quinion, the term first appeared in the *Journal of Medical Ethics* in October 2002 (Quinion 2007). It has gained increasing currency, particularly since the high-profile Hashmi case in the House of Lords, which provides the focus of this chapter. Babies conceived in this way differ from those labelled 'designer babies' which are designed to meet a range of parental specifications rather than created for the specific purpose of healing an ailing sibling (Quinion 2007). The difficulty with attaching such 'catchy' terminology to this situation is that other (less favourable) labels inevitably also become attached besides the more favourable 'saviour sibling' label. These may encompass the notion of 'spare parts' children, which reflects the criticism that such uses of reproductive technology enhance the further 'commodification' of infants in a highly commercial age. While recognizing the current pervasiveness of the term 'saviour sibling' (to the extent that the *Guardian Weekly* (Watt 2008, 17) so labels the relevant section of the United Kingdom's Human Fertilisation and Embryology Bill 2008), we suggest it is timely to review the terminology. For the very use of such emotive labels may in itself be a danger, hinting at religious and moral judgements that may endure well into the future and burden the child – whether negatively as 'spare parts' or positively as 'saviour' – with a sense of long-term responsibility. Through this continuing characterization, we argue, the emotional umbilical cord will be difficult to cut.

Law as Mediator Between Parents, Children and Technology

Throughout the common law world, the law is being kept busy mediating the respective interests of parents and infants in the light of ever accelerating scientific developments. As Lord Phillips MR quoted in the Court of Appeal in this context two decades ago:

> It is not often that Parliament has to frame legislation apt to apply to developments at the advanced cutting edge of science (*The Queen on the Application of Quintavalle and the Human Fertilisation and Embryology Authority*, per Lord Phillips MR at para 25, citing White Paper, Human Fertilisation and Embryology: A Framework for Legislation, 1987).

Such technology includes not only the familiar In Vitro Fertilization (IVF) but also pre-implantation genetic diagnosis (PGD) which enables embryos to be screened to ascertain whether they carry a genetic disease, and Human Leukocyte Antigen (HLA) which is a form of tissue typing to determine the tissue-compatability of embryos with a living person. Parents may use these technologies to give birth to a child who may then donate the needed tissue to the ill child. In such cases the label 'saviour sibling' is on the surface an apt one, as the child is brought into being partly, although it must be reiterated by no means exclusively, to benefit and even 'heal' the ill sibling. Without resort to the reproductive technology, there is no guarantee that a child born into that family will have the matching tissue that is needed to save the ill child. With the aid of the technology, a specifically selected new family member can offer their sibling the hope of health in the future.

The use of this technology was challenged in *Quintavalle (on behalf of Comment on Reproductive Ethics) v Human Fertilisation and Embryology Authority* [2005] UKHL 28 (hereafter *Quintavalle v HFEA*), the 'classic' saviour sibling scenario, where the technology was, pursuant to a licence from the Human Fertilisation and Embryology Committee (HFEA), resorted to in order to provide a donor for critically ill six-year-old Zain Hashmi.

Reproduction and Intervention: *Quintavalle v Human Fertilisation and Embryology Authority*

The House of Lords decision in *Quintavalle v HFEA* is the most prominent higher court decision of the common law world dealing with the specific and classic scenario of the 'saviour sibling': the case of an embryo that will become a newborn infant specially selected to provide tissue for an ailing sibling. The case arose because, as Lord Hoffmann sympathetically explains, six-year-old Zain Hashmi, on whose behalf a licence had been sought, suffers from a serious genetic disorder, beta-thalassaemia major. Due to this his bone marrow fails to produce enough red blood cells and his health, as a result, is 'often very poorly' with the need for daily drugs and regular blood transfusions for survival (*Quintavalle v HFEA,* per Lord Hoffmann at page 2 of 15). Having sought a compatible donor both from outside and within the family, including two more pregnancies and one birth, the parents turned to the HFEA so they could desist 'from having to play dice with conception' (per Lord Hoffmann at page 2 of 15). And, by obtaining a transplant of stem cells from a suitable tissue donor, the ill child would be, in the words of Lord Hoffman's leading judgement in the case, '... restored to normal life'. The license was granted by the Human Fertilisation and Embryology Authority specifically to use a relatively new technology called pre-implantation genetic diagnosis (PGD). The question that arose for consideration was whether a cell biopsy technique to test for tissue-compatibility, at that time permissible only in the United States, could lawfully be also used in the United Kingdom. The creation and use of the embryos for the purpose of bearing a 'tissue-compatible child' (per Lord Hoffmann at page 3 of 15) required the granting of a licence from the HFEA and the Authority granted a licence to permit both PGD and HLA typing. The parents had two attempts to produce a child by the IVF treatment involving the PGD and tissue typing, and 15 embryos were produced, with the only one that was an exact tissue match also carrying the disease. With the second attempt, ten embryos were produced of which two were disease free and had a match with their ill son. One was implanted but a pregnancy did not result. Any further attempt was then delayed by the challenge to the power of the Authority to issue such a licence [2003] EWCA Civ 667. The challenge was brought by the director and founder of a group dedicated to absolute respect for the human embryo, known as Comment on Reproductive Ethics (CORE). It was thus that their spokesperson, Josephine Quintavalle, became a party to the proceedings. The challenge is of interest in itself, representing another example of intervention by often very 'tenacious' campaigners opposed to the potential inherent in modern reproductive technologies (Millns and Sheldon 1999). In the common law world, those interventions make public property of what might otherwise have remained within the province of private, autonomous family reproductive decisions. While such privacy and reproductive autonomy is the exclusive province of most parents, no matter how ill-advised, ill-timed, inappropriate, inattentive or inadvertent their decisions (Jackson 2002), it is not the province of those who fall foul of zealous campaigners opposed to such uses of technology for reproductive purposes.

The Dilemmas of the Family

The privacy of family reproductive decisions is widely acknowledged as a bioethical tenet that complements the principle of autonomy. Little would have been known of the parental decision to resort to IVF technology to produce a 'saviour sibling' for their ill son, had the rights campaigner not decided to challenge the decision of the competent authority to grant a licence. The challenge at first succeeded, with Justace Kay endorsing in 2002 the narrow reading of the legislative text such that tissue typing was not necessary or desirable for the purpose of assisting Mrs Hashmi to carry a child (Gavaghan 2007, 147). The Court of Appeal took the contrary view and it was then to the House of Lords to determine whether to reinforce the narrow or broad reading of the legislation. This required that the House consider the licensing powers granted to the HFEA, which is the body established in 1990 that regulates all research and treatment involving the use of IVF embryos in the United Kingdom. The objection to the licence centred around an objection to the reproductive ethics or as it was perceived, lack thereof, inherent in the decision. With the objection to the license, the respect for the embryo group not only made very public the bioethical dilemma of the family but also demonstrated Selgelid's contention that bioethicists are:

> … kept so occupied by discussion of religious objections to things like abortion, euthanasia, cloning, stem cell research, and so on that they give only limited attention to infectious diseases (Selgelid 2006, 18).

What were the parents to do? They were fully aware that the chances of finding a suitable tissue donor for their son, who was not his sibling, were extremely low. They attempted to conceive another sibling who would be a compatible donor with their son. Biology both thwarted and assisted them. One foetus conceived, their fifth, also suffered from beta-thalassaemia major. They aborted. Their next child born did not possess the necessary compatible tissue. They embarked upon an unsuccessful worldwide search for a donor (Sheldon and Wilkinson 2004, 138). To be spared 'from having to play dice with conception', the metaphor chosen by Lord Hoffmann, they sought, through their fertility clinic for approval to use PGD on embryos: this being a new use of the technology which had hitherto become accepted as allowing for the screening out of particular kinds of genetic disorders (Sheldon and Wilkinson 2004, 138) but not for specific conception of a suitable donor child.

Short of reproducing sufficient healthy children to produce a suitable donor, the reproductive options open to the family were few. They sought approval from HFEA according to the proper authorized channels. Under the Act, they did not seek the more straightforward PGD but HLA tissue typing, which was not so clearly within the licensing power of HFEA. The difficulty was that the Act permits HFEA to license certain activities in the course of providing treatment services which means, according to the Act, 'medical, surgical or obstetric services provided to the public or a section of the public for the purpose of assisting women to carry children'. Therefore, it fell to the British court system to determine whether both PGD and HLA typing could lawfully be authorized as activities to determine the suitability of the embryo for implantation within the meaning of the Act. Pointing again to the rapid developments in the science, at the time of the enactment in 1990, PGD was 'expressly foreseen' (Lord Brown, para 47) whereas tissue typing was not. Tissue typing fell into the category of 'unforeseen possibilities' (Lord Brown, para 47) and as such, the House of Lords would have to determine:

> ... whether by the 1990 Act, Parliament was conferring power upon the newly created authority to take whatever decisions arose from such unforeseen possibilities as tissue typing, or whether Parliament must rather have been contemplating the need for further primary legislation to deal with whatever ethical questions arose out of such future discoveries (per Lord Brown, para 47).

With the HFEA having granted a license for the tissue typing, albeit with several restrictions,[1] the dilemma facing the family seemed resolved. With the intervention and challenge to the licence and the power of HFEA, broad bioethical matters were at stake, but the legal issues were narrow: the case concerns an '… important, but limited, question' (per Lord Brown, para 42), which is whether HFEA created by the Act had the power to license tissue typing where the eventual aim of the procedure was to treat a sibling with blood from the baby's umbilical cord, which might extend to bone marrow later in life. Hence in Lord Brown's view: 'Your Lordships' sole concern is whether the Act allows the authority to license tissue typing were it in its discretion to think it right to do so' (per Lord Brown, para 46).

Resolution of the Narrow Legal Question

While adhering to the resolute judicial articulation of the narrowness of the legal question at issue, Lord Brown also acknowledges that the ethical questions raised in the process of decisions as to licensing tissue typing are so 'profound' (para 43), as to hardly need to be stated. Reflection on those questions includes consideration of whether selection of certain preferred genetic characteristics is permissible, and whether it is acceptable to follow a procedure resulting in the birth of a child designed to secure health for a sibling, who is thus intended to donate tissue to that sibling (para 43). Lord Brown acknowledges how 'troubling' such questions are, and the extent to which Zain's condition is 'wretched, his prospects uncertain'(para 44) due to his 'serious blood disorder' (para 44).

Such reflections remind us of the extent to which law has failed to keep apace with the speed of scientific progress and Lord Brown was fully cognizant of the extent to which: 'IVF treatment is a fast moving medical science' (para 47).

Yet the law in this case required only a narrow response, as Lord Justice Mance had also observed in the Court of Appeal:

> The facts of this case excite great sympathy. But the issue is one of law. It involves the construction of the Human Fertilisation and Embryology Act 1990,

1 Lord Brown notes at para 45 that the licence was made subject to conditions which the authority had laid down on 13 December 2001 when announcing a policy decision to permit tissue typing in cases where pre-implantation genetic diagnosis (PGD) was already necessary to avoid passing on a serious genetic disorder. Included among the conditions were that the sick sibling's condition should be severe or life threatening; of a sufficient seriousness to justify the use of PGD; that the embryos should themselves be at risk of that condition; that all other possibilities of treatment and sources of tissue for the sick sibling should have been explored; that the technique should not be available where the intended recipient is a parent; and that the intention should be to take only cord blood for the purposes of the treatment.

> in the context of scientific developments which go beyond any specifically envisaged at the time of the Act (*The Queen on the Application of Quintavalle and the Human Fertilisation and Embryology Authority*, para 99).

The Warnock Committee provided the genesis and design of the HFEA which granted the family their licence. It reported in 1984 and the '… centrepiece of the committee's recommendations was the creation of a statutory licensing authority to regulate all research and treatment which involved the use of IVF embryos' (per Lord Hoffmann at para 6). The recommendation was given effect with the Human Fertilisation and Embryology Act (HFEA) 1990, establishing HFEA, a body with wide-ranging membership, although the establishment of HFEA was preceded by a White Paper entitled Human Fertilisation and Embryology: A Framework for Legislation (per Lord Hoffmann at para 20, citing Cm 259, published November 1987). Despite the input from such eminences, the Act has been characterized by Margaret Brazier as one with 'little conceptual depth' (Brazier 1999, 167) and presaging the perpetual analysis of '… the same issues in different guises' (Brazier 1999, 188).

So it is that in his analysis, Lord Brown observes that his initial inclination was that PGD was acceptable and 'properly licensable' under the 1990 Act (para 51). In contrast, tissue typing posed a 'completely different concept and [was] impermissible' (para 51), and:

> It is one thing to enable a woman to conceive and bear a child which will itself be free of genetic abnormality; quite another to bear a child specifically selected for the purpose of treating someone else (para 51).

While noting that the ethical issues raised by the latter are of 'quite a different order' from those raised by straightforward PGD screening, Lord Brown conceded that several possible interpretations exist with respect to the statutory wording. One interpretation is that the 1990 Act permitted PGD screening only as required to eliminate gene and chromosome defects such as would affect the child and enable the woman to carry the child to full term (a viability of the foetus interpretation). Another interpretation is that the 1990 Act allows PGD screening to eliminate gene and chromosome defects such as may affect that child (or be carried by that child to future generations), but does not extend to tissue typing (an exclusion of unforeseen possibilities interpretation). The third interpretation is that like PGD screening, tissue typing can be licensed because it provides information about the characteristics of the embryo which is relevant to the woman's decision whether or not to carry the child. The House was concerned with the power accorded the authority: hence Lord Brown interpreted: 'suitability is for the woman, the limits of permissible embryo selection are for the authority'.

The Fine Lines in the Sand Drawn by the HFEA

Part of the difficulty with the discretionary power accorded the HFEA is that it must inevitably proceed on a case by case basis. The incremental nature of the decision-making authority drew lines in the sand between the situation for the family against whom Quintavalle objected to the issuing of the licence, the Hashmi family, and that of another family, the Whitaker family, who sought to have another child with matching tissue type to that of their son, who suffered from a rare form of anaemia (DBA). This family went to the US in order to realize conception of a 'saviour sibling'. Like the Hashmis, they maintained they did want another child and not solely as a source for sibling-compatible tissue. So why the difference? In incisive comments on these cases, Sheldon and Wilkinson critique the outcomes for the two families, arguing that any distinctions between them are 'misguided' and 'unjustifiable' (Sheldon and Wilkinson 2004). In their view, the HFEA simply 'got it badly wrong' in dealing with the Whitaker case (Sheldon and Wilkinson 2004, 160). Similarly, bioethicist Crystal Liu has reinforced that the drawing of a distinction between PGD with HLA tissue typing and pre-implantation HLA tissue typing is inconsistent from both an ethical and comparative policy perspective, as there is little real distinction between them (Liu 2007). In Liu's opinion, the HFEA had inadvertently reinforced the artificial nature of the distinction between the parents allowed to use PGD/HLA and those not so permitted by distinguishing the motivation of the parents who seek access to the technology – and particularly whether the parents made an application on the basis that they were at risk of transmitting the disorder – thus ignoring the transplant needs of the child (Liu 2007). Hence, in Australia too, in Liu's characterization, the situation could arise where parents with a child afflicted with Fanconi Anemia are eligible to use PGD with HLA typing due to the hereditary nature of the illness and risk of transmission, whereas parents with a child afflicted with Diamond Blackfan Anaemia as a result of spontaneous mutation would be prohibited due to not being at risk of transmission (Liu 2007). However, in the United Kingdom, the HFEA subsequently changed its policy to ameliorate the distinction drawn between the situations of the Hashmis and Whitakers, the protracted efforts that each family had to pursue in order to obtain a match for their ill child and the publicity that each received, attests to the tenacity of each family, and it is worth noting by way of conclusion to this overview of Quintavalle that in the Hashmi case no intrusive surgical procedure was at issue: the tissue was to be taken from 'discarded umbilicus' (Gavaghan 2007, 153). This contrasts with a donation that concerns the harvest of bone marrow or involves the transplantation of a non-regenerative organ such as a kidney, where the case of *Re Y* (mental incapacity: bone marrow transplant) [1997] Fam 110, (1996) 35 BMLR 111 provides authority for the proposition that here the donation must clearly be in the child's best interests.

The Case Law in Australia

There have been applications in Australia to use IVF techniques to screen an embryo in the manner of the Hashmi quest. Spriggs and Savulescu note a couple in the State of Victoria who obtained approval from the Infertility Treatment Authority to use pre-implantation genetic diagnosis with tissue typing in order to provide a match for their daughter, suffering from Fancon's anaemia (Spriggs and Savulescu 2002). More recently a mother announced she would continue to have children 'naturally' till she conceived a 'saviour'. In the absence of a direct Australian higher court equivalent to *Quintavalle (on behalf of Comment on Reproductive Ethics (Appellant) v Human Fertilisation and Embryology Authority (Respondents)* [2005] UKHL 28), there are related cases dealing, for example, with 'a willing and knowledgeable child' and one more recent case concerning infant cousins. Perhaps the most instructive is the decision of Hannon J in *Re GWW v CMW* ([1997] 21 Fam LR 612). Here, the Family Court of Australia, sitting in Hobart, was confronted with a proposed medical procedure on a 10-year-old child, denominated B, who to adopt the terminology, could be characterized as the 'saviour' of an adult aunt. The procedure involved a bone marrow harvest or peripheral blood collection for the benefit of this third party family member. The application to the court for approval authorizing performance of this procedure had been made by the parents of the child. Here the proposed procedure was the harvesting of the child's cells. Rather than being performed for the benefit of a near relative like a sibling or parent, it was for the benefit of a third party: in this case, the maternal aunt to B, Mrs R. The law here confronts a family relationship incarnation of the familiar contractual dilemma as to who is 'privy' to the family, and in tort who is 'proximate': how is law to determine how close a relationship is required: how close is 'close enough' to provide a relational peg to justify the provision of bone marrow within a family and how broadly ought family be construed? Mrs R was aged 26 and mother of three young children, and had been diagnosed with leukaemia. Without a transplant, the prognosis was terminal and urgency was apparent. Mrs R's siblings and their spouses had not proved fully matching, whereas B had been tested for compatibility and identified as the only fully matched relative donor. This meant that if B donated the tissue, then the success rate for Mrs R would be in the vicinity of 25 to 40 per cent; if an unrelated donor were selected, then the success rate would be in the vicinity of 20 to 30 per cent. Given that the application for this procedure was not for the benefit of the child but for that of a third party, Hannon J considered it necessary that the child be made a party to the proceedings, as well as separately represented, and arrangements were made accordingly.

On the jurisdictional issue, the court decided that a decision as to this matter lay within the welfare jurisdiction of the court and the procedure was determined. Hannon J considered that the court had jurisdiction, particularly given that the application was brought by the parents of the child themselves, in their capacity as parents with the duty to protect the child, emphasising that to hold otherwise would be to interpret too narrowly the court's welfare jurisdiction.

Hannon J described the proposed medical procedure in some detail, noting its invasive features, and emphasizing that it was not being undertaken for the benefit of the child himself but for that of the third party. The judge's yardstick for consideration of this surgical procedure, albeit less grave, is the well-known High Court decision concerning a proposed parental sterilization of a seriously disabled girl: *Secretary, Department of Health and Community Services v JWB and SMB [Re Marion].* (1992 FLC 92–293;(1992) 175 CLR 218. The principles laid down in this well-known case were confirmed in *P v P* (1994) FLC 92–462; (1994) 181 CLR 583). In confronting the proposed sterilization of an intellectually disabled 14-year-old girl, the joint judgement articulated the 'right of each person to bodily integrity' (per Mason CJ, Dawson, Toohey and Gaudron J), referring to the right to choose what occurs with respect to one's own person. The majority in *Re Marion* noted the uncertainty within the common law as to whether minors can consent to medical treatment in any circumstances. They followed the House of Lords decision in *Gillick v West Norfolk and Wisbech Area Health Authority* [1986] AC 112, which determined that a minor is capable of giving informed consent when they achieve sufficient understanding or intelligence to enable them to understand fully what is proposed.

Mrs S, a psychologist, provided expert evidence in *Re GWW v CMW* and in the words of Hannon J, 'assisted' the court with evidence of the opinion that B possessed an understanding of the proposed procedure. However, his depth of understanding was not sufficient that he could be considered 'Gillick competent' in terms of informed consent. Hence Hannon J determined it necessary to consider whether this was a 'special case outside the scope of a parent's power to consent to or on behalf of his or her child' (citing *Re Marion* (FLC at 79, 171–79; CLR at 232)). In *Re Marion* it had been considered necessary to obtain court authorization as 'in essence a procedural safeguard' given the risk of making a wrong decision and because the consequences of a wrong decision were particularly grave. Passages in the judgement in *Re Marion*, in Hannon J's view, indicate that it is not only sterilization that constitutes special cases outside the scope of parental power to consent. The foundations for the intervention of the court lie in the interests of the state in protecting the rights of minors. Hannon J noted the emphasis that had been placed upon the fact that this proposed procedure was not for the child's own benefit but for that of a third party. He considered this an important factor given that the situation concerned invasive surgery that would be invasive of the bodily integrity of a child 'of tender years'.

Having determined that this was indeed a 'special case', and that the responsibility of the court to protect children justified an intervention, Hannon J then discussed the relationship between the child and the aunt for whom he was to undergo the invasive procedure. On that relationship, in Hannon J's view, the interests of the child donor were paramount, to the exclusion of the aunt's needs: 'It cannot be emphasized too strongly that although the court has great sympathy for the plight of the aunt, as a matter of law her interests are not a relevant consideration.' Rather: 'the sole consideration in the determination of the application is the best interests of the child' ((1997) FLC 92–748).

Hannon J then turned to the crucial matter of the welfare of the child, which under the relevant section enables the court to have regard to any other fact or circumstance that it considers relevant, the court is required to consider any wishes expressed by the child and any other factors such as the understanding or maturity of the child, that the court considers relevant in attaching weight to the wishes of the child. The words of the Full Court in *H v W* ((1995) FLC 92–598) consider the weight to be attached to the wishes of children. Cited with approval are 'recent social forces have indicated that more realistic weight should be attached to the wishes of the children than may have been the practical realities in years past'. In ascertaining the wishes of B in the instant case, Hannon J refers again to the evidence of Mrs S, and her opinion reached after comprehensive interviews. This is considered together with the positive wishes expressed by B, and the evidence of Mrs CW, B's mother, to the effect that both she and her husband had originally tried to dissuade B from participating in the procedure, and that B had remained steadfast in his wish to be a donor. With the child as the lynchpin to the ultimate decision and accorded autonomy, Hannon J attached 'significant' weight to the child's willingness to be a donor to his aunt.

The other key relevant factor: to which the court ought have regard is the relationship between B and Mrs R. In this case, no special relationship exists between B and Mrs R or Mrs R's children (who are much younger than he) although the relationship between all members of the extended family is considered 'extremely close'. A further matter arose out of the evidence of Mrs S to the effect that preventing B from taking part in the procedure would be likely to produce negative consequences. To refuse would in fact 'directly contradict his personal value of "helping"'. Mrs S had even hypothesized that the confusion and puzzlement that might arise from a refusal could later manifest itself as lack of respect for authority and for the court system in particular. Accordingly, Hannon J authorized the performance of a bone marrow harvest to collect bone marrow cells or alternatively a peripheral blood collection to collect peripheral blood stem cells from the child for the purposes of a transplant and the further administration of any drug which may be incidental to or necessary for the procedures. The parents were therefore authorized to consent to the performance on the child. The decision of Hannon J was followed by Frederico J in *E v E* [1999] FamCA 2403.

Further insights into judicial understandings of the significance of the family ties in the resolution of this issue were provided by the recent decision of Cronin J in the Family Court of Australia in *Re Inaya* (Special Medical Procedure) [2007] FamCA 658. Here a close Muslim family sought a bone marrow transplant between infant cousins: the donor thirteen months old and the recipient seven months old. The procedure would have been prohibited under the Human Tissue Act 1982 (Vic), which provided a prohibition against removal of tissues from children. However the legislation despite this seemingly absolute prohibition also provided thus: 'A parent of a child may give his consent in writing to the removal from the body of the child of specified regenerative tissue for the purpose of the transplantation of the body of a brother, a sister or a parent of that child.' Cronin J considered the issues to be 'similar if not more stark, because of the two very young and oblivious children' to those that confronted Hannon J in *Re GWW v CMW*. Again, as in that case, the issue of consequences for the family – possible antisocial developments of the child – if the procedure were not to take place was canvassed, and it is noted that the physical risks to Inaya are low. Given it is considered within the realm of parental responsibility, it is observed that the relationship between the two very young children is 'of particular importance' as the families of the children live together and they will 'grow up closely together'. Hence it is portrayed almost as a sibling–sibling relationship, and further that 'It is in the interests of Inaya that this relationship be preserved if possible'. With this emphasis upon a broad understanding of family, reference is also made to the father of Inaya considering it 'almost [his] duty to do anything to assist' and his support (but it is emphasized, not pressure) from the Muslim community. Therefore, Cronin J allows the procedure as being in the best interests of Inaya.

Two other cases provide further illumination of the Australian position. In *Northern Sydney and Central Coast Area Health Service v CT (by his tutor ET)* [2005] NSWSC 551, the situation was one of an intellectually disabled adult proposed as the donor of blood stem cells to his brother. The question for the court was whether it was in the best interests of the donor to authorize the transplant procedures to the brother: Nicholas J in the Supreme Court of New South Wales found that it was in CT's interests if his brother's life was saved, and recognizing the minimal risks involved, allowed CT to be a donor of blood stem cells for his brother's benefit.

In what has been heralded as 'the first "savior sibling" to be born in Australia', in 2004 a couple from Tasmania used pre-implantation genetic diagnosis (PGD) with tissue typing in order to ensure that their second baby would be free from the specific genetic condition (Hyper IgM syndrome) that affected their first child, and who could provide matched tissue for their afflicted child (Biotechnology Online 2008). It appears that representatives of the Catholic Church again voiced concerns as to the fate of the embryos with the genetic condition and of those who did not constitute a match, just as there was only very recently pro-life anger over a stem cell baby to help an ill brother in Spain (*Times Online* 2008). The destruction of embryos was of paramount concern. The Australian Medical Association however took the view that it is acceptable for parents to seek PGD and tissue typing to avoid a genetic disease, and to choose a tissue matched embryo, whereas it is not acceptable where PGD is sought for tissue typing alone (*BioNews* 2004). The fine line comes from the conviction that a decision to have a child ought to be made with that individual child's best interests at heart.[2]

2 See (www.mirror.co.uk/news/tm_objectid=15861809&method=full&siteid=94762&headline=my-little-brother-was-born-to-save-my-life--name_page.html) accessed 31 August 2005.

Goold (2005) laments that human tissue use in Australia is regulated in a fragmented and conflicting fashion, more in response to specific uses of the tissue than as a coherent jurisprudential approach to potential future uses (Goold 2005, 62). Cases like *Quintavalle (on behalf of Comment on Reproductive Ethics (Appellant) v Human Fertilisation and Embryology Authority (Respondents)* [2005] UKHL 28, might be dealt with differently in Australia, depending upon the precise wording of State IVF laws.[3] Some States have no specific legislation and rely at present upon guidelines despite calls for appropriate and uniform legislation, while others have enacted quite detailed legislation (Hocking and Guy 2005). There is an argument that eligibility criteria are more restrictive in the statutory jurisdictions and that this may mean that the non-statutory jurisdictions are more amenable to detecting tissue compatibility even if the parents are not at risk (Smith 2007).

Bioethical Dilemmas and the Best Interests of the Child in Sweden

Sweden is not a common law country and primarily uses legislation to deal with the many bioethical issues confronting modern law. For a long time no law on the subject of 'saviour siblings' existed, but recently such a law was passed (Lag 2006, 351, om genetisk integritet m.m. Act on Genetic Integrity). Before its passage, no authority existed to grant permits when it came to PGD/HLA; there were only guidelines. However, the Swedish parliament approved the guidelines after a recommendation by the social committee more than 10 years ago (1994/95: SoU18, 13).

The guidelines show that PGD was supposed to be used very restrictively and only on couples who had hereditary dispositions toward a certain sickness or deviation regarding chromosomes. The diagnoses would be aimed at serious, progressive, hereditary sicknesses, with no cure or treatment and where the child would die prematurely. A medical reason would have to be evidenced to allow for sex-determination (1994/95: SoU18, 13).

The absence of an authority to grant permits led inevitably to a lack of clarity as to the status of the guidelines. This meant that the hospitals themselves had to make the decisions in accordance with science and reliable experience (statement of opinion on Pre-implantation Genetic Diagnosis (PGD) 2004–01–23, 10).[4] When the guidelines were approved, however, it was determined that the National Board of Health and Welfare (Socialstyrelsen) would, on the government's assignment, supervise the development and give reports (1994/95: SoU18, 13).

---

3 Note those of Victoria, South Australia and Western Australia in particular.

4 See (www.smer.se/Uploads/Files/5.pdf) (8 May 2008). Note also further reference to Letter from the National Board of Health and Welfare to Magnus Nordenskjöld, Head of Department at Karolinska University Hospital, Reg. no. 11570/2001.

In hindsight, the guidelines worked out well. They seem to have been assimilated into medical practice (SOU 2004: 20, Genetik, integritet och etik, 293). In 2004, however, recommendations were presented that suggested changes in the guidelines regarding PGD in order to make the guidelines somewhat more lenient (SOU 2004: 20 and 301–305). This was also the case in the subsequent bill which suggested that the prerequisites to use PGD were to be determined by law (Prop. 2005/2006: 64, Genetisk integritet m.m., 100–107). One reason to make the legislation more liberal seems to be the quite different rules that are applicable on prenatal diagnosis. A diagnosis aimed at aborting the fetus has been quite common in Sweden for some years even where the condition is not serious enough to allow PGD (SOU 2004: 20 and 293). When it comes to PGD/HLA, however, the recommendations failed to offer a clear standpoint, but instead referred to the Swedish National Council on Medical Ethics (SMER)[5] (SOU 2004: 20, 301–305). PGD/HLA did not seem to have been performed in Sweden at that point, even if there was no absolute law against it.[6] One could say that it derived from the guidelines on PGD. In the recent bill, however, it was suggested that the use of PGD/HLA to try to get a child who would be a suitable donor of blood stem cells to a very ill sibling could be allowed if the National Board of Health and Welfare could find extraordinary reasons to be at hand and thus would issue a permit (Prop 2005/2006:64, 100–107), which later was stated in the law (Act on Genetic Integrity, Chapter 4, Section 2).

For a long time SMER did not take any stand with respect to PGD/HLA typing, even though it also did not rule out the possibility of using it.[7] In its response to the recommendations in SOU 2004: 20, the council declared that it could consider a certain, precautious application of the method. The council furthermore stated that the risks, even though they were not in any way to be neglected, are not sufficiently obvious or far-reaching to lead to a total prohibition of PGD/HLA where the method can save lives (Prop 2005/2006: 64, 102).

Intersections Linking the Approaches of the Three Jurisdictions

In leaving the matter to the National Board of Health, the approach of Sweden is to keep the issue out of the courts, a side effect of which is that it is more difficult to ascertain the basis of decisions. In contrast, in the United Kingdom and Australia the common theme to both the cases and legislation is a balancing of interests weighing up the rights and interests of the donor child and the ill

5 Statens medicinsk-etiska råd (Advisory board to the Swedish Government) (www.smer.se) 8 May 2008.

6 Cf. Statement of opinion on Preimplantation Genetic Diagnosis (PGD) 23 January 2004, (www.smer.se/Uploads/Files/5.pdf) 8 May 2008, pp. 2 and 10.

7 Statement of opinion on Pre-implantation Genetic Diagnosis (PGD) 23 January 2004, (www.smer.se/Uploads/Files/5.pdf) 8 May 2008, p. 2, SOU 2004: 20, 305.

child. It is of further note that in both the common law countries, a significant role questioning law and policy has been played out by lobby groups, such as CORE, whose website contained statements such as 'PGD is purely and simply another example of modern eugenics practiced even earlier on developing human life' (Gavaghan 2007, 147).

Consideration is given in each jurisdiction to the balance to be struck between natural and artificial conception. As Lord Brown observes, it is quite another thing to bear a child solely for the purpose of healing another child rather than to use the technology to make sure you have a healthy child (para 51). In the balancing act, the House of Lords acknowledges the difficulty of the Hashmi family to find a suitable donor other than a sibling of their son. Yet they are also clearly somewhat 'spooked' by fears as to how this technology will be used in the future. It is abundantly apparent to all affected parties that the advancing capacity of reproductive technology will only augment the bioethical dilemmas.

It is our view that this dilemma is best resolved by placing the best interests of the specific individual unborn child at the forefront of the balancing act, and this includes engagement with the long-term psychological impact of the procedure on the 'saviour' child. Strings are attached to the so-called gift of life. Had the donor child not been an infant, perhaps this engagement would have ensued in the House of Lords analysis. By way of comparison, the Australian common law approach to this use of IVF technology stems from a case concerning an older child donor. This takes full cognizance of the centrality of the rights of the 'saviour' child while building procedural safeguards into a relatively flexible view of the child's wishes where they are capable of consenting to tissue donation. In the case of the child asked to harvest bone marrow for his maternal aunt, the court decided that since the child was so steadfast in his conviction, the parent should be allowed to consent on the child's behalf. This outcome shows clearly that a child of sufficient age may give consent, and thus – provided the procedure is not risky – even at an age as young as 10 years old. Were the procedure to be risky, however, then this would factor more strongly in the balancing act that must be adopted by a court.

There is merit in Jackson's argument that principles derived from family law are not appropriate to inform decisions in this area (Jackson 2002). The extent to which children's welfare ought always provide the central pivot in such cases has been contended by Jackson on the basis that there are 'several compelling reasons to be skeptical about the welfare principle's colonization of reproductive choice' (Jackson 2002, 176). Yet an unresolved dilemma concerns the situation of ongoing demands upon the 'saviour' child as they reach physical and emotional maturity and the impact of those demands when they have a greater maturity and heightened understanding of the concept of medical autonomy and informed consent. What should be the court's position in attempting to arrive at an outcome to such a demanding balancing act? We concede that the 'child welfare filter' (Jackson 2002, 177) is riddled with inconsistencies, ambiguities and 'collective blindness' (Jackson 2002, 177), and that we ought not to violate individual autonomy in parental decision-making. However, this is one of the few occasions on which the modern state, through the law, can scrutinize parental 'procreative decision-making' (Jackson 2002, 177) or 'pre-conception decisions of adults' (Jackson 2002, 178). There is an inherent tension between such scrutiny in a modern liberal democracy, which is uncomfortable with intrusions that appear to fly in the face of the established principles of medical autonomy and informed consent. It is for this reason that we advocate the rolling back of the 'saviour sibling' label. It places too pressing a burden should a 'saviour sibling' later choose to no longer be a donor. Psychologically, it is easier for the donor to refuse consent when he or she has never been classified a 'saviour' at any stage of the process. Without such linguistic baggage, it is also easier for the bioethicist to consider the complexities involved. As the most recent report into this matter, that of the Human Genome Research Project at Otago University, concluded, it may only be public understanding that is hindering the science, and the benefits from this particular incarnation of genetic testing may outweigh potential harm.

Related Matters of Bioethical Complexity

This specific biological dilemma sits with many others pressing at the boundaries to the law. Sheldon has canvassed many others in her many writings in this area. Another particularly poignant recent example is that of *Evans v Amicus Health Care* [2003] EWHC 2161 and *Evans v Amicus Healthcare Ltd* [2004] EWCA (civ) 727, where both the United Kingdom's High Court and Court of Appeal agreed with Howard Johnston's assertion of the right to deny Natalie Evans access to embryos stored when they were a couple, with their mutual consent, now the subject of bitter discontent. In resolving the intractable conflict, the courts accepted that his consent could not be 'frozen' at the initial point of agreement (Sheldon 2004). He was entitled to choose not to father a child despite his decision meaning it was unlikely she would ever become a mother. Ms Evans was not able to convince any of the judges that she had been discriminated against in enjoyment of Convention rights due to her infertility (Sheldon 2004), and the media again picked up on the case, situating it, in Sheldon's view, as often with unusual fact situations, 'within a broader narrative of "long simmering gender wars"'(Sheldon 2004, 310). The European Court of Human Rights has also upheld a 300-year-old French tradition allowing mothers to give birth anonymously and hence denying the child the right to discover the identity of their biological parents (Henley 2003). The court decided the children and mothers' interests were almost incapable of reconciliation and considered both equally valid (Henley 2003).

Implications for our Understanding of the 'Family'

These essentially and traditionally autonomous family dilemmas – decisions about reproduction – have been elevated into the public sphere. The Hashmi family suffered such publicity through the intervention of the CORE campaigner. For that family this has meant that their very private decision as to how to best to nurture their critically ill son became headline news as they sought to obtain a compatible or suitable tissue donor for him from within their own family. Their actions offended pro-embryo spokespeople, concerned with the reproductive ethics implications. They were not concerned with their son's health. Yet as Lord Brown poignantly noted: 'His condition is wretched, his prospects uncertain' (para 44). Was it really necessary that we should know? Or was it necessary so that we can consider how best to protect the 'saviour' itself? Thomas expresses well the conflicting ethical issues: 'Although it could be argued these procedures fall within the procreative liberty of the parents and so should be unregulated, such is the vulnerability of the donor child that it is suggested that it is necessary to have adequate procedures to safeguard the child' (Thomas 2004, 3).

Thomas's insight is reflected in the Australian approach, although it is also balanced against the rights of a third party to invade privacy in order to object to a proposed use of IVF. This is the core privacy issue in such situations, and could prompt us to question further the seemingly utilitarian logic to the decision in the case. Is there any compelling moral logic such that the law should deny to parents in those situations the possibility of embryo screening so they can procure through nature a 'cure' for the wretched condition of their offspring? Is such utilitarianism really 'treating the offspring to be born as a commodity' as Lord Winston maintains?[8] Does it really cheapen the 'worth' of the selected child and render him or her little more than a reservoir of spare parts?[9] If it does, our moral aversion is already enshrined in the law, for example, through the refusal across the common law world, to countenance recovery of damages in negligence based on for child rearing costs in 'wrongful conception' actions. This aversion is 'based on the dignity or commodification of the child' (Nolan 2007, 71).

It does not seem productive to second-guess motives for parenthood, for it is hardly a science. There are many persuasive arguments as to the cohesive nature of various family formations, with or without biological connections. The modern family is not decomposable into rigid identities but rather fluid. Members are defined by emotional as well as biological connections (Thomas 2004, 5). Indeed, anthropologists have noted over the last thirty years that the traditional family as ideally portrayed (two cohabiting parents of opposite sex with a marriage contract) is fairly novel in human history, being peculiar to the agricultural phase of economic development (Tiger and Fox 1971). Hunting-gathering societies are matrilineal and, from current trends, so too may be post-industrial societies. Many of our fundamental assumptions about familial interconnections and biologically 'attuned' behaviour and relationships in this new reproductive environment are under challenge. These challenges remind us of Gavaghan's pertinent reflection

8 Per Lord Brown at para 43, citing 'the celebrated geneticist, Lord Winston'.

9 See Justine Ferrari, 'Born to Save your Sister' *Weekend Australian*, 28–29 October 2000, p. 31.

that: 'It is interesting to speculate on the extent with which the courts are likely to replace the legislature as the primary forum within which bioethical disputes will be played out' (Gavaghan 2007, 146).

At the conceptual level, these scenarios prompt reflection upon our understanding of 'family' and the 'contested concept' (Day Sclater et al. 1999, 1) of parenthood. The contest emerges from technological capacities which include an increasing capacity for 'artificial' reproduction, scanning for prenatal deformity or disease, and 'engineering built-in genetic characteristics or even disabilities' (Ferrari 2000). The contest compounds with a deeper understanding of 'family' and 'parenthood' afforded from evolutionary psychology and changes in relationship patterns in adult life. The cases reviewed here illustrate the dilemmas that arise from tissue donation while also alerting us to the distinctions in each of those cases. In an era when so much is 'valued' *sensu economica,* one suspects that profit will eventually enter more directly into the scenarios described. Commercialization will be explosive inasmuch as the donor group are, mostly, young or infant children who are extremely vulnerable. The extent to which those children ought to be rendered identifiable and effectively public property by virtue of a legal challenge to the reproductive situation and decision of their parents within the family unit is highly contestable.

Conclusion

Donations within families are commonplace. The more familiar monetary donations may be emotionally fraught but they are more amenable to legal resolution than matters of tissue donation in life and death situations. The resolution of collective family good *vis-á-vis* individual rights are always unique to that family, but there are prevailing fundamental human rights that may assist in resolution where emotional or bodily autonomy are at issue. It is therefore disappointing that *Quintavalle (on behalf of Comment on Reproductive Ethics (Appellant) v Human Fertilisation and Embryology Authority (Respondents)* [2005] UKHL 28, was channelled into a decision solely on the power of the licensing authority, which meant that 'human rights arguments are notable by their complete absence in this judgment' (Sheldon 2005, 403). It provided a catalyst for debate and may well have influenced the proposed legislative changes in the United Kingdom but it did not prompt soul-searching for the optimal expression of the human rights of the unborn 'saviour' or their ailing sibling, whether in infancy or as they proceed within that family and into adulthood. In that they have concerned older children, the balancing of interests in the Australian cases has pivoted around the primacy accorded the welfare of the child donor, while situating that within a broad understanding of extended familial relations. We accord with Jackson that the welfare principle and the principles of autonomy and informed consent have only a limited place where a parental decision to find a 'saviour' is made prior to conception (Jackson 2002). The age at which children can decide for themselves clearly varies but one could presage a 10–15 years rebuttable presumption and 15–20 years informed consent framework, somewhat along the lines of the criminal law's conceptual approach, with decreasing influence of parental autonomy depending on age/infancy.

Although we have resorted to the widely used terminology ourselves, we argue by way of conclusion that as law catches up with science, such terminology may ascend into the heavens of the lexicon. In our view, the label has not been instructive as it has implied a prejudgement of parental emotions and a subtle continuing moral imperative upon the infant or child donor. We could note the related objections to the use of the language of commerce in the context of another bioethical dilemma concerning unplanned pregnancies: 'As modern medicine has placed the male seed in the language of the market – sperm "bank" and "donor" – it is little wonder men are arguing that semen is property and women that ejaculation is a freebie' (Prasad 1999). Our concluding argument is to therefore cease to use the highly charged 'saviour' label and to recast the terminology even where dealing with infant donors: separate church, state and sibling; this will enable the donor to step out of '… the shadows of the sibling they were born to save' (Liu 2007), and reinforce that within close families, the gift of life has no strings attached.

References

Albrechtsen, J. (2005) 'Mothers Must Tell the Truth', *The Australian*, 23 March, 15.

BioNews (2004) '"Saviour Siblings" Debate Down Under' 249, 15 March.

Brazier, M. (1999) 'Regulating the Reproduction Business' *Med. L. Rev.* 166.

Buxton, J. (2007) 'Unforeseen Uses of Preimplantation Genetic Diagnosis – Ethical and Legal Issues' in K. Horsey and H. Biggs (eds) *Human Fertilisation and Embryology: Reproducing Regulation* (London and New York: Routledge-Cavendish) 109–34.

Day Sclater, S., Bainham, A. and Richards, M. (1999) 'Introduction' in A. Bainham, S. Day Sclater and M. Richards *What is a Parent? A Socio-Legal Analysis* (Oxford: Hart Publishing).

Dayton, L. (2006) 'Adult Stem-cell Bonanza', *The Australian Higher Education*, 17 May, 40.

Douglas, G. (2001) *An Introduction to Family Law* (Oxford: Oxford University Press).

Ferrari, J. (2000) 'Born to Save your Sister', *Weekend Australian*, 28–29 October, 31.

Gavaghan, C. (2007) *Defending the Genetic Supermarket* (London and New York: Routledge-Cavendish).

Gearty, C. (2006) *Can Human Rights Survive?* (Cambridge: Cambridge University Press).

Goold, I. (2005) 'Sounds Suspiciously Like Property Treatment: Does Human Tissue Fit Within The Common Law Concept of Property?' in *The Mind, the Body and the Law* no. 7 UTS Law Review (2005) and no. 4 *Santa Clara Journal of International Law* (2006) 62–86.

Healy, D. (2002) 'Review of Rahul K. Dhanda, Guiding Icarus: Merging Bioethics with Corporate Interests' (New York: Wiles-Liss IABN 0-471-22380-8) in [2004] 23 *Monash Bioethics Review* (no. 1) 47–50.

Henley, J. (2003) 'Court Rules Against Those Who Seek Parents', *Sydney Morning Herald*, 15–16 February, 18.

Hocking, B.A. and Guy, S. (2005) 'Desperately Seeking Donors: The "Saviour Sibling" Decision in *Quintavalle v Human Fertilisation and Embryology Authority (UK)*', *Australian Journal of Family Law*, 19(2): 144–52.

Jackson, E. (2002) 'Conception and the Irrelevance of the Welfare Principle', *The Modern Law Review* 65: 2, 176–203.

Lag (2006: 351) om genetisk ingegritet m.m. (Act on Genetical Integrity).

Liu, C. (2007) 'Saviour Siblings? The Distinction Between PGD with HLA Tissue Typing and Preimplantation HLA Tissue Typing', *Journal of Bioethical Inquiry* (accessed 4 June 2007).

Millns, S. and Sheldon, S. (1999) 'Delivering Democracy to Abortion Politics; *Bowman v United Kingdom*' (European Court of Human Rights, Case no. 141/1996/762/959, 19 February [1998] 26 E.H.R.R.1', *Feminist Legal Studies*, 7: 63–73.

Morgan, D. and Veitch, K. (2004) 'Being Ms B: B, Autonomy and the Nature of Legal Regulation', *Sydney Law Review*, 26, 6.

Nolan, D. (2007) 'New Forms of Damages in Negligence', *The Modern Law Review,* 70: 1, 59–88.

Picoult, J. (2005) *My Sister's Keeper* (Sydney: Allen & Unwin).

Prasad, R. (1999) 'The Sperm that Turned.' *The Guardian* 11 February, 2.

Quinion, M. (2007) World Wide Words (www.worldwidewords.org/turnsofphrase/tp-sav1.htm) accessed 12 January 2008.

Seddon, N. (2003) 'Contract and the Executive', *Federal Law Review* (www.austlii.edu.au/cgi-bin/disp.pl/au/journals/FedLRev/2003/14.html?query=+%28%28%28%28contract+law%29+and+%28on%29%29%29+and+%28on%29%29#disp85) accessed 8 March 2006.

Selgelid, M. (2006) 'Ethics and Infectious Disease', Chapter 1 of M. Selgelid, M.P. Battin and C.B. Smith, *Ethics and Infectious Disease*, 3–19 (Malden, MA: Blackwell Publishing).

Selgelid, M. and Battin, M. (2005) 'Ethical Issues in Infectious Disease', Editorial introduction to *Bioethics*, 19: 4, iii–vii.

Sheldon, S. (2004) 'Gender Equality and Reproductive Decision-Making', *Feminist Legal Studies*, 12: 303–16.

Sheldon, S. (2005) 'Saviour Siblings and the Discretionary Power of the HFEA', *Medical Law Review*, 13: 403–11.

Sheldon, S. (2006) 'Sperm Bandits', Birth Control Fraud and the Battle of the Sexes', *Legal Studies*, 21 (3): 460–80.

Sheldon, S. and Wilkinson, S. (2004) 'Hashmi and Whitaker: A Misguided and Unjustifiable Distinction', *Medical Law Review*, 12(2): 137–63.

Smith, M. (2007) 'Reviewing Access to Assisted Reproductive Technology for the Creation of "Saviour Siblings": Limits on the Basis of Genetic Disposition?' Queensland University of Technology Conference paper.
Spriggs, M. and Savulescu, J. (2002) 'Saviour Siblings', *Journal of Medical Ethics*, 28, issue 5, p. 289 – doi: 10.1136/jme.28.5.289.
Thomas, C. (2004) 'Pre-implantation Testing and the Protection of the "Saviour Sibling"', *Deakin Law Review*, 5.
Tiger, L. and Fox, R. (1971) *The Imperial Animal* (New York: Holt, Rinehart and Winston).
Times Online (2008) 'Pro-life Anger over Stem Cell Baby to Help Ill Spanish Brother', 21 October (www.timesonline.co.uk).
Watt, W. (2008) 'MPs Vote in Favour of Hybrid Embryos and Savior Siblings.' *The Guardian Weekly*, 23 May 2008, 17.

Cases

The Queen on the Application of Quintavalle and the Human Fertilisation and Embryology Authority, Court of Appeal United Kingdom [2003] EWCA Civ. 667.
Quintavalle (on behalf of Comment on Reproductive Ethics) v HFEA [2005] UKHL 28 (www.austlii.edu.au/cgi-bin/sinodisp/au/cases/cth/FamCA/2007/658.html?query=tissue%20donation) accessed 1/5/2008.
Re Inaya (Special Medical Procedure) [2007] FamCA 658 (27 June 2007).
In re Marion (No 2) [1994] FLC 92-448; 17 FamLR 336.
Secretary, Department of Health and Community Services v JWB and SMB (Marion's case) [1992] HCA 15; [1992] flc 92-293; [1992] 16 ALJR 300; [1992] 106 ALR 385.
Re: GWW and CMW [1997] FLC 92-748; 21 FamLR 612; [1997] 136 CLR 421.
E v E [1999] FamCA 2403.
Re Y [1996] 2 FLR 787.

Government Reports

Report of the Committee of Inquiry into Human Fertilisation and Embryology (Cmnd 9314), July 1984 and White Paper, Human Fertilisation and Embryology: A Framework for Legislation, November 1987 (Cmnd 259).

Swedish Preparatory Work

Bet. 1994/95: SoU18.
SOU 2004: 20 Genetik, integritet och etik.

Prop. 2005/2006: 64, Genetisk integritet m.m.

Other Material

Statens medicinsk-etiska råd (Advisory board to the Swedish Government), www.smer.se, 8 May 2008.
Statement of opinion on Preimplantation Genetic Diagnosis (PGD) 23 January 2004 (www.smer.se/Uploads/Files/5.pdf) 8 May 2008.

Chapter 2
I Sing of Arms and the Doctor: What Role for Law When Biology is Called to War?

Piero P. Giorgi, Scott Guy and Barbara Ann Hocking

Summary

Welfare, not warfare, is the customary pursuit for the doctor. Yet man's seemingly relentless pursuit of war frequently calls upon medical knowledge and capability, whether to alleviate the suffering of those injured or to devise biological means of waging war. Little wonder that the battle against war has long preoccupied philosophers and physicians. In this chapter we seek to explore some of the important biomedical and legal issues that arise from the ever-present, pervasive, harmful and yet fundamentally avoidable human activity that we label war.

We discuss the types of biomedical knowledge utilized in the pursuit of war, and the manner in which certain chemical and biological weapons have been, inconsistently, deployed, forbidden, controlled and tolerated, under a façade of ethical and legal principles. It is in this context of the use of chemical and biological weapons that we seek to discuss the role performed (and that can potentially be performed) by international law in preventing the onset of war and containing its severity and intensity when it occurs. As part of this discussion, attention is also focused on the strategies employed by governments and corporations to circumvent legal and ethical barriers and what can be done to prevent this in the future. We also discuss the victims of war and chemical, as well as biological, warfare and the various means employed to counter the illegal pursuit of war. The law of armed conflict has developed as a *lex specialis* (Stephens and Lewis 2005), but recent events in world affairs, as well as recent advances in the disciplines of biomedical, peace, ethics and legal studies, justify a new multidisciplinary discussion on the vitally important issue of the control of military weapons, particularly chemical and biological weapons. In this regard we will seek to undertake a reconsideration of the relationship that currently exists between the law and biological warfare, while recognizing that our arguments reflect our own 'moral compass' and that this may be attendant upon our own cultural values (Stephens and Lewis 2005).

Introduction

The notion of imposing legal constraints on war has endured through the ages, even as war has endured through the ages. It is perhaps one of the most curious anomalies of humankind: the fact that aspects of war can be unlawful but, as Mathews and McCormack explain, it has ever been so for we both pursue and abhor war, so: 'The notion of legal constraint upon the waging of war is as old as the earliest extant history of the conduct of war' (Mathews and McCormack 1999, 65).

During the First World War, the use of chemical weapons was 'particularly severe' (Mathews and McCormack 1999, 76) and this extensive use of toxic chemicals in the context of war prompted the International Committee of the Red Cross to take a stand in 1918 (Mathews and McCormack 1999, 76).The primary modern means of controlling war and uses of certain weapons through law is the reliance upon principles of international humanitarian law and arms control (Mathews and McCormack 1999, 65). Through those principles, we seek to limit the destructive potential of warfare. Besides those, we have developed the 'order' of international law through a law of armed conflict, such as the Hague Conventions, which have been characterized as among the first 'human rights' orientated treaties recognizing rights of soldiers (and civilians) *vis-á-vis* the state (Stephens and Lewis 2005). Yet their optimistic and seemingly 'civilizing' aspects as underpinning the development of the law of armed conflict during European expansion was in one view in essence 'an article of faith' and 'reservoir of inspiration' (Stephens and Lewis 2005).

Only 80 years ago representatives of various nations that witnessed the horror of chemical warfare in the First World War signed and ratified the *Convention on the Prohibition of the Development, Production and stockpiling of Bacteriological (Biological) and Toxin Weapons and on Their Destruction*, usually referred to as the Biological Weapons Convention or BWC. The Convention opened for signature in April 1972 and entered into force in March 1975, prohibiting parties to develop, produce and stockpile biological and toxin weapons. However, it is the purposes to which the weapons may be put that are prohibited.

The further development of the Convention as a tool for minimising the destructive impact of war has been hindered in more recent times when the Republican Administration headed by George W. Bush rejected a draft protocol (that had been in negotiation since 1995) enabling the monitoring and detection of biological and chemical weapons. Inevitably, a disarmament agreement without the legal power of monitoring and verification is effectively useless and has left nations, such as Iraq, immune from international control. Further gaps – or loopholes – in the principles of international humanitarian law may in the future enable the continuing use and exploitation of these biological and chemical weapons, which are already pervasive. They range from nuclear devices to relatively simple (but deadly) instruments, such as anti-human land mines.

The 1925 Geneva Protocol and the Changing Nature of Warfare

The first very significant contemporary legal instrument that purported to confine the destructive potential of biological and chemical warfare was signed in 1925 (in Geneva) and this was the *Protocol for the Prohibition of the Use in War of Asphyxiating, Poisonous or other Gases and of Bacteriological Methods of Warfare*. This particular protocol sought to regulate (and to restrict) how nations entered into, and conducted, international warfare. It should, however, be noted that there are additional international sources that seek to limit how nations enter into, and conduct, international warfare: these include the United Nations Charter, the various Geneva Conventions and the Hague Convention. Significantly, the United States was among the first signatories of the 1925 Geneva Protocol. Despite this, the United States Congress ratified this agreement only fifty years later in 1975 – well after the use of Agent Orange and other defoliants in Vietnam. By comparison, the Australian Federal Parliament ratified the Geneva Protocol in 1930. It only did so, however, on the condition that it reserved the right to utilize poisonous gases against possible enemies that had not in turn ratified the agreement (McCulloch 1984, 37).

These ambiguous and contradictory positions enabled Australia and the United States to develop active CBW programmes with quite serious consequences, the prime contemporary example of which was the subsequent use of prohibited weapons during the various wars fought in Iraq.

The Vietnam War and the Legacy of Agent Orange

The Vietnam War – waged by the United States from the 1960s – is often spoken of as the first war where the environment influenced, and featured so strongly in, the battle ground and military action. Given the (non-ratification) stance adopted by the United States in relation to the 1925 Geneva Protocol, it is not surprising that during this war, they systematically gassed the underground tunnels that were used by Vietnamese insurgents. Destruction of the environment was viewed as crucial to winning the war, resulting in blitzes against that environment, as Ham recounts in his recent book on the Australian engagement in the war:

> The defoliation of one heavily wooded area … involved 101 crop-dusting sorties, which sprayed 83,000 gallons of herbicide, fired 85,000 rounds of ammunition and dropped 760 tons of bombs (chiefly napalm, diesel fuel and white phosphorus) (Ham 2007, 143).

> The weapons chosen to destroy the environment included a '… chemical saturation of the Iron Triangle in the first massive application of herbicides, including Agent Orange, ordered by Westmoreland in late 1964' (Ham 2007, 143).

Like so many other potentially harmful substances, what became known as Agent Orange represents an adaptation of a substance originally deployed in seemingly benign situations: adapted for the purposes of extensive and destructive military deployment, Agent Orange was not considered to be a weapon in the 1960s. Rather, it was being used throughout the world to clear unwanted shrub in urban and agricultural areas and it presented itself in liquid form, not as the gas targeted by CBW agreements.

Agent Orange – n-butyl esters of the phenoxy-acetic acids 2,4-D and 2,4,5-T – was the most used (11 million gallons) herbicide and defoliant delivered by aerial spray by United States troops in Vietnam from 1962 to 1970. The object of this was to destroy farmers' crops in rebellious regions and to eliminate bush land where guerrilla troops were hiding. The actual biological action on plants was one that produced an inappropriate facilitation of growth, consequently causing an impact similar to cancer, much of which was graphically depicted in Oliver Stone's movie, *Apocalypse Now*.

Initially, the potential deleterious effect of Agent Orange on animals and humans was not a concern for authorities nor was it, indeed, perceived as a serious ethical breach in itself. The first criticism was expressed in 1966 from American scientists, citing starvation among the civilian population in Vietnam (McCulloch 1984, 32). The issue regarding the exposure of American and Australian troops to Agent Orange subsequently followed, but this was with mixed impact. The spraying of Agent Orange was discontinued in 1970 following publication in various medical journals of evidence relating to its danger to humans (McCulloch 1984, 3). Despite this, other chemical agents continued to be used in Vietnam until 1972.

Like various other types of dioxins, Agent Orange can produce chloracne on the skin. It can also produce liver dysfunction, severe personality disorders, cancers and birth defects. The allegations of birth defects were the first to be raised, but the most decisive evidence would only come after the Vietnam War (Smith 1994, 366). A causal relationship between Agent Orange and cancer has always been potentially present but the difficulties of proving direct causal links even to a balance of probabilities, drawing upon epidemiological data, have bedevilled plaintiffs since *Daubert v Merrill-Dow Pharmaceuticals, Inc*, if not before.[1]

The difficulty with medical investigation in relation to the effects of Agent Orange has been that serving army personnel in the field were only indirectly exposed to spraying. Hence, the pathologies or the medical conditions of non-Vietnamese personnel were statistically more difficult to detect than more traditional forms of injury. While the media was more interested in serving personnel being injured, it would have been sufficient, in this respect, to investigate the health

1 113 S. Ct. 2786 [1993]. The case concerned the alleged link between birth defects and the anti-nausea drug Bendectin, produced by Merrill-Dow. The plaintiffs relied on epidemiology, the 'study of the cause and effects of disease on large populations' (Houck and Siegel 2006, 639).

history of peasants directly targeted by massive amounts of Agent Orange to unravel the causal relationship. As a consequence, forty years later illness and congenital conditions are being passed on to third-generation Vietnamese farmers, as well as to children of children who have no responsibility for these conflicts and who are experiencing the consequences of the reckless decisions made in that war. In fact, the Diem regime of the Republic of Vietnam supported the spraying of defoliants by United States troops on its own rebellious farmers. The plight of subsequent generations is due to the fact that Agent Orange acts on the developing reproductive system of foetuses and young children and primordial germ cells can pass on defects after they have become mature eggs and sperm cells.

The case of Agent Orange as a cause of cancer and psychiatric disorders among Vietnam veterans is difficult to prove, because of the concomitant occurrence of post-traumatic disorders. Stress and depression – common complaints of veterans – tend to reduce the capacity of the immune system to control cancer, while they promote psychiatric conditions. A more realistic study of returning soldiers of both sides exposed to Agent Orange – together with civilians exposed to various chemical poisoning – in Europe and the United States have clarified these specific pathologies. There is very little doubt that Agent Orange *is* responsible for increased cancer among exposed people and the various ailments among their descendants (Appy 2007, 141). It is worth noting these words about health in Vietnam in our overview of the tyrannies of colonialism and the devastating effects of Agent Orange during the Vietnam War, for they suggest what was achieved in the hiatus between tyrannies and what might have been achieved had not further tyranny intervened: 'Since 1954, and the expulsion of the French, North Vietnam has been transformed into a country which is remarkably modern and seems to develop despite the tremendous amount of bombs and shells that have been inflicted upon it for more than two years. It is said that illiteracy had been essentially eliminated at the end of 1958, after four years of peace. Through large-scale vaccinations and a nation-wide campaign for better hygiene, small pox, cholera, plague and many other diseases have been eradicated' (Takman and Hojer 1968, 173).

The worst example of the effect of Agent Orange was the accident at Seveso, Italy, in 1976, when the overheating of a vat at the ICMESA factory (a subsidiary of Hoffman-La Roche) released a large cloud of trichlorophenol over a surface of land inhabited by 5,000 farmers (McCulloch 1984, 130–34). Other accidents concerning heavy metal poisoning have occurred in Mexico, California, New York State; in 1984 in Bopahl, India, an explosion at a Union Carbide factory poisoned thousands of people.

The Vietnam Veterans

By January 1973 peace negotiations entered into their initial stage and the majority of the troops were withdrawn. Casualties have been estimated as 58,000 for the US and two million for the Vietnamese (Davies et. al. 1998, 133). The remaining

Australian contingent in Vietnam was withdrawn in 1972, soon after the election of the Labor Government of Gough Whitlam. Subsequently, American troops were withdrawn at the conclusion of the war in 1975. In spite of several reports of health problems among troops exposed to Agent Orange during the war, the first clear indications of the effects of Agent Orange emerged in 1977 with the death in Chicago of the returned soldier, Charles Owens.

Indications of similar effects in Australia became evident one year later in the Yarram district of Victoria, where extensive spraying of Agent Orange had been used for sometime to reduce ragwort and blackberry bushes. Local health practitioners noticed an unusual rate of birth defects and many veterans soon manifested health problems similar to those experienced in Vietnam. Rather than a vigorous investigation, a pattern of denial was pursued through a sequel of public and legal manipulations to defend governmental authorities and chemical companies. The relentless attempt at redefinition and denial is documented in the concluding sections of Jock McCulloch's 1984 book *The Politics of Agent Orange* (McCulloch 1984). In this regard, it has been suggested that Vietnam veterans have been, in effect, betrayed twice. First, by being forced to fight an unjust war; second, by being denied natural justice after developing consequent physical and psychological traumas. This raises the issue as to how the use of Agent Orange could be rationalized or justified on the part of the relevant corporation; Dow Chemical revealed its underlying rationale for Agent Orange in its defence statement:

> To offset ambush attacks and protect allied forces, the US military sought to defoliate combat areas by developing and using the herbicide Agent Orange. U.S. military research developed Agent Orange, and the product was formulated on the basis of precise military specifications … Public concern over Agent Orange has centred not over the product itself, but an unavoidable by-product that was present in only trace levels of one of the product's ingredients. The unavoidable trace by-product was the dioxin compound 2,3,7,8-TCDD … As a nation at war, the US government compelled a number of companies to produce Agent Orange under the *Defence Production Act*. The government specified how it would be produced and controlled its use … The scientific investigation on Agent Orange has gone on since the Vietnam War and continues today. There have been extensive epidemiological studies of those veterans most exposed to Agent Orange. Today, the scientific consensus is that when the collective human evidence is reviewed, it does not show that Agent Orange caused veterans' illnesses (see www.dow.com/commitments/debates/agentorange).

The Supply of CBWs to Saddam Hussein

Industrialized oil-consuming countries have continually interfered with the internal affairs of oil producing countries in the Middle East. In the tradition of Machiavelli, the United States, for example, have been allies and then opponents of the same Muslim country to promote their own hegemonic plan. Their relationships with Iran and Iraq, indeed, are also consistent with such an interpretation.

When in 1979 the new theocratic government of Iran developed a clear and obvious hostility toward the United Sates, a brutal and ambitious secular leader in Iraq, Saddam Hussein, was accorded by the United States and some European countries sufficient resources to then prompt an attack on Iran in 1980. Western firms then supplied both biological and chemical weapons to Hussein when the fortunes of war turned in favour of the Iranians (Shultz 1993). A precursor to mustard gas was sold to Saddam Hussein's regime and was, in fact, used in the March 1988 gas attack against the Iraqi Kurdish town of Halabja. More than 5,000 people were killed, 7 to 10,000 were injured and thousands more suffered long-term effects in what the Human Rights Watch defined as an act of genocide and the largest-scale gas attack directed against a civilian populated area in history. In this respect, then, intrinsically innocuous chemicals were converted into military weapons and these played an important and crucial role during all the wars fought by Iraq.

Eight years after the 1980 attack to Iran, the balance of power between Iran and Iraq hardly changed, except that they had drained their own manpower and resources. A badly indebted Hussein invaded oil rich Kuwait and his former western allies exploited this opportunity with the 1991 Gulf War and its post-war control agreements. Ten years later, after the events of 9/11, the illegal chemical and biological weapon material (previously supplied by the West) fed the fear of 'Weapons of Mass Destruction' that justified the invasion of Iraq. One can conclude that confusing Protocols and Conventions, lack of verification, illegal sales and convenient lies caused millions of deaths in the Middle East.

During the Iraq–Iran war the West made available to Iraqi scientists a degree of technical know-how in biological warfare, in case such knowledge might then ultimately prove necessary to avoid an invasion by Iran. In this respect, Saddam Hussein did, indeed, possess CBWs before the invasion of Kuwait, but he was forced to destroy these facilities for building weapons of mass destruction and their delivery systems after the Gulf War. Accordingly, it eventuated that '... Iraq was invaded with lower US losses than had been expected by those of us who thought it was more likely than not that Iraq still had some chemical and biological weapons (and that if Saddam had kept them, he would use them)' (Braithwaite 2006, 96). The availability of chemical weapons in Iraq during the Gulf War later fuelled speculation concerning the so-called Gulf War syndrome, as discussed below.

> Ethics is not just about rights. It is also about justice in the distribution of public health burdens, and about social justice in access to opportunities and goods. It is about normative responsibilities to redress inequalities, to care for those most at risk of public health harms, to redistribute goods so that all members of the population have an equal opportunity to survive a public health disaster. And few plans address these issues (Martin and Hocking 2009).

The Use of Chemical Weapons in the Gulf War

Unlike the poisoning of Vietnamese and American soldiers with Agent Orange, uncertainty and vagueness still remain on the issue of the so-called 'Gulf War syndrome'. As an example of the policy adopted by the United States Central Intelligence Agency (CIA) to obstruct information, former CIA officer, Patrick G. Eddington, did send a letter to the Acting Director of Central Intelligence, George Tenet, as well as to Senators Arlen Specter and John D. Rockefeller referring to an internal CIA memorandum dated 21 April 1995 (*The Coastal Post*, 7 February 1997). It explicitly stated that the CIA did not plan a review of the information on the Gulf War syndrome, such as troop testimony, medical records and operational logs. Furthermore, the CIA refused to debrief Gulf War veterans or to review thousands of pages of captured Iraqi intelligence that discussed the employment of chemical and biological weapons. It should also be remembered that the press was not allowed to accompany troops, the so-called embedded journalists, during Gulf War operations.

The veterans' claim is that Iraqi troops did, indeed, use of chemical and biological weapons in an attempt to hold back the American advance. Had the CIA evaluated this information in 1994–95, two years of delay could then have been avoided and the veterans' suffering might have been consequently lessened. The fact that this type of high-level cover-up does in fact occur in a country purporting to promote democracy, is a demonstration that international laws on war and their implementation are urgently needed.

Legal and Ethical Views about Atomic Weapons

The Association of International Physicians for the Prevention of Nuclear War (IPPNW), which was awarded the Nobel Prize for Peace in 1985, has attempted for several years to have nuclear weapons banned by an international convention. The contention was that their very nature and their potentially harmful consequences for human beings would make them even more unethical than CBWs. Atomic weapons act in two associated ways: a sudden and enormous liberation of heat, which could be compared to an extremely large bomb, and a radioactive fall out, which is unique and difficult to control.

The bomb-like effect can be controlled and predicted by determining the location on the ground and the height of detonation. The radiation fall out is unpredictable and can extend over long distances depending on various environmental factors. The consequence of this is that on the ground it would be almost impossible to distinguish one side from the other – after the destruction of civil/military targets in enemy territory, it would be necessary to wait too long a time before effectively securing the zone with ground troops. This is precisely why retired generals have recently stated that they would have little or no idea on how, in fact, fighting or planning a nuclear war would work.

From a study on civilians hit by an atomic bomb in Hiroshima and Nagasaki, it is common knowledge that medical consequences of exposure to nuclear radiation are similar, in fact, to those that are caused by Agent Orange: long-term induction of cancer and developmental abnormalities at the expense of subsequent generations. Unfortunately the banning of nuclear weapons on the basis of international laws on war – the Protocols and Conventions signed and ratified between 1925 and 1997 – is impeded by semantic and/or scientific issues (Price 1995, 73).

For example, what do we mean precisely by the term 'chemical war' and 'biological war'? A thermonuclear reaction does belong in the realm of physical chemistry, but it also has obvious biological effects. It is unclear, in this respect, whether one should classify weapons on the basis of their nature or their effects. The aim of IPPNW and of the International Campaign against Nuclear Weapons (ICAN) is to have a specific international convention on nuclear weapons, which can then be enforced and verified (Ashford and Dauncey 2006). The arguments in favour of banning nuclear weapons are similar to those already accepted by world nations to ban CBWs, which raises the point as to why they have ever been accepted? It has been suggested that nuclear weapons are not military tools and serve, in effect, purely political purposes, that is, they are used to distinguish strong players in the international arena (the 'nuclear club') from other ordinary nations that, therefore, have fewer privileges. There are three arguments to exclude outright nuclear weapons from the category of military tools: they cannot be used on the battle field (Leber and Press 2006, 42); they cannot distinguish between combatants and civilians; and a nuclear exchange of any size would irreversibly change world climate (Office of Technology Assessment 1979).

The Failure of Negotiations over the Compliance Mechanism for the Biological Weapons Convention

The object of the Chemical Weapons Convention is arguably 'the elimination of the use of chemical weapons', and further 'the elimination of the possibility to use chemical weapons' (Sztucki 2006, 50). In the United Nations General Debate of the UN First Committee on 8–17 October 2001, the matter of biological and chemical weapons was discussed. The European Union emphasized the importance of the obligation of destroying specific items indicated in the Chemical Weapons Convention. New Zealand pointed out that the matter of a compliance mechanism for the Biological Weapons Convention has been in negotiation for approximately a decade, and a draft Protocol Evidence of non-compliance with the Convention's prohibition has failed to eventuate. New Zealand commented that it regretted this failure of the negotiations, noting that bio-defence measures are essential and are, indeed, consistent with the implementation of the Convention. In addition to this, the Vatican representation at the United Nations pointed out that the protocol would have required all signatory states to declare industrial facilities capable of manufacturing bioweapons. In this respect, Canada observed that the potential links to terrorism are 'clear and disturbing'. The urgency of the compliance Protocol lay in the need to deter biological weapons proliferation and 'reduce the risks of the weaponization of disease' (www.acronym.org.uk/un/2001cbw.htm), as discussed below.

The Weaponization of Disease

The possibility of utilizing diseases as weapons is a further dimension to our overview of medical–military intersection. A 2003 editorial in *Nature* stated that, while the world may have celebrated the containment of the outbreak of the severe acute respiratory syndrome (SARS), '... the epidemic has revealed gaps in our defences against emerging viral diseases and the ever-looming threat of a flu pandemic' (*Nature*, 10 July, vol. 424, 6945, 113). There are increasing fears of the possible use of diseases as weapons of bioterrorism, with medical opinion asserting that: 'Naturally occurring diseases such as SARS offer valuable lessons in preparation for a deliberate release of biological agents by terrorists' (Weber et al. 2004, 483).

In this respect, bioweapons could be used for germ warfare and two are feared as possible agents of weaponized disease in the early twenty-first century: anthrax and smallpox.

Anthrax

Anthrax is a particularly severe bacterium, one which can be transferred from the carcasses of animals to humans, but not so readily from human to human. Hence it is unlikely to specifically cause or facilitate an epidemic. Where the anthrax virus is raised it is usually associated with the occasional farm or abattoir worker contracting it. However, the 'anthrax scare' of September 2001 provoked renewed fears as to its wider uses in a bioterrorist context.

Five years subsequent to this, Debora Mackenzie featured a special report on bio-defence titled 'Fortress America' in *New Scientist* (Mackenzie 2006, 18). Soon after 11 September 2001, anthrax spores were sent through the mail to journalists and to politicians (5 people died and 17 got sick), and the American government organized a very expensive and, arguably, inappropriate attempt to protect the country from a possible large-scale biological attack involving anthrax, botulism and smallpox.

Project Bioshield

Project Bioshield was thus eventually launched on 21 July 2004 and involved the spending of $5.6 billion by 2014 to store drugs in a Strategic National Stockpile. It essentially provided new tools to improve medical countermeasures protecting Americans against a chemical, biological, radiological or nuclear attack. The Project seeks to make available modern, effective drugs and vaccines to protect against attack by chemical, biological, radiological or nuclear attack. As a consequence of the Project Bioshield legislation, the Administration has already commenced the process of acquiring several new medical countermeasures which include:

1. 75 million doses of a second generation anthrax vaccine to become available for stockpiling;
2. new medication treatments for anthrax directed at neutralizing the effects of anthrax toxin;
3. polyvalent botulinum antitoxin;
4. a safer second generation smallpox vaccine; and
5. initial evaluation of treatments for radiation and chemical weapons exposure.

It would appear that this is one further step taken by the United States Government to combat biological warfare – whether it is, indeed, successful remains to be seen …

During this time contracts were awarded to small bio-companies both to develop and test vaccines and new remedies. By 2006 about $44 billion was spent in a project that, according to experts, was scientifically flawed and wasteful due to inefficient management. Project Bioshield was designed, in this respect, to turn small drug companies into defence contractors.

As to the legal aspects, the anthrax scare caused a fundamental reverse in American policy on intellectual property. Patents held by German company Bayer, on two key necessary ingredients in the antibiotic Cipro (ciprofloxacin) were ultimately overturned in the interests of public health (side effects of quinolone products). However, neighbouring Canada found its own solution, as Permarker explains:

> The United States was not the only country that feared bio-terrorism. On October 18, the Canadian Minister of Health made an agreement with another pharmaceutical manufacturer, called Apotex, for the production of Cipro. Since Bayer claimed that it was not possible to produce the adequate supply of Cipro, the national health care system of Canada, Health Canada, then had to use generic products equivalent to Cipro (Permarker 2004, 142).

The links between patents and warfare are waiting to be explored, and it is interesting to recall that the US could not enter the Second World War until patent pooling in relation to aircraft made that entry feasible.

Smallpox

Smallpox, caused by the *Variola* virus, is especially feared in the context of the weaponization of diseases and is, in fact, allegedly the most destructive of human life in history (Selgelid 2006). Following a massive global campaign by the World Health Organisation (WHO), its eradication has been lauded as one of the most successful public health programmes ever to be initiated. After the elimination of this agent, reserve stocks of the vaccine were preserved by the WHO and only two laboratories retained known *Variola* stocks during the Cold War – one in the United States and the other in Russia (Koplow 2003, 146). Concern has arisen that the stocks from the USSR have not been adequately safeguarded. Furthermore, the smallpox eradication by the mid-1970s has meant that no one has been vaccinated against it since the 1960s, with the consequent risk that we have lost our 'herd immunity'. Should smallpox be used as a bioterrorism agent, it could lead to the killing of hundreds of millions of people and it has thus been treated with great trepidation in the news.

We can presage the way in which a government might have to respond to such a threat by looking at the responses to SARS, particularly the Canadian response (Hocking 2005). A meeting in relation to the Biological Weapons Convention (BWC) was held in 2004 which strengthened surveillance for infectious disease and this does support the purposes of the BWC. The two Conventions offer the potential of controlling war even as the Security Council is called to sanction invasion in the interests of that control. For it is worth noting that, as one view puts it: 'The scope of the CWC is much wider than that of the BWC for biological weapons for it also includes a commitment never under any circumstances to use chemical weapons' (Myjer 2006, 62). In this respect: 'A complete disarmament of this category of weapons is foreseen as States which possess such weapons will have to destroy all the existing chemical weapons as well as the production facilities' (Myjer 2006, 62).

Scientists and Doctors Caught Up in Post-9/11 Sensitivities

The events of 9/11 intervened dramatically in the halting developments to control weapons and war discussed thus far. The 'war on terror' that has since ensued has been described as 'an international constitutional moment' (Slaughter and Burke-White 2002, 2). Indeed, the responses to the terrorist acts of 11 September 2001 have been characterized by Joseph Camilleri as instituting 'the globalization of insecurity' (Camilleri 2002, 7). The 'war on terror' has prompted extreme legal responses to the threat on a concerted scale, demonstrating the extent to which the Canadian and British models of human rights protection 'leave some scope for the legislature to enact laws that are contrary to human rights standards' (Charlesworth 2002, 73). The result of this has been the enactment of 'draconian' federal legislative responses that undermine civil rights (Michaelsen

2003, 13). This has been particularly criticized in the Australian context, given that country's absence of a federal bill or charter of rights (Williams 2004, VIII). In this security environment, the lines between the 'war on terror' and the 'war on Iraq' became blurred. There are changes to the very nature not only of the terminology or discourse of war but also to the ways in which it is waged and, in fact, constituted on the ground. This blurring of what constitutes 'war' again puts pressure in international human rights instruments: to take just one example, the Second Optional Protocol to the International Covenant on Civil and Political Rights, aiming at the abolition of the death penalty (adopted by General Assembly resolution 44/128 of 15 December 1989) permits of no reservation except for a reservation mage at the time of redification or accession that provides for the application of the death penalty in time of war pursuant to a conviction for a most serious crime of a military nature committed during wartime.

In the current continuing climate of heightened security awareness, scientists may be called upon to provide knowledge for 'national security purposes' whether by governments or private security agencies. The entire spectrum of science and technology thus becomes vulnerable to security scares, espionage, and in most extreme incarnations, under threat of the law relating to treason in the event of any alleged misuse of potentially sensitive data. The United States has already foreshadowed controls on the dissemination of research, particularly concerning cutting edge microelectronics (Lane 2001, 80). And in 'one of the most explosive espionage cases in US history' (Lee 2001, 26), Los Alamos scientist, Wen Ho Lee, pleaded guilty to a lone felony count of mishandling nuclear secrets, thus raising memories of the trial of the Rosenbergs for treason at the height of the Cold War.

The prosecution of high profile scientist, Thomas Butler, provides a background to Ho Lee's prosecution, which has been analysed as a *cause célèbre* for those who felt that the government was using him to scare scientists into obeying strict new bioterror prevention laws (*Science* 2003, 2054). However, in spite of this, the government was advised to drop the case since pursuit of the action would force scientists out of bio-defence research and undermine, rather than promote, national security.

Other scientists have provoked fears of bioterror from biotechnology. For example, it was recently revealed that a US virologist obtained a genetic blueprint for the polio virus from the internet, requesting strips of DNA from a biotechnology company, and reassembling it in his laboratory – 'like kids assembling LEGOs' (Kalb 2005, 69). *Newsweek* expressed the fears in this way: 'If the polio virus can be made in a New York lab, what's next? Mail-order smallpox?' (*Science* 2003, 2054). The same *Science* report also recalled the 'frightening precedent' from Australia, where in 2001 researchers attempted to create a contraceptive vaccine for mice by using mousepox as a conduit. *Newsweek* also claims that 'purely by accident they created a killer strain of the virus, which destroyed the animals' immune systems'.

Besides these inadvertent incursions into the military domain, mentioned above, rumours circulated that the anthrax terrorist scare emerged from weaponized anthrax that had been developed in the US's own military research laboratories. In this security environment, the role of the research bioscientist assumes increasing political significance. In fact, the Royal Society Welcome Trust recently stated: 'The threat of advances in the life sciences being used for harmful purposes is a real one' (Royal Society Report 2004). The Trust also warned that '... this needs imaginative thinking as the vast majority of work falls into the grey area of having some potential for misuse' (Royal Society Report 2004, Policy 29). Fraser and Dando have thus articulated the fears for the genomic industry that:

> ... the revolution in biology could be misused in offensive biological weapons programs directed against human beings and their staple crops or livestock (Fraser and Dando 2001, 253).

A specific policy response has been advocated by Shane K. Green and colleagues in a special feature on bioethics and war, where they articulate guidelines to prevent malevolent use of biomedical research (Green et al. 2006). Noting the seven classes of 'experiments of concern' itemized by the National Research Council (NRC) in its *Biotechnology Research in an Age of Terrorism: Confronting the Dual Use Dilemma*, the authors suggest, given the elusiveness of categorical classifications, that all biomedical researchers be ethically assessed. Bioethicist Michael Selgelid takes the debate further, looking at the sensitive issue of the censorship of science, arguing that awareness of the potential for 'dual use' discoveries may at times warrant government censorship of certain scientific endeavours (Selgelid 2006, 446).

The fate of government scientists in this security climate raises related concerns as to the ambiguities of science in a heightened security environment. In the United Kingdom, David Kelly was an Oxford-educated microbiologist who became embroiled in a media frenzy as to whether he was the source or the 'mole' for a BBC story on biological weapons (*Today* programme, 29 May 2003) and the inspections in search of weapons of mass destruction in Iraq. He had been scientific adviser to the proliferation and arms control secretariat for more than three years and was an expert in arms control, working as a weapons inspector in Iraq between 1991 and 1998, following the first Gulf War. He had been a senior adviser on biological warfare for the UN in Iraq from 1994, holding the post until 1999. Despite being widely regarded as dealing well with the media pressure, it was alleged that he became increasingly depressed when the story broke out and took his own life shortly after in 2003. One could question the responsibility to protect scientists acting in these positions, perhaps?

Protection from Bioterrorism as a Health Issue

The problem of bioterrorism should mainly be regarded as a public health issue and not simply as a militaristic concern, along the lines of Physicians for Social

Responsibility. In this respect, we should reconceptualize the entire problem to understand the notion of biological warfare and its public health implications. As Scaiarrino argues:

> The greatest scandal in the government's preparations for a response to biological terror is how … the military has been getting the lion's share of monies while public health remains in the cold. Whatever rationale such a division of spoils may have in relation to other types of terrorist attacks, this is unconscionable in relation to biological warfare where almost all major steps, from identifying what pathogen is in use, to treating casualties, and preventing the spread of the epidemic (in the case of a contagious disease) would be in the hands of public health agencies (Scaiarrino 2006, 458).

This imperative is all the more urgent given that even in Vietnam, 'disease exacted a far greater casualty than combat' (Ham 2007, 724). An associated issue here is the need to formalize access to essential medicines for those engaged in combat, an issue concerning humanitarian law and complex decisions as to whether to triage solders, victims, medical personnel, aids workers and volunteers.

We also need to develop more cooperative and collaborative responses to biological terrorism between the different levels or tiers of government, also in view of the fact that in countries with a federal structure health is largely a responsibility of the individual States. In this respect, there is a need to focus greater attention on the strategies of cooperative and collaborative federalism. This has been said of the United States, but it applies equally to Australia and Canada. As Buchsbaum therefore argues:

> … it is critical for States to work together and closely coordinate their response efforts. While each State's public health system is different, States need to collaborate with one another and with the federal government to determine ways in which they can mutually strengthen their response efforts. Collaboration must be contemplated and planned for ahead of time, not in response to an emergency after it has begun (Buchsbaum 2002, 17).

In addition, in order to develop more effective legal strategies against the underlying threat of biological terrorism, attention should be paid to developing more effective quarantine measures (Ries 2005, 531). Confronting biological terrorism requires both policymakers and legislatures to consider this problem, not simply either from a militaristic or from a public health perspective. Rather, in order to facilitate an effective response, policymakers should develop a response that is integrated and one that takes into account *both* perspectives. Further, when considering biological terrorism from a public health angle, policymakers need to consider this as an essentially collective and public, as opposed to a private 'one to one', issue. As Richard Danzig argues:

> One of the challenges of bioterrorism is that it forces us to think about those issues not as acts of health but as acts of warfare. This demands a new paradigm for the military, which has great difficulty adjusting to it. It also forces new thinking in other parts of our society. Health care has traditionally been something that is dealt with on a local basis through retail (one by one), largely private, interactions, classically between doctor and patient. Now we need to deal with it in the mass in the hypothesised situations, which are, alas not so hypothetical. This is a challenge for all of us. Now the conceptual boxes of warfare, policing, and health all run together. Methods of thought that previously were sufficient are no longer sustainable (Danzig 2003, 1508).

As part of developing underlying theoretical strategies to combat bioterrorism, attention further needs to be accorded to its *prevention* and how policymakers and legislators should go about deterring people from committing bioterrorism. One misconception here is that bioterrorists act irrationally. Yet there is a subjective, political and cultural context to interpret their actions that has been subjected to critique (Hocking 2005), and in light of this, policymakers may need to give some attention to the complexities of 'stigmatizing' and to 'criminalizing' such behaviour. As Danzig argues:

> … sociologists have also very usefully observed that most of us do not commit crimes just because of a calculus about capture and punishment. We also refrain from criminality because we want to avoid the stigma of regarding ourselves as criminals … This perception about deterrence suggests that the stigmatisation part of our ability to deter may be all the more significant. Terrorists do not, by and large, act irrationally. They do not act indifferently. While they frequently have the appearance of mere individuals, like the loan suicide bomber, they are typically acting in the context of a larger constituency that they care deeply about and which they wish to animate. They care a lot about their standing in the eyes of that constituency. We all know that terrorists in the Palestinian-Israeli context care very much about their standing with those they represent in their acts. My question, therefore, is whether it is possible to evolve some form of international understanding, which includes Islamic constituencies that condemns biological weaponry and regards it as an act of ungodliness (Danzig 2003, 1503–504).

Assumptions about the Inevitability of War

We have raised issues of contemporary interactions between law, war and biomedical sciences while recognizing that modern warfare has placed real pressures upon principles developed for traditional armed conflict where enemy personnel are targeted (Stephens and Lewis 2005, 14 of 31). In this brief conclusion we would like to frame this information into conceptual and ethical dimensions by asking crucial questions. We hope that the reader will find practical cases and supporting evidence in the text already offered above.

Our central concern is of the significance of international Protocols and Conventions that establish the proper way of killing each other. They are so necessary, yet they raise many troubling ethical issues. For example, how is it that blowing up enemies with bombs dropped from the sky is acceptable, while gassing them on the ground is forbidden by a Convention? One cannot escape the idea that we consider war as an inevitable destiny, and it makes us feel better if we can render such a human curse more humane. This word pun should make us wonder whether the initial assumption is correct. In fact, during the last twenty years or so many scientists have, indeed, cast serious doubts about the inevitability of human violence and war, but the relevant information is being kept well away from public knowledge (Giorgi 2001, 2007, 2008a, 2008b). The socio-political interests that maintain such selective information, even in so-called free democracies, may be the same that bypass people's profound desire for peace and even undermine or circumvent the few Protocols and Conventions designed to limit the horror of war. A discussion about the nature of these interests and how they operate is beyond the scope of this work but remain out there for further consideration.

Conclusion

So, what is the role of law when biology and medicine are called to war? The answer to this question depends on the basic premises one starts from. But first one should realize that contemporary social values apply to all endeavours: professions, private life, public life and international relations. If social values are degenerated by the recent acceptance of individualism, greed and competition as the driving forces of humanity, the hope for improvement is slim. To close on a positive note, let's see two specific premises and their possible aims.

If we embrace the *pessimistic view of human nature*, whereby we are compulsively greedy and carry violence in our genes, we should set short-term and long-term aims on such a premise. For short-term results, we can work on the clear, demonstrable facts that military solutions do not resolve international disputes any more, cost too much money and do not make us any safer (Preparing for Peace 2005, xv): tax payer will respond to political candidates offering cheaper and safer alternatives, such as negotiations preventing arm conflicts and real international justice. Appealing to the social pride and ethical strength of professionals may provide results, as discussed above. For long-term results, relieving children from the pressure exercised upon them by the commercial world and from the obsession for money would allow them to express their human potentialities (Galtung 1969) and become strong citizens with some values. If combined with in-depth programmes of civil education, this would produce citizens less vulnerable to bribing and less naïve in front of political gimmicks. If we embrace, instead, the optimistic view of human nature, whereby we have been conceived by a bio-cultural process of natural selection to live in solidarity and non-violence and started only recently (about 8,000 years ago) to oppress, wound and kill members of our own species (Giorgi 2001, 2008a), we should set short-term and long-term aims on such a premise. For short-term results, the strategies would not differ much from those suggested above and based on a different premise, as the adult generations would still operate on a structurally violent culture. However, there are educational programmes guiding adults through the acquisition of non-violent conflict resolution methods and disintoxication from individualism, greed and competitiveness. For long-term results there would be the opportunity of initiating a slow, non-violent revolution by offering to children (from birth) a new structurally non-violent environment (Giorgi 2007). Such a programme would take about two generations and should be first attempted in small townships, where strong collaborative axes can be established between young families and school, and between citizens and local administration. While recognizing that this proposal rests upon our own ideological postures and beliefs as to the origins of structural and direct violence, we argue that it is not conceivable to eliminate CBW and nuclear war without removing war itself from the pedestal of respectability and admiration it currently enjoys; in turn this cannot be obtained without removing structural violence from our daily life. We conclude that while the law of armed conflict is indeed 'a testament to humanity's determination to eviscerate the horrors and suffering of war'(Stephens and Lewis 2005, 1), it remains the case that resort to national sovereignty still allows powerful nations to wage war unrestricted and unlimited by even minimal rules and standards, and there are powerful arguments that recent wars, notably that on Iraq, have been illegal (Simpson 2005, 1). It remains of enormous imperative therefore that the global community, as well as the individual within small communities, act now to stem the potential of bacteriological and toxic warfare, wherever the battleground and actively promote the healing power of medicine.

References

Appy, C.G. (2007) *Vietnam – The Definitive Oral History Told from All Sides*. (London: Ebury Press).

Ashford, M. and Dauncey, G. (2006) *Enough Blood Shed* (London: New Society Publisher).

Braithwaite, J. (2006) 'Pre-Empting Terrorism', *Current Issues in Criminal Justice*, 17(1): 96.

Buchsbaum, L. (2002) 'The US Public Health Response to Bioterrorism: Need for a Stronger Legislative Response', *Journal of Medicine and Law*, 1: 7.

Camilleri, J. (2002) 'Terrorism, Anti-Terrorism and the Globalisation of Insecurity', *Arena* 19: 7.

Charlesworth, H. (2002) *Writing in Rights Australia and the Protection of Human Rights* (Sydney: UNSW Press).

Chinkin, C. (1999) 'Women: The Forgotten Victims of Armed Conflict?' in H. Durham and T. McCormack (eds) *The Changing Face of Conflict and the Efficacy of International Humanitarian Law* (London: Kluwer) 23–44.

Danzig, R. (2003) 'Academics and Bioterrorists: New Thinking About the New Terror', *Cardozo Law Review*, 24: 1497.

Davies, P.J., Ryan, D., Brown, D. and Mendel, R. (1998) *The History Atlas of North America* (US: Macmillan).

Fraser, C.M. and Dando, M.R. (2001) 'Genomics and Future Biological Weapons: The Need for Preventive Action by the Medical Community', *Nature Genetics* 29: 253.

Galtung, J. (1969) 'Violence, Peace and Peace Research', *Journal of Peace Research* 6: 167–91.

Gardam, J. (1997) 'Women and the Law of Armed Conflict: Why the Silence?', *International and Comparative Law Quarterly*, 55.

Giorgi, P.P. (2001) *The Origins of Violence by Cultural Evolution,* second edition. (Brisbane: Minerva S&E). A few copies of this second edition can still be obtained from (www.365bookmark.it). While waiting for the third edition the text can be downloaded at (www.pierogiorgi.org). A similar updated edition in Italian is P.P. Giorgi (2008a) see below.

Giorgi, P.P. (2007) 'Countering with Nonviolence the Pervasive Structural Violence of Everyday Life – The Case of Three Small Italian Townships' in R.V. Summy (ed.) *Nonviolent Alternatives for Social Change*. Part of the *Encyclopedia of Life Support Systems (EOLSS)*, realized under the patronage of UNESCO, Eolss Publishers, Oxford (UK) (www.eolss.net). About a neotopia-based on a slow, non-violent, legal revolution, see <www.neotopia.it>.

Giorgi, P.P. (2008a) *La violenza inevitabile – Una menzogna moderna* (Inevitable violence – A modern lie) (Milano: Jaca Book).

Giorgi, P.P. (2008b) 'The Origins of Violence – New Ideas and New Explanations Affecting Terrorism' in R. Summy and S. Ram (eds) *Nonviolence – An Alternative for Defeating Terror(ism)*, second chapter (Hauppauge, NY: Nova Science Publishers).

Green, S.K., Taub, S., Morin, K. and Higginson, D. (2006) 'Guidelines to Prevent Malevolent use of Biomedical Research', *Cambridge Quarterly of Healthcare Ethics*, 15: 432–9.

Griffith, P. (2003) *Agent Orange: Collateral Damage in Vietnam* (London: Organic).

Ham, P. (2007) *Vietnam The Australian War* (Pymble, N.S.W.: Harper Collins).

Hocking, J. (2005) *Terror Laws* (Sydney: University of New South Wales Press).

Houck, M.M. and Siegel, J.A. (2006) *Fundamentals of Forensic Science* (London: Academic Press).

Kalb, C. (2005) 'New Threat in the Lab', *Newsweek*, *Special Issue*, Summer, 69.

Koplow D. (2003) *Small Pox as a Biological Weapon* (Berkeley: University of California Press).

Lane, N. (2001) 'The Openness Imperative', *Foreign Policy*, Washington, DC: March/April 2001, 123: 80.

Leber, A. and Press, D.G. (2006) 'The Rise of U.S. Nuclear Primacy', *Foreign Affairs*, March/April 2006, 42–55.

Lee, A. (2001) 'Making A Case for Los Alamos's When Ho Lee', *George*, December/January 2001.

Mackenzie, D. (2006) Debora Mackenzie featured a special report on bio-defence titled 'Fortress America' in *New Scientist*.

Martin, R. and Hocking, B.A. (2009) 'Disease and (In)Security', Paper for the IALMH Congress, July

Mathews, R.J. and McCormack, T.L.H. (1999) 'The Relationship Between International Humanitarian Law and Arms Control' in H. Durham and T. McCormack (eds), *The Changing Face of Conflict and the Efficacy of International Humanitarian Law* (London: Kluwer), 65–98.

McCulloch, J. (1984) *The Politics of Agent Orange* (Richmond, Victoria: Heinemann).

Melson, A. (2004) 'Bioterrorism, Biodefense and Biotechnology in the Military: A Comparative Analysis of Legal and Ethical Issues the Research, Development, and Use of Biotechnological Products on American and British Soldiers', *Albany Journal of Science and Technology*, 14: 497.

Michaelsen, C. (2003) 'International Human Rights on Trial – The United Kingdom's and Australia's Legal Response to 9/11', *Sydney Law Review*, 13.

Myjer, E.P.J. (2002) 'The Organisation for the Prohibition of Chemical Weapons: Moving Closer Towards an International Arms Control Organisation?', 7 *Journal of Conflict and Security Law*, 5.

Office of Technology Assessment (Congress of the United States) (1979) *The Effects of Nuclear War* (Totowa, NJ: Rowman and Allanheid).

Permarker, M. (2004) 'Compulsory Licensing Hybrids in the United States' in H. Lidgard (ed.) *Transferring Technology to Developing Countries* (Master of European Affairs) 131.

Preparing for Peace (by asking the experts to analyse war) (2005) Westmorland General Meeting, Religious Society of Friends, known as Quakers (Westmorland General Meeting, London).

Price, L.B. (2007) 'Nuclear Weapons Don't Kill People' (44) *International Politics*, 232–249.

Ries, N. (2005) 'Infectious Disease: Quarantine and the Law: The 2003 SARS Experience in Canada', *Alberta Law Review*, 43: 529.

Robbins, I. (2005) 'Anthrax Hoaxes', *American University Law Review*, 54: 1.

Royal Society Report (2004) Welcome Trust meeting held at the Royal Society on 7 October.

Scaiarrino, A. (2006) 'The Grapes of Wrath and the Speckled Monster, Part III: Epidemics, Natural Diseases and Biological Terrorism – The Federal Response', *Journal of Medicine and Law*, 10: 429.

Schultz, G. (1993) *Turmoil and Triumph: My Years as Secretary of State* (New York: Scribner).

Science (2003) 'The Trials of Thomas Butler', vol. 302, 19 December, 2054.

Selgelid, M. (2006) 'Commentary: The Ethics of Dangerous Discovery', *Cambridge Quarterly of Healthcare Ethics*, 15: 444–7.

Simpson, G. (2005) 'The War in Iraq and International Law', *Melbourne Journal of International Law*, 7.

Slaughter, A.M. and Burke-White, W. (2002) 'An International Constitutional Moment' 43 *Harvard International Law Journal*, 1.

Smith, F.B. (1994) 'Agent Orange – The Australian Aftermath' in B.G. O'Keefe, *Medicine at War* (St Leonards: Allen and Unwin).

Stephens, D. and Lewis, M. (2005) 'The Law of Armed Conflict – A Contemporary Critique', *Melbourne Journal of International Law*, 3.

Sztucki, J. (2006) 'Methods of Resolving Conflcts' (59), BYBIL, 100.

Takman, J. and Hojer, A. (1968) 'Bombardment of Civilians in North Vietnam' in J. Duffett (ed.) *Against the Crime of Silence* (Bertrand Russell Peace Foundation: O'Hare Books) 165–74.

Weber, S.G., Bottei, E., Cook, R. and O'Connor, M. (2004) 'SARS, Emerging Infections and Bioterrorism Preparedness', *The Lancet Infectious Diseases* vol. 4, August 2004, 483.

Williams, G. (2004) 'Foreword' in J. Hocking, *Terror Laws* (Sydney: UNSW Press).

Chapter 3

Indigenous Peoples and Genetic Population Research: Reflections on a Culturally Appropriate Model of Indigenous Participant Consent

Helena Kajlich

Introduction

Genetic population studies, such as the Human Genetic Diversity Project (HGDP), have captured the attention of the scientific community and the imagination of the wider public. Such studies tap into the public's growing fascination with the use of genetic technology to piece together individuals' genetic ancestry. Family histories are fascinating on an individual scale, but genetic population research awakens public fascination on a grander scale and has wider collective implications. It attempts to locate and map the genetic make-up unique to diverse populations and through this work reveal the history of humanity's global migration and even trace the human species' genetic evolution back to shared ancestors. Proponents argue that such research would demonstrate humanity's fundamental connectedness and, as a result, may even bring an end to racism.[1] Yet at its core, this use of biological information raises important questions about whether research ethics may be blind sighted to cultural difference and seemingly straightforward biological research may be underpinned by cultural insensitivities.

The aim of genetic population research is to pursue the alleged benefits of the human species interconnectedness, and in pursuit of that aim, genetic population research has focused its attention on the unique genetic information held by remote indigenous populations. It is argued that as a result of their geographical isolation, indigenous populations have not experienced the same level of 'admixture' as non-indigenous populations, that is, genetic variation caused by population migration and interbreeding (TallBear 2007, 356). Such research assumes, however, that the human genome contains genetic variations that are unique to indigenous peoples and that these variations can be used to identify an individual's 'indigenousness'

1 For a discussion of the HGDP and narratives of race and racism through the HGDP: Wald (2006).

or 'Aboriginality'. Many academics have, however, challenged the highly problematic and questionable scientific basis of such assumptions.[2]

While this issue of the biological determinability of 'Aboriginality' is vitally important, this chapter focuses instead on an important methodological problem emerging from genetic population studies, that is, the form of consent that should be obtained from indigenous peoples. In order to identify some of the issues associated with this problem, two recent examples will be critically considered. First, the consent methodology adopted by the first and arguably most controversial genetic population study, the HGDP, and second, the methodology adopted by an independent researcher sampling Aboriginal Tasmanians as part of an international genetic population study.

In both examples consent is conceptualized as a single act or event and while the consent protocol adopted in the HGDP attempts to recognize the cultural situatedness of indigenous peoples, neither consent methodology establishes mechanisms by which indigenous peoples can participate in decision-making about their continued involvement in these projects. As commentators have recently observed, projects that involve genetic information being stored in databases or biobanks over long periods of time require consent to be reconceptualized, consent in these contexts needs to be approached as a dynamic and ongoing process (Kaye 2004, 131; Chalmers and Nicol 2008, 545). For indigenous peoples, this capacity to make decisions about how their genetic information is used and their ongoing involvement in such projects is intimately tied to indigenous peoples' rights to maintain, control, protect and develop their biological resources as recently affirmed in the *United Nations Declaration on the Rights of Indigenous Peoples* (UN Declaration).[3]

This chapter argues, therefore, that a dynamic and culturally appropriate consent methodology must include mechanisms by which indigenous peoples are able to make decisions about the use of their genetic resources throughout the life of the project. As an element of this, genetic population studies must set clear procedures by which indigenous participant consent may be withdrawn. Reconceptualizing consent as an ongoing process moves towards greater consistency with the UN Declaration. It also ensures that genetic studies meet the standards set under recent international and domestic protocols regulating genetic research in Australia. The chapter concludes by briefly outlining current international and domestic protocols operating in Australia that specifically relate to indigenous research participants

---

2 See Wald (2006); Barker (2004); and M'charek (2005).

3 The General Assembly adopted the *United Nations Declaration on the Rights of Indigenous Peoples* on 13 September 2007. Article 31 states that 'Indigenous peoples have the right to maintain, control, protect and develop … manifestations of their sciences, technologies and cultures, including human and genetic resources … They also have the right to maintain, control, protect and develop their intellectual property over such cultural heritage, traditional knowledge, and traditional cultural expressions'.

and considers whether these protocols reflect this dynamic and more culturally appropriate model of consent.

The Human Genome Diversity Project

In 1991, the first global genetic population study, the HGDP, was announced (Cavalli-Sforza et al. 1991). The project was developed in response to the Human Genome Project, which had commenced in 1990 and by 2003 had sequenced and mapped the first composite human genome. Proponents of the HGDP argued that this composite genome did not account for the genetic diversity of the entire human species as it was constructed using predominantly European genetic samples (Barker 2004, 575).[4] In contrast, the aim of the HGDP was to create a database that could be used by the international scientific community that included samples from populations around the world representing the genetic variations of the entire human species.

It was claimed that isolated indigenous populations would best be able to assist this research as they had not been greatly affected by admixture as a result of migration and population interbreeding (TallBear 2007, 356). Unlike non-indigenous populations that tended to be more historically mobilized and now urbanized, indigenous populations were seen to have maintained their geographical isolation and historical connection to land as well as maintaining their linguistic and cultural distinctiveness (Cavalli-Sforza et al. 1991, 490).

Due to the threats to the continuing isolation of many indigenous peoples and the threats to their survival as a result of high incidences of disease, poverty and extreme forms of political and cultural discrimination, there was also a great sense of urgency surrounding the work. It was felt that the loss of these unique populations would risk 'destroying irrevocably the information needed to reconstruct our evolutionary history' (Cavalli-Sforza et al. 1991, 490). Proponents of the project called upon geneticists and public and private agencies to act urgently 'to preserve our common heritage' (Cavalli-Sforza et al. 1991, 490).

Through an initial series of conferences in the early 1990s, the HGDP's objectives, methodology and ethical guidelines were finalized and proponents sought to attract the interest of international geneticists, anthropologists, linguists, archaeologists and ethicists (Barker 2004, 580). At these initial conferences indigenous representatives and indigenous organizations were not invited to attend, but experts were invited from relevant academic disciplines (Barker 2004, 580). Those involved were asked to identify possible target groups and to determine

4 Amade M'charek argues that the materials that were used to sequence the composite genome were not homogenous, but that researchers had relied upon race and sex-differences in its construction. M'charek argues that the genome became not only a 'standardized, but also a naturalized technology' and, as a result, its own complex history and origins were ignored (M'charek 2005, 165).

the number of participants required from each group. Due to genetic similarities between the world's total populations, by the end of the conference, participants had narrowed the number of populations to be studied to 722 (Barker 2004, 574–5 and 582).

Almost from its inception the HGDP faced strong opposition from indigenous peoples and international indigenous organizations. Many indigenous organizations felt it was inappropriate that indigenous peoples had not been consulted or involved in defining the objectives, methodology and research ethics for a project that would ultimately rely upon indigenous peoples' biological resources. Indigenous organizations called for a stop to the project until proponents developed 'appropriate domestic and international policies that protect the best interests of indigenous peoples' (Harry 1995, 3). In 1995 UNESCO's International Bioethics Committee (IBC) expressed concern regarding the HGDP's failure to include representatives of indigenous groups and reaffirmed the importance of ensuring their inclusion in every stage of the project including facilitating the representation of the multiplicity of indigenous experiences (IBC 1995, 60). Growing international criticism surrounding the HGDP's research methodology ultimately led to the failure of the project to secure ongoing federal funding and proponents were forced to abandon the project (Barker 2004, 598).[5]

Models of Consent: HGDP

Introduced after the Second World War, the Nuremburg Code was the first international code regulating scientific research involving human beings. The first principle of the Nuremburg Code requires that an individual's voluntary consent be obtained and that the individual has, before providing this consent, been given sufficient knowledge and comprehension of the elements of the research to understand and make an informed decision as to whether or not to participate.[6] Thus, informed consent has become, since the Second World War, the central means by which researchers ensure individual autonomy is respected. For genetic population research involving indigenous peoples, however, group consent is

5 In April 2005, the Genographic Project recommenced research into the evolutionary genetic origins of humanity. As with the HGDP, the Genographic Project has attracted much criticism from indigenous peoples and indigenous organizations but has attempted to distance itself from the HGDP by broadening its research scope. The Genographic Project insists that it is interested in researching not only indigenous peoples, but the peoples of the world, including urbanized and non-indigenous peoples. It promotes 'do it yourself kits' that individuals may purchase online and use to take their own genetic samples that can be sent to laboratories for testing.

6 The principles of the Nuremburg Code are available at: United States National Institutes of Health, Office of Human Subjects Research. *Regulations and Ethical Guidelines: The Nuremburg Directives*. (http://ohsr.od.nih.gov/guidelines/nuremberg.html) accessed 7 February 2008.

often more relevant than individual consent. Informed consent, in the context of genetic population research, can be reconceived as a means of respecting and acting consistently with not only individual autonomy, but also indigenous peoples' group autonomy and it is this broader understanding of group consent that was adopted in the HGDP.

The *Model Ethical Protocol for Collecting DNA Samples* (HGDP Protocol) adopted by the HGDP's North American Regional Committee intended to guide sampling done in North America. It was also intended to guide researchers associated with the HGDP collecting samples internationally. The HGDP Protocol requires not only that individual consent be obtained, but also that the indigenous community, as a group, provide their collective consent. The proponents of the HGDP stated that because the research would involve the study of indigenous populations, it was essential that the population's consent be obtained (Section IV(A)(2)). The HGDP Protocol went so far as to privilege group consent over individual consent. The HGDP Protocol states that if a group does not consent to be involved in the HGDP, individual members of that group cannot override the collective decision and are, therefore, not permitted to participate (Section IV(A)(2)).

The methodology for obtaining group consent is also set out in the HGDP Protocol. It states that, if at all possible, group consent should be obtained 'through [the population's] culturally appropriate authorities where such authorities exist' (Section IV(A)(2)). In determining a group's 'culturally appropriate authority', this will be determined on a case by case basis (Section IV(A)(2)). As a general guide, however, researchers are to consider the cultural context of the group or community being studied. If there are no culturally appropriate authorities identifiable, researchers need to obtain the consent of the entire community through consensus or by consensus where this is the culturally appropriate means (Section IV(A)(2)).

The consent must be recorded in some formal manner, however, this also needs to be culturally appropriate (Section IV(D)). The HGDP Protocol observes that it is a federal requirement in the United States that all participants in genetic research must sign written consent forms (Section IV(D)). The HGDP Protocol recognizes, however, that for some international indigenous peoples that do not have similar legal requirements, there may be strong reluctance and suspicion to sign such forms as a result of historical experiences where such documents were relied upon to legitimate the wrongful taking of land and resources. It may, in these instances, be more culturally appropriate to use other methods, such as video recordings of the consent process or audiotapes (Section IV(D)).

The HGDP Protocol takes important steps in recognizing that consent must take into account the cultural situatedness of each indigenous community. There are, however, important limitations associated with projects, such as the HGDP, that obtain genetic samples for broad and largely unknown purposes (such as to research 'human genetic evolution' or 'genetic diseases'). In such situations the concept of informed consent is deeply flawed as it is impossible to meet the standard of *informed* consent when the participant cannot know how their samples will be used and so, consent to it being taken and used in an informed way (Siminoff et al. 2004, 54).

An important means by which researchers can ensure that the samples are used in a manner that is consistent with the individual and community's original consent is by following up with participants to keep them informed of future uses as they become known and to provide them with the opportunity to continue to be involved or alternatively, to withdraw their consent. Consent in this context is reconceived not as a single act or event, but as an ongoing process requiring the researcher to follow-up and obtain a renewal of consent (Chalmers and Nicol 2008, 544). Should participants wish to withdraw their consent, Chalmers and Nicol identify three degrees to which consent may be withdrawn (2008, 546). First, a participant may wish there to be 'no further contact' which requires that the participant not to be contacted, but may allow their health and genetic records to continue to be accessed. Second, a participant may wish there to be 'no further access' which requires that the project not only cease to contact to the participant, but their records are also not to be accessed. Finally, a participant may decide to withdraw their consent and require 'no further use' which requires that the project cease all contact with the participant as well as stop using and accessing the participant's records and destroy any of the participant's information and samples held as part of the project.

The HGDP Protocol is, however, silent on the issue of withdrawal of consent. The Protocol is concerned with ensuring that the process of obtaining consent is culturally appropriate and takes account of the cultural distinctiveness of indigenous peoples, but fails to provide an important mechanism by which participants may determine their ongoing involvement throughout the life of the project. In late October 1997, the National Research Council of the United States found that the failure to establish a process for participants to withdraw their consent was one of the reasons the project should fail to obtain further federal funding (Barker 2004, 598).

Consent Process: Aboriginal Tasmanians

The second consent methodology to be considered is a recent sampling of Aboriginal peoples that occurred in Tasmania, Australia. In 2002 a Tasmanian individual identifying as Aboriginal sought to have their Aboriginal heritage determined through genetic testing. This 'proof' of Aboriginality was sought in order to qualify for candidature for election to the Regional Council of the Aboriginal and Torres Strait Islander Commission (ATSIC). ATSIC was the federal representative voice of indigenous Australian interests and was subsequently abolished by the federal government under former Australian Prime Minister John Howard.

A private international researcher, who claimed association with the University of Arizona (University), took the individual's genetic samples, as well as samples from other individuals all seeking to have their Aboriginality confirmed. These samples were then sent back to the United States on the basis of consent having been given. The participants argued that they had consented to the samples being taken on the understanding that they were to receive the results of the tests determining whether they were, in fact, Aboriginal. After not receiving the results for some months, the participants contacted the University. The University had obtained eight samples, but was unaware of the undertaking given by the researcher to return the results to the participants (Johnston 2002b). When contacted by the Australian Broadcasting Corporation, the director of the University research laboratory stated that there was never any intention to send the results back and that the intended purpose had always been to use the samples as part of research into genetic evolution and to 'look for the markers that we would normally extract from such samples, and put the DNA in the database' (Johnston 2002b).

Reports state that the participants had in fact signed two consent forms (Johnston 2002a). The first stated that the samples would be destroyed after testing for Aboriginality had been carried out and the second, produced by the University, was a consent form to allow genetic information to be extracted and stored in a research database as part of genetic evolutionary studies. Despite the participants having signed these consent forms, the participants maintained that the intended purpose had not been adequately explained to them. Once made aware of the participants' concerns, the University offered to return the results and samples to those participants who requested them (Johnston 2002b).

This experience exposes a basic failure to achieve mutual understanding. The participants claimed to be completely unaware of the purpose for which their involvement was solicited and the implications of their involvement. It is questionable the extent to which this consent could be deemed satisfactory as the participants were not given sufficient information to make an informed decision. While it is alleged that the consent form contained details regarding the University's intention to store the samples in an international database and to use the samples for genetic population studies, the participants argue that this had not been explained to them. There was, quite obviously, a complete disconnect between the actual intention of the researcher/University and the explanations given to the participants. The further issue is that presaged by Gesche, who notes that there are two important limitations to such a process: first the biological limitations as to appropriate population-specific alleles, and second the sociocultural limitations, given the 'complex understanding of family in Aboriginal life' (Gesche 2006, 231).

As to the complexities of consent itself, this Tasmanian experience demonstrates the problems associated with approaching consent as an event rather than ongoing process. It ignores the complex fields within which the consent process takes place and by ignoring these, the methodology of consent is unable to anticipate and respond to the possibilities for miscommunication or conflicting expectations. Further, as with the HGDP, once the individual's consent is obtained, there is no longer any responsibility placed upon the researcher or research institution to consult with the participants. There is no mechanism established by which participants may find out when their samples may be used for specific purposes that they may not have consented to or withdraw their consent if they decide they no longer wish to participate in the project.

For indigenous peoples there may be additional concerns about the importance of exercising control over their genetic samples as there is the possibility that this information could be used in ways that may have discriminatory consequences. While the participants themselves sought to use the genetic testing to prove their Aboriginality, genetic information could be used by third parties, without the knowledge or consent of the individual, to determine the 'authenticity' of an individual's claim to group membership as an Aboriginal person. In Tasmania, this is a critical issue as group belonging is intensely contested and there may be exclusionary consequences in terms of determining an individual's eligibility to participate in political spheres as well as to access economic benefits which attach to a person's Aboriginality in Australia.

Both the HGDP and Tasmanian incident highlight the importance of a culturally appropriate model of consent. This model of consent must move beyond the requirement of informed consent, which is highly problematic in the context of genetic databases, to require that researchers, particularly those involved in long running projects, such as genetic population studies, establish mechanisms that allow for the ongoing involvement of indigenous participants and, as part of this, create procedures that enable participants to withdraw their consent.

International Protocols

In October 2005, the General Conference of UNESCO adopted the *Universal Declaration on Bioethics and Human Rights* (UNESCO Declaration). The UNESCO Declaration establishes a legal framework by which member states are required to regulate ethical issues associated with human genetic research.

Article six of the UNESCO Declaration deals with this issue of consent. It states that any person involved in human genetic research must give their 'prior, free and informed consent … based on adequate information' (Article 6(1)). In determining whether adequate information is provided to the participant, it must be 'provided in a comprehensible form and should include the modalities for withdrawal of consent' (Article 6(2)). Importantly, consent 'may be withdrawn by the person concerned at any time and for any reason without disadvantage or prejudice' (Article 6(1)).

The UNESCO Declaration also addresses the issue of group and individual consent stating that:

> In appropriate cases of research carried out on a group of persons or a community, additional agreement of the legal representatives of the group or community concerned may be sought. In no case should a collective community

> agreement or the consent of a community leader or other authority substitute for an individual's informed consent (Article 6(3)).

As with the HGDP Protocol, the UNESCO Declaration recognizes that consent must be culturally appropriate in order to be adequate. Unlike the HGDP Protocol, however, it goes further and reconceptualizes consent not as a single formal act or event, but as an ongoing process. It affirms the participants' ability to withdraw consent at any time without the threat of being discriminated against for doing so.

Australian Protocols Regulating Consent

In Australia, there are currently two national regulatory protocols that govern genetic research involving indigenous peoples: the *National Statement on Ethical Conduct in Research Involving Humans* (National Statement) and the *Values and Ethics: Guidelines for Ethical Conduct in Aboriginal and Torres Strait Islander Health Research* (ATSI Guidelines). The National Health & Medicine Research Council (NHMRC) requires all institutions or organizations that receive NHMRC funding to establish a Human Research Ethics Committee and be subject to ethical review. There are additional laws at both federal and state level that may apply to genetic research on humans, however, the National Statement and ATSI Guidelines endeavour to meet a higher standard than any relevant state or federal laws.

According to the National Statement, there are two conditions that must be satisfied in relation to a participant's consent to be involved in human research: it must be voluntary, and 'based on sufficient information and adequate understanding of both the proposed research and the implications of participation' (NHMRC 2007, 19). What is required to satisfy these conditions will be considered on a case by case basis and 'may be affected by the requirements of the … cultural sensitivities of the community' (NHMRC 2007, 19). For participation to be on a voluntary and informed basis, a participant must understand the 'purpose, methods, demands, risks and potential benefits of the research' (NHMRC 2003, Guideline 2.2.2). The National Statement states that the process of communicating information and seeking consent is not a matter of satisfying a formal requirement, but should aim to achieve 'mutual understanding' (NHMRC 2003, Guideline 2.2.4).

As with the UNESCO Declaration, obtaining participant consent is not about the signing of a consent form, but establishing and maintaining a process that 'may need to be renegotiated or confirmed from time to time, especially where projects are complex or long-running, or participants are vulnerable' (NHMRC 2003, Guideline 2.2.8). Further, onus is placed on the researcher to contact and inform participants if the terms to which they originally agreed are altered and given opportunity to withdraw their consent (NHMRC 2003, Guideline 2.2.8). As with both the HGDP Protocol and UNESCO Declaration, the National Statement recognizes that consent may not only involve an individual, but it may also involve a group and that researchers may be required to engage with this group (NHMRC 2003, Guideline 2.2.13).

The ATSI Guidelines have been developed in Australia to assist researchers who are working specifically with indigenous peoples. There are six core principles that inform the ATSI Guidelines: spirit/integrity, reciprocity, respect, equality, survival/protection and responsibility. In demonstrating the principle of respect, the ATSI Guidelines state that researchers should consider the following:

- Whether the proposal responds to the diversity of Aboriginal and Torres Strait Islander Peoples and communities, including the way decisions are made.
- How the proposal acknowledges the individual and collective contribution of Aboriginal and Torres Strait Islander Peoples.
- How the researchers propose to minimize the effects of difference blindness on and in the research process.
- How the research proposal engages with Aboriginal and Torres Strait Islander Peoples' knowledge and experience.
- Whether appropriate agreements have been negotiated about ownership and rights of access to Aboriginal and Torres Strait Islander Peoples' intellectual and cultural property.
- Whether the processes of reaching agreement demonstrate engagement with the values and processes of participating communities.
- Whether the participating communities have expressed satisfaction with the research agreement and decision-making processes.
- Whether in reaching agreement with participating communities all relevant issues including management of data, publication arrangements and the protection of individual and community identity have been adequately addressed (NHMRC 2003, 12–13).

These guidelines demonstrate a commitment to ensure researchers understand the unique social, cultural and historical situatedness of indigenous peoples. It moves away from the researcher/subject dichotomy to involve indigenous peoples as research partners by securing their involvement in negotiating the terms of ownership and rights to their biological resources.

This brief survey of the regulatory frameworks as they relate to human genetic research in Australia demonstrates an awareness of the importance of adopting a methodology that is culturally appropriate. It demonstrates increased awareness that, in relation to the issue of participant consent, it is not exclusively a matter of respecting individual autonomy, but may also involve group autonomy. It also makes clear statements that to adopt a 'best practice' approach requires that researchers provide participants with the opportunity to withdraw their consent. This is particularly relevant for projects, such as genetic population studies, where it is proposed that the genetic samples be held over a long period of time and for purposes that may not be known at the time of collection.

Conclusion

The recent interest in indigenous peoples as custodians of unique genetic information for genetic population studies raise important issues for researchers and regulators. The survey of the regulatory frameworks that exist in relation to indigenous participant consent reveals that there is awareness of the importance of reconceptualizing consent not as a single event, but as an ongoing process. Features of this process must contain, as a minimum and as now required under the National Guidelines and ATSI Guidelines in Australia, the mechanisms for withdrawing consent. Moving beyond this requirement, however, this process should more broadly establish creative and innovative methodologies by which indigenous peoples can maintain, control, protect and develop their biological resources.

References

Barker, J. (2004) 'The Human Genome Diversity Project', *Cultural Studies*, 18: 4, 571–606.

Cavalli-Sforza, L., Wilson, A., Cantor, C., Cook-Deegan, R. and King, M.-C. (1991) 'Call for a Worldwide Survey of Human Genetic Diversity – A Vanishing Opportunity for the Human Genome Project', *Genomics*, 11: 2, 490–91.

Chalmers, D. and Nicol, D. (2008) 'Human Genetic Research Databases and Biobanks: Towards Uniform Terminology and Australian Best Practice', *Journal of Law and Medicine*, 15: 538–55.

Gesche, A. (2006) 'Protecting the Vulnerable: Genetic Testing and Screening for Parentage, Immigration, and Aboriginality' in M. Betta (ed.) *The Moral, Social, and Commercial Imperatives of Genetic Testing and Screening: The Australian Case* (Amsterdam: Springer), 221–36.

Harry, D. (1995) 'The Human Genome Diversity Project and Its Implications for Indigenous Peoples', Indigenous Peoples Council on Biocolonialism, Information about Intellectual Property Rights, no. 6, (www.ipch.org/publications/briefing_papers/files/hgdp.html) accessed 5 February 2008.

Human Genome Diversity Project (HGDP) (1997) 'Proposed Model Ethical Protocol for Collecting DNA Samples North American Regional Committee', *Houston Law Review*, 33: 5, 1431–73.

Johnston, N. (2002a) 'Tasmanian DNA tests halted', *The World Today* (transcript) (www.abc.net.au/worldtoday/stories/s666117.htm) 3 September 2002 (accessed 15 November 2007).

Johnston, N. (2002b) 'Tasmanian DNA test controversy grows', *Radio National* (transcript) (www.abc.net.au/pm/stories/s667275.htm) 4 September 2002 (accessed 15 November 2007).

Kaye, J. (2004) 'Abandoning Informed Consent: The Case of Genetic Research in Population Collections' in R. Tutton and O. Corrigan (eds) *Genetic Databases:*

Socio-Ethical Issues in the Collection and Use of DNA (London: Routledge), 161–80.

McGregor, J. (2007) 'Population Genomics and Research Ethics with Socially Identifiable Groups', *Journal of Law, Medicine and Ethics*, 35: 3, 356–70.

M'charek, A. (2005) 'The Mitochondrial Eve of Modern Genetics: Of Peoples and Genomes, or the Routinization of Race', *Science as Culture*, 14: 2, 161–83.

Morrissey, P. (2005) 'Trust, Truth and Fatuity' in B.A. Hocking, *Unfinished Constitutional Business? Rethinking Indigenous Self-determination* (Canberra: Aboriginal Studies Press).

NHMRC (2003) *Values and Ethics: Guidelines for Ethical Conduct in Aboriginal and Torres Strait Islander Health Research* (Canberra, 5 June).

NHMRC (2007) *National Statement on Ethical Conduct in Human Research* (Canberra, March).

Siminoff, L., Caputo, M. and Burant, C. (2004) 'The Promise of Empirical Research in the study of Informed Consent Theory and Practice', *HEC Forum*, 16: 1, 53–71.

TallBear, K. (2007) 'Narratives of Race and Indigeneity in the Genographic Project', *Journal of Law, Medicine and Ethics*, 35: 3, 412–24.

UN (2007) *United Nations Declaration on the Rights of Indigenous Peoples*, sixty-first session of the General Assembly.

UNESCO (1995) International Bioethics Committee. *Bioethics and Human Population Genetics Research*, Proceedings of the Third Session, Chapter 3.

UNESCO (2005) *The Universal Declaration on Bioethics and Human Rights* (Oxford: Blackwell Publishing).

United States National Institutes of Health, Office of Human Subjects Research. *Regulations and Ethical Guidelines: The Nuremburg Directives.* (http://ohsr.od.nih.gov/guidelines/nuremberg.html) accessed 7 February 2008.

Wald, P. (2006) 'Blood and Stories: How Genomics is Rewriting Race, Medicine and Human History', *Patterns of Prejudice*, 40: 4, 303–33.

Chapter 4
The SARS Epidemic in Hong Kong 2003: Interplay of Law, Medicine and Ethics

Edwin Hui

Introduction

In 2003, Hong Kong was seized with a nameless, unknown but highly infectious disease. By the time it was over, a total 1,755 residents including 386 (22%) health care professionals (HCP) developed what was later called Severe Acute Respiratory Syndrome (SARS), among whom 300 died, including eight health care workers. Not only were the health care system and its personnel put under great stress and their resilience tested under vigorous and difficult conditions, but most importantly the epidemic also exposed the inadequacies of existing legislations and moral frameworks to deal with issues and dilemmas that manifested themselves as disharmonies and alienations in human relationships involving SARS and non-SARS patients, their families, health care workers, government agencies and the public at large. This chapter attempts to show that the resolution of the issues surfaced by SARS necessitated a paradigmatic shift in the community's fundamental understanding of health, illness and health care with concomitant changes in societal values, ethics, laws and public policies. This must take place in order to meet the challenges of other epidemic outbreaks in the future including pandemic influenza and the Bird Flu.

Individual and Public Interests in Collision

In an epidemic, not only the health of individual citizens is being threatened, the welfare of the public at large is also affected. During the SARS outbreak in Hong Kong, a number of contentious issues arose that were due to conflicts between individual autonomy and rights *vis-à-vis* the welfare and interests of the community. This raises the issue of the priority of individual interest versus public interest, and involves not only medical ethics but also public health ethics (Gostin 2002). Public health ethics considers the conditions under which the individual interest has to give way to public interest, and some of the more common individual interests at stake include curtailment of freedom of movement, privacy, property use and so on (Veatch et al. 1996). In a 'westernized' and modern city like Hong Kong where individual rights and interests are ordinarily deemed more important than the 'common good', the SARS outbreak revealed many individuals' reluctance to yield to the welfare of the society as a whole. Under these circumstances, the law plays a critical role in trying to resolve these difficult ethical dilemmas and to adjudicate the priority of individual and communal rights in different situations.

During the SARS outbreak in Hong Kong many parents insisted on sending their children to school with flu-like symptoms that were difficult to distinguish from the early stages of SARS, when from the public health point of view and for the safety of other classmates, the children should have been kept at home until their symptoms subsided. Yet, for a variety of self-regarding reasons including fear that their children would fall behind in their studies, or due to parents' own reluctance to stay home with their children, or to incur 'babysitting' expenses, etc., many parents refused to keep their children from school, and there was no legislation that would force parents to keep their unwell children at home. The government eventually was forced to declare a school closure on 29 March 2003 which lasted over one month, with secondary students returning to school first, and primary school students and handicapped students returning last. Many parents took this as an affront to their individual autonomy and rights, and accused the government of acting paternalistically.

During the SARS outbreak in Hong Kong, many non-emergency medical and surgical services were suspended to make room for the large number of admissions of confirmed and suspected SARS patients in the public hospitals. For example, shortly after the outbreak in Prince of Wales Hospital on 13 March 2003, the hospital suspended all non-emergency surgical operations. Many operations such as cataract removal, haemorrhoidectomy, nasal polypectomy, arthroscopy and so on had to be postponed, even though many of these patients had been waiting for years to have the surgery. Services such as liver transplantation services were also suspended and it was reported that before the SARS outbreak, an average of one liver transplant was performed each month in PWH. But for six months since the outbreak, no liver transplant was performed since the ICU was entirely reserved for patients with SARS. Two patients on the waiting list died during this period (Chui et al. 2004). The hospital also suspended all day services and the cardiac specialist outpatient clinic and drove some cardiac patients to panic as they needed to either renew or adjust their medications. Non-atypical pneumonia emergency patients in distress who were brought to the hospital emergency department were not seen but diverted to nearby Alice Ho Miu Ling Nethersole Hospital and North District Hospitals. Even though these hospitals were close by and took no more than ten minutes to get to, for patients in distress the ten minutes might seem to be forever. Eventually on 19 March the hospital closed its A & E department completely. One study on the impact of SARS on the Emergency Department (ED) of PWH reported that there was a significant drop in the overall number of patient visits to the ED, trauma cases and other minor cases after the outbreak of SARS (Man et al. 2003). It may be speculated that non-SARS patients were either afraid of not getting timely services in the ED since priority would be given to SARS patients or of contracting SARS in the ED. Either way they were displaced. In other hospitals, medical resources such as beds and equipments were distributed in favour of SARS patients and their families. Surgical specialists were called upon to back up their medical colleagues as their workload drastically increased and many of them even fell sick due to the infection.

All these curtailments of service betrayed the fact that the health care system in Hong Kong failed to include a comprehensive contingency plan, particularly an adequate surge capacity in hospitals, to deal with public health emergencies or major outbreaks. The result was an unwelcome competition between SARS patients and non-SARS patients for medical services that both desperately needed. The problem cannot simply be resolved by a balancing act to reallocate resources and restore justice in distribution. Whether health-related resources should be distributed to those with the greatest need, or to where they can have the greatest impact on the well-being of the community is a question often asked but seldom answered. To a certain extent it depends on the local community's ideology, values and wishes (Charlene and Galarneau 2002) but the starting point in dealing with the problem is to find the root causes in the asymmetry between clinical and public health medicine.

Controlling SARS and Curtailing Individual Rights

During the SARS outbreak in Hong Kong, a number of contentious issues arose in relation to privacy and confidentiality. Initially in mid-March, the debate was centred on whether there was a community outbreak of the disease. The government was quite ambiguous about the matter and information released by the government insinuated that the outbreak was confined to hospitals without spreading to the community. The media charged the government with downplaying the seriousness of the outbreak and for delaying the necessary legislative amendment to make SARS a notifiable disease.

In Hong Kong, the legal framework for the prevention and control of infectious diseases that threaten the public is the Quarantine and Prevention of Disease Ordinance (Chapter 141 of the Laws of Hong Kong). Adding SARS to the list of notifiable diseases would provide the government with statutory powers to deal with the epidemic by mandating notification of SARS cases, medical surveillance, compulsory quarantine of households and close contacts, and other public health measures necessary to control the spread of the disease in the community. However, in mid-March, the government was more concerned about issues of civil liberty and public acceptability, and only at the end of March when more than six hospitals reported admission of patients with SARS-like symptoms, including 15 suspected SARS cases from seven households from a private housing estate known as the Amoy Gardens, was SARS added to the list of infectious diseases specified in the First Schedule to the Quarantine and Prevention of Disease Ordinance (Chapter 141 of the Laws of Hong Kong).

Before SARS became a notifiable disease, all close and household contacts of SARS patients were contacted by telephone and advised not to go to school or work. After 27 March, it became compulsory for all close contacts of both suspected and confirmed SARS patients to remain at home with no visitors allowed. They were to report to one of the four designated medical centres on a daily basis (Regulation 9 of Cap. 141B) for a period of ten days where they underwent health screening and temperature checks and were barred from leaving Hong Kong during the quarantine period. If contacts were symptomatic and suspected of developing SARS, the law also empowers the medical officer to admit them to hospitals (Regulation 10 of Cap. 141B) where they could be detained until, 'in the opinion of the medical officer in charge ... such person is no longer infectious' (Regulation 12 of Cap. 141B).

During the SARS outbreak, a large housing complex named 'Amoy Gardens' was involved. The Department of Health was notified of a probable SARS outbreak in the housing complex on 26 March when members of seven households in Block E were admitted to a hospital as suspected SARS cases. By 30 March, there were a cumulative total of 190 suspected and confirmed SARS cases, with 107 coming from Block E alone. Many residents of Amoy Gardens panicked and started to move out of the housing estate. Empowered by Regulation 24 of Cap. 141B, the government put the whole of Block E in isolation for ten days and forbade its residents to come out of the block or visitors to go in. Households that had moved out before the government's imposition of the isolation order were successfully contacted with assistance from the Police and subject to medical surveillance. Two days later when it was found that the vertical spread of SARS cases in Block E might have been caused by the poorly maintained sewage and drainage system, the government issued a 'Removal Order' under Regulations 10 and 12 of Cap. 141B and evacuated Block E and moved all its residents to three government holiday camps for a ten-day period of quarantine and medical surveillance, and disinfected individual flats of the entire Block E (Regulation 19 of Cap. 141B). The government felt justified to take the drastic action because there were sufficient reasons to believe that among the residents there were both infected and uninfected patients, and both could exhibit symptoms indistinguishable from early SARS. If these people were allowed to move in and out of the building, the rest of the general population would be exposed to further jeopardy.

Since the Amoy Garden outbreak was widely publicized by the media, residents from other blocks of the estate continued to move out to avoid stigmatization and discrimination (see below). Since not all 19 blocks of the Amoy Gardens were involved with SARS cases, the owners' committee urged the government to release the names of blocks that were affected by SARS. At the same time, the public and press media also put pressure on the government to disclose the names of buildings in Hong Kong with SARS cases. On the other hand, many were against such disclosure as an invasion of privacy. Eventually the government was swayed in favour of disclosing the names of buildings with SARS patients admitted to hospitals within the past ten days on a government website, believing that the benefits of alerting residents of affected buildings to step up preventive public health and personal hygienic measures out-weighed the harms of intrusion of privacy, stigmatization and discrimination. Two weeks later, the disclosure of names of buildings was also extended to those with suspected SARS cases.

The SARS outbreak also highlighted deficiencies in public health legislation that is necessary to guard its borders with mainland China and the rest of the world. The Hong Kong Government responded to this need by passing new legislation (Prevention of the Spread of Infectious Diseases (Amendment) Regulation 2003) on 15 April 2003 which empowers authorized persons to take the body temperature of persons arriving or departing Hong Kong (Regulation 27C (1) of Cap. 141B), and if necessary to perform medical examination to ascertain the presence or absence of SARS (Regulation 27C (2) of Cap. 141B). The new legislation also empowers health officers to stop a person believed or suspected to be 'suffering from a specified disease [SARS], has been exposed to the risk of infection of a specified disease [SARS] by contact with a person suffering from that disease; or is a carrier of a specified disease [SARS] … from leaving Hong Kong …' (Regulation 27A (1) of Cap. 141B).

Disclosure of SARS cases and/or buildings with SARS cases came with a price in the form of reported discrimination against persons with a spouse, family members or relatives either suspected of SARS, confirmed with SARS, working in hospitals treating SARS patients or living in a building with known SARS cases. Health Care Providers (HCPs) working with SARS patients were given suspicious stares or kept at a distance from or refused to ride in the same lift with HCPs and bystanders from other non-SARS wards. It was a very trying time for the HCPs because they were perceived to be a potential source of infection for other people in the community. The hurt they felt was particularly deep and heart rending because they were ostracized and discriminated against for risking their lives to help SARS patients. Some SARS patients who were convalescing at home received letters of dismissal from their employers. Many family members of SARS patients reported experiences of being stigmatized and ostracized by other family members, colleagues at work and friends. The wife of a SARS patient lost her career as a saleslady because all her clients avoided her. Another patient's spouse had her working hours reduced with a salary cut because she was not considered suitable to return to work. As expected, Amoy Garden residents, particularly those of Block E, experienced a variety of stigma and discrimination. One study reported that residents indicated that SARS deeply affected their daily life (88%), social relationships (79%), work (71%) and family life. Over 40 per cent of surveyed residents reported that they were rejected for dining or visiting with friends during the outbreak; over 30 per cent were refused household maintenance or home delivery services; and over 48 per cent of those employed perceived discriminating treatment by employers including being asked to work at home, to produce evidence of good health, to take unpaid leave or to be fired. One employer required an employee to move out of Amoy Garden before he would be allowed to return to work (Lee et al. 2005). Many employees who were not infected with SARS and were not household or close contacts with suspected or confirmed patients were likewise discriminated against. Some were asked not to report to work by their employers even when they produced doctor's certificates that they were uninvolved. Others were asked to sit in separate areas in restaurants and by the end of March 2006, the Equal Opportunity Commission (EOC) had received more than 520 complaints from the public of possible discrimination related to SARS (SARS Expert Committee Report 2003, 156–7).

The implementation of all of the above public health measures by the government of Hong Kong required a delicate balance of a number of intertwining factors including health care needs, legal powers and ethics. The ferocity of the SARS epidemic demanded 'early detection, swift contact tracing, prompt isolation and quarantine, and effective containment' (SARS Expert Committee Report 2003, 96) in order to limit the spread of the disease, but this required the decisive deployment of available legal powers to implement public health measures that protect public interest and that often conflict with human rights and civil liberties that the community has valued. In the face of an epidemic that threatened to kill hundreds and thousands in a short time, compulsory restrictions might be necessary components of public health maintenance. Such coercive restrictions, properly carried out under the law, are considered legitimate measures under international human rights law. After all, it may be argued that measures taken by a government to control an epidemic are themselves acts to protect citizens' human right to health as provided by UN's International Covenant on Economic, Social and Cultural Rights (ICESCR 1976; Davis and Kumar 2003). In Hong Kong, both the Basic Law and the Bill of Rights Ordinance of the Hong Kong Special Administrative Region recognized that it is sometimes necessary to restrict individuals' rights in the interest of public health and safety. Hence in carrying out the public health measures the Hong Kong Government was careful to calibrate the measures as precisely as possible to well-defined risks they intended to contain, to limit citizens' private rights to those that were absolutely necessary to achieve the goal, and to use the least intrusive and restrictive measures with the highest sensitivity to individual liberty and dignity. The SARS epidemic was therefore a brilliant display of the intricate interactions between medicine, ethics and law. In this regard, the role played by public education was found to be particularly important to convince the public that in an epidemic, personal interests often have to give way to public interests for the good of all. In this regard, more public education in Hong Kong to enhance the community's collective moral consciousness of the common good *vis-à-vis* individual rights will be important as part of the community's preparation for future epidemics.

SARS and Medical Professionalism

The public health measures adopted during the SARS outbreak illustrate the dual obligations held by the medical profession. On one hand, HCPs owe fiduciary duties to individual patients as their advocates and this is sometimes called the 'micro-ethics' of the medical profession. On the other hand, the medical profession is also bound by a 'macro-ethics' in the form of a collective commitment to the welfare of the entire community (Hui 2005) and in the circumstances of an epidemic to act as the 'social lifeguard'. In considering the art and science of medical ethics in new emerging infectious diseases, it is of paramount importance for individual HCPs and the medical profession as a whole to recognize the distinction between the two different levels of ethics that must be properly applied and delicately balanced. These two levels of ethics do not normally conflict with each other, but as we will discuss below, in the midst of an epidemic a degree of flexibility must be allowed in order for the two levels of ethics to accommodate each other to attain a specific standard of care that serves the interests of both the public and patients. We now turn to discuss four situations that were found during the SARS outbreak in Hong Kong in which HCPs encountered dilemmas that challenged their professionalism and tested the limits of the laws.

1. SARS and the Elderly Patients Suspected to Have SARS

During the SARS outbreak, due to inadequate resources specifically needed to deal with epidemics, isolation procedures in Hong Kong hospitals exposed patients to high risks of cross-infection. Many patients who developed symptoms suspicious of SARS, for instance, persistent fever, dry cough and/or diarrhoea were promptly admitted to the hospital for isolation and observation. Due to the large number of these so-called 'SARS-suspicious' patients and the virtual absence of private rooms in local hospitals, they were put in large wards each capable of housing 20 to 40 patients (dubbed as 'fever wards' by Hong Kong media). These overcrowded and outdated wards were later considered by the SARS Expert Committee to be 'inappropriate for the management of communicable diseases' (SARS Expert Committee Report 2003, 122–3). Many patients, especially elderly patients living in residential care homes who unfortunately developed flu-like illnesses, were admitted to the hospital and became victims of cross-infection by SARS patients (invisible SARS patients) isolated in the same 'fever wards'. This accounts for the fact that in Hong Kong over 70 per cent of elderly SARS patients were hospital acquired (Kong et al. 2003).

This sequence of events has raised some serious ethical issues. To begin with, the decision to take patients with flu-like symptoms out of the community (and particularly from the residential care homes for the elderly) and put them in the hospital was made with the purpose of protecting both the patient and the public (and particularly asymptomatic residents in elderly homes and their care providers) so that just in case the 'SARS suspect' was proven to be a real SARS patient, the number of people that would be exposed in the residential homes and the community could be minimized. Yet when these patients were hospitalized for the purpose of 'isolation', they were put in an environment with a much higher risk of contracting SARS if they turned out to be non-SARS patients and their SARS-like signs and symptoms were caused by other conditions (Lee 2003). The segregation rather than genuine isolation of SARS suspects also turned Hong Kong hospitals into the most efficient 'amplifier' of the SARS epidemic as the number of hospital acquired SARS cases accounted for over 40 per cent of all SARS cases. Ideally, 'SARS suspects' would be isolated in single rooms with bathroom facilities to prevent cross-infection, and since this type of isolation facility was generally unavailable in Hong Kong public hospitals, patient care suffered and patients were exposed to unwarranted risks. Since many of these SARS suspects were elderly patients from residential care homes, most of them were poorly informed of the nature of SARS and were not even aware of the risks involved in being hospitalized (Tse et al. 2003).

Did HCPs betray the trusts and interests of these elderly patients during the SARS epidemic? Furthermore, most of these elderly residential care home patients came from lower socio-economic classes, and the SARS epidemic has underscored the suboptimal conditions under which they have been cared for, especially in the context of an epidemic caused by emerging infectious diseases. Ordinances that focused on the welfare of the elderly were few and none was found to be able to protect the elderly during the SARS outbreak. It was for this reason that, after the epidemic was over, the SARS Expert Committee Report (2003) has emphasized the importance of a population-based concept of health promotion so that the specific health needs of special sections of the community, such as the elderly, would be identified and attended to. It raises a much needed ethical discussion that residential care home patients as a whole can no longer be treated simply as regular patients needing geriatric care; instead, as a class of patients, there are specific personal and public health issues that need special attention. This raises the issue of justice in the allocation of medical resources for chronic diseases in the health care budget, as well as institutionalized forms of discrimination against the elderly in the community. The SARS epidemic should have awakened ethicists and lawmakers to this important concern as the society rapidly ages.

2. SARS Patients and the Fiduciary Duty of the HCP

During the SARS outbreak in Hong Kong, it became clear to HCPs that treating SARS patients posed a real and serious risk to themselves. By the end of the outbreak in June 2003, among the total number of 1,755 Hong Kong residents confirmed with SARS, 386 (22%) were HCPs and among the 300 deaths, eight were HCPs. Although all necessary precautions were taken to prevent HCPs from being infected by patients they were treating, it was still very unnerving to see the number of HCPs, coming down with and being killed by SARS, continue to rise. There were several reasons for the vulnerability of HCPs including close contact with patients for long durations, lower index of suspicion of elderly SARS patients presenting with atypical and 'innocuous appearing' clinical signs and symptoms (dubbed as 'invisible SARS patients' by people in Hong Kong), a shortage of personal protection equipment and a high exposure to the SARS virus

in aerosol-generating procedures (see below) (Koh 2003). In the Prince of Wales Hospital outbreak, the index patient was put on nebulizer treatment for a week without droplet precautions and was subsequently found to have infected 50 HCPs through direct contact with them. As fear in the health care community increased, some private hospitals refused admitting patients with fever and some private practitioners closed their clinics. To protect themselves and their family members, a small number of HCPs employed by public hospitals used 'sick leave' and 'casual leave' to avoid reporting to duty. Some argued that to expose themselves or their families to risks of infection went beyond their call of duty since HCPs have obligations to themselves and their families, and, in the case of the pregnant HCPs, their yet to be born children. We will argue that with the exception of pregnant HCPs and HCPs with pre-existing chronic respiratory diseases, such as chronic asthma, all HCPs did not have the right not to treat patients either suspected of or confirmed as having SARS. In the Hong Kong SARS outbreak, these latter two categories of HCP were deployed to other low-risk services in the hospital.

In the best tradition of medical professionalism in many countries of the world, primacy of patient interest has been taken as the cornerstone of an ethical patient–professional relationship (PPR). This in turn entails a fiduciary duty on the part of HCPs who are obligated to set aside their own interests in favour of patients' interests, including health-related interests. A modern example of fiduciary duty for HCPs in the context of treating patients with a potentially lethal infectious disease can be found in the injunction not to refuse treating HIV-positive or AIDS patients. The justification to impose fiduciary duties on HCPs has been discussed in detail elsewhere (Hui 2005). Briefly, it is founded on the basis that due to the asymmetry in knowledge and power between HCPs and their patients, the latter are left without a choice but to trust the former. The superiority in knowledge and power, and the acquisition of virtual monopoly to practise medicine by HCPs render helpless patients entirely dependent and vulnerable. In order for the medical profession to merit the trust placed in it by the society, as well as not to betray the trust of individual helpless patients who must depend on HCPs to meet their health care needs, society rightly expects from the medical profession the fiduciary obligation to safeguard patients' interests. In short, it is the asymmetry of superiority, power and monopoly possessed by HCPs on one hand, and trust, dependency and vulnerability of patients on the other that is inherent in the patient–HCP relationship that imposes the fiduciary obligation on HCPs. To meet the fiduciary standard, individual HCPs cannot abandon their patients infected by a highly infectious disease even when there is a high risk to the HCP of acquiring the infection from the patient. For an HCP to refuse to treat a SARS patient is to put his/her health interests ahead of the patient's interests and this violates the principle of the primacy of patient interests. In the true spirit of medical professionalism anchored in the fiduciary principle, altruism and self-sacrifice are obligatory rather than supererogatory and in many common law countries, fiduciary laws have been put in place to regulate the patient–doctor relationship (Hui 2005).

In the Chinese tradition, such a duty is called the 'heavenly mandate' (*t'ien zhi*) of the HCP. This may explain why during the outbreak in Hong Kong, when the public applauded the performance of HCPs as heroic, the latter felt that they were merely fulfilling their duties. Hong Kong HCPs, particularly those working in the public sector, exemplified the highest form of medical professionalism and fiduciary standard by risking their own lives in their fight against the SARS epidemic. On the other hand, this position does not condone the practice which allegedly took place in some countries of 'quarantining' HCPs in the hospital as a way to force them to take care of SARS patients. Such a practice violated the HCPs' basic human rights. If HCPs refused to take care of SARS patients, they should have resigned, or been asked to resign, their posts. Once the HCP is no longer part of the medical profession, they no longer has the fiduciary obligation to patients.

3. Elderly SARS Patients and the DNR (Do Not Rescuscitate) Order

One of the most unusual features of the SARS pandemic in Hong Kong and elsewhere was the large number of HCPs becoming SARS patients. Despite rigorous implementation of safety protocols, in Vietnam, Canada, Singapore and Hong Kong, HCPs accounted for 57, 43, 41 and 22 per cent of SARS patients respectively. Among the several reasons for the vulnerability of HCPs, one of the most significant reasons for the high rate of infection was due to the high viral load presented to HCP who directly participated in endotracheal intubation (ET) of SARS patients. In a study conducted in Toronto hospitals, physicians performing ET had a 3.8 times greater likelihood of subsequently developing SARS than physicians who cared for SARS patients but did not perform the procedure. Three of the five nurses who assisted in ET for SARS patients developed SARS (Fowler et al. 2004). The risk of HCPs acquiring SARS from intubating patients can be reduced or avoided by either (a) electively intubating patients with impending but not actual respiratory failure so that HCPs are better prepared for the event in terms of infection control, or (b) executing a DNR order for some SARS patients based on age and the presence of pre-existing medical conditions that predispose them to have low CPR success rate. Elective intubation was not a practical option in an epidemic that could claim hundreds of victims in a matter of days, and it might not meet the required medical standard of practice. The second option may be considered since studies have shown that age and co-morbidity were the top two most important prognostic factors for SARS mortality (SARS Expert Committee Report 2003, 78–83), although it raises the quandary of the moral permissibility of adopting a new set of criteria for the DNR order for elderly SARS patients. There may be two possible justifications for such a proposal: (a) on the basis of these patients' poor survival rate even when CPR and ET were given; and (b) to reduce the number of HCPs acquiring SARS who became agents to further disseminate the virus in the community.

Several studies in Hong Kong have shown that elderly SARS patients had considerably higher mortality rates (50–75%) for several reasons including: (a) delay in confirming their SARS status due to their atypical clinical presentations; (b) their decreased reserve capacity in vital functions resulting in difficulty to maintain homeostasis; and (c) presence of multiple co-morbidities. These factors caused elderly SARS patients to develop rapid clinical deterioration after diagnosis, increased their requirement for critical care and mechanical ventilation, and ultimately led to a greater than 50 per cent mortality rate (Au 2004). For elderly patients greater than 80 years old, the mortality rate was reported to be as high as 75 per cent (Dai et al. 2004). Arguably, if one sets the clinical goal of performing CPR to a 70 per cent chance of discharge from hospital, one can justify withholding CPR on the basis of medical futility from most elderly SARS patients over 75 years old with limited reserved capacity and multiple co-morbidities. However, such a clinical judgement stretches both the clinician's acumen and conscience, especially if the patient's family is not supportive of the DNR order. To stop the chain of transmission of the disease from elderly patients needing intubation to HCP can also be defended, given the significant proportion of HCPs afflicted with SARS in the epidemic. As we have discussed earlier, in traditional public health ethics, it is thought to be legitimate, under certain circumstances, to ask members of a community to set aside their own individual interests for the collective good of the community (Veatch et al. 1996). But the sacrifice members of a community may be asked to make for the public good hardly goes as far as to the point of giving up the chance to stay alive on behalf of the community. This is probably unprecedented in the history of medicine. On the other hand, it may be argued that since SARS and other highly infectious diseases with high efficiency in person to person transmission represent extraordinary situations, it may possibly be justified to deliberately limit the HCP's fiduciary duty, not so much for the benefit of the HCP involved, but for the benefit of the general public. This raises the possibility that in an epidemic of emerging infectious diseases, utilitarian considerations may act to circumscribe fiduciary duties that are usually required of HCPs and accepted in medical ethics as normative on a deontologic basis. Ultimately whether a DNR should be ordered for an elderly SARS patient should be decided jointly by the HCP, the patient and or the family as well as a member of the hospital ethics committee. The SARS epidemic challenges the limit of medical skills and professionalism. To meet the challenges of emerging infectious diseases in the future, guidelines should be drawn up to provide duties and standards of care, not only on the basis of the patient's medical condition, but also on the vulnerability of the HCP attending to the patient as well as the interests of the public. Duties of care will likely differ from patient to patient, and may be different in different phases of disease in the same patient. Hence the time when HCPs may limit and resume their duties should be established in order to avoid unwarranted situations of breach of duty and professional negligence or malpractice.

4. Use of Non-evidence-based Therapeutic Modalities for the Prevention and Treatment of SARS

In clinical ethics developed in the West, the most overriding consideration in medical decision-making is the patient's wishes and preferences, which reflects the principle of self-determination or autonomy. HCPs are expected to make the most objective and evidence-based judgements about the risks and benefits of certain therapeutic interventions efforts, and prioritize them on the same basis. Their own personal preferences play a relatively minor role in their patients' medical decision-making. Rather, they are morally obligated to respect their patients' wishes, preferences and treatment choices, based on their own beliefs, values and traditions. In this sense, patients are said to be 'qualified' to make independent medical decisions for themselves. However, in dealing with unknown new emerging diseases, like SARS or the Bird Flu, the repertoire of armamentaria that are evidence-based is very limited. At the beginning of the epidemic when little was known about the disease, clinical management included selective broad-spectrum antibiotics that have been effective in the treatment of some atypical pneumonia of known bacterial etiologies. But they were found to be ineffective against SARS. A regimen consisting of corticosteroids combined with broad-spectrum antiviral agents, such as ribovirin, was introduced with significant improvement in patient responses, but the effectiveness was subsequently cast in doubt because after the SARS coronavirus was isolated, it was found that ribavirin did not exhibit significant *in vitro* activity against the pathogen. At the same time, reports from hospitals in mainland China indicated that traditional herbal Chinese medicine was of significant uses both in the prevention and treatment of SARS, either alone or in combination with western medicine (Lau et al. 2005a; 2005b). Some HCPs were enthusiastic about combining the use of conventional western therapy with remedies of the time-honoured Traditional Chinese Medicine (TCM), whereas others were sceptical, but the majority were wary of the legal implications of using remedies that are not scientifically proven for their patients. But the media as well as most Chinese people, including many SARS patients' family members were in favour of using Chinese herbs largely because of their Chinese cultural roots. On the other hand, most of the SARS patients were too sick to make autonomous decisions and to make an informed request for the use of TCM, and in Hong Kong family members are not allowed to act as proxies for 'incompetent' family members unless appointed by the court to become legal guardians. HCPs felt that they were left alone to make an unconventional decision and to shoulder all the responsibilities for the decision made.

In an epidemic caused by a largely unknown disease and where conventional (western) therapy could not be counted on to deliver assured beneficence and the patient's autonomy was suspended, the HCP become the sole advocate for and defender of patients' interests. Unquestionably, this means a large increment of 'responsibilities' and 'risks' for the HCP involved. In a medical crisis, due to an epidemic without a name, medical decisions are confounded by a degree of uncertainty that would never be tolerated in more ordinary circumstances, and the four biomedical principles neatly developed by Beauchamp and Childress for less urgent and chaotic circumstances are less useful to guide clinical decision-making. In an epidemic, an ethic of 'responsibility' assumes a more important role than the others. 'Responsibility' first and foremost implies an action of being 'responsive'. HCPs are responding to the real situation of dying patients desperately fighting for their lives. 'Bravery' in taking risky actions, and 'courage' to bear the responsibility of taking risks are essential for this ethic. In the SARS outbreak in Hong Kong, many HCPs exhibited the moral character of being responsible, brave and courageous in their choice of using alternative and innovative therapeutic interventions, and unless there were clear contraindications, many chose to use TCM to supplement available conventional western therapies to benefit their patients, at the risk of being charged for acting paternalistically. Fortunately, to date, no HCP in Hong Kong has been sued for being courageous enough to try new therapies in an attempt to help SARS patients.

What Have We Learned and What Has to be Changed?

Based on what we have highlighted above, the SARS outbreak in Hong Kong has inflicted extensive damage to different aspects of life in this city, including individual human lives, families, relationships and institutions. Naturally many lessons can be learned and many things have to be changed so that when and if SARS or other emerging infectious diseases reappear, things will be done better. On our part we are most interested to know precisely what lessons are to be learned and what needs to be changed from the ethical point of view. In this chapter, we have made moral assessments on some of the events that took place during the SARS outbreak in Hong Kong. But on the whole, we believe that most of the difficulties the community encountered during the outbreak, including inadequate preparation of the health care system to respond to an epidemic, poor communication and coordination between departments, agencies and institutions involved in health care, tension between SARS and non-SARS patients, opposition to school closure and other quarantine procedures and discriminatory behaviour against HCPs, SARS patients and their family members, etc., were due to a medical culture that has been mistakenly informed about the nature of medicine and medical practice, or more precisely, a medical culture that has been amnesic of certain vital aspects of medicine and medical practice. Consequently, what needs to be changed is fundamentally a proper understanding of medicine and a reformation of the culture of medical practice in Hong Kong.

It is often said that medicine is both a science and an art, and the 'art' of medicine refers to the humanistic, experiential, relational, social and communal aspects of medicine. In the past, before the science of medicine was elevated to the top of the pedestal by modern biotechnology, the art and science of medicine were happy partners, like the two hands of a person. But in the last century or two, advances in the science of medicine has gone so fast and far that the art of medicine has been left beyond, or perhaps worse still, forgotten as something that can be dispensed with. Consequently, modern medicine is understood as a technology – a scientific discipline, and HCPs are specialists with expertise to use technology – a technician/scientist. In this context, the main agenda of medicine is to eradicate diseases and the main responsibility of medical practitioners is to intervene when a person becomes a patient. Since this 'biomedical' model of medicine has disease as its main focus, the patient is nothing more than a passive 'carrier' of diseases and human health is understood in the negative sense as the absence of disease. In this model, the science of medicine is the only 'hand' that counts, and the other hand, the 'art' of medicine is dispensable. In contrast, a more holistic approach to the concepts of health and medicine is to put the human person centre stage and to recognize that the human person does not have an atomistic existence but is a 'person in relations' to self, others, communities and environment that are inseparably and interdependently related. People are healthy if their body stays in homeostatic balance, at peace with themselves, relatives, friends and the surroundings, and disease is primarily due to a breakdown of a person's multiple relationships leading to a disturbance of their 'bio-psycho-social' milieu. Hence, 'bio-psycho-social' medicine understands its main task as assisting people to build up their various relationships that are integral to their personhood, and as such it is primarily concerned with the prevention of disease and maintenance of personal and communal health. In turn, it prescribes a practice of medicine that focuses on people's psychosomatic well-being (personal health), social relationships (psychological health) and the living environment (public health), reserving therapeutic interventions to dispel pathogenic factors only for acute conditions caused by breakdowns in a person's relationships (Hui 2002). In this context, both the science and the art of medicine are crucial for the practice of medicine.

In light of the differences between 'biomedical' and 'bio-psycho-social' models of medicine, it is not surprising that Hong Kong, which has adopted the former model of medicine for nearly a century, was thrown into utter chaos during the SARS outbreak. 'Biomedical' medicine that specializes in intervention and eradication of disease(s) for individual persons is particularly impotent in dealing with emerging infectious diseases for at least two reasons. First, when a novel infectious disease first attacks, its identity is unknown. The 'science' of medicine is deprived of a target for it to analyse and apply its therapeutic rationale when the pathogenic agent is unknown and without a name. This was exactly what had happened in the early phase of the SARS outbreak in Hong Kong. Second, of all diseases that are known to afflict humanity, infectious disease is most 'social' or 'relational' in the sense that its very existence depends on its ability to pass 'interpersonally'. The transmission of the SARS coronavirus from the Guangzhou professor who stayed in a local hotel in Hong Kong to two other persons who were in the same hotel and led to two hospital outbreaks involving a total of 260 persons, together with another 14 persons who acquired SARS in the same hotel who managed to spread the virus to Canada, Singapore, Vietnam, Philippines, USA and mainland China to turn it into a global epidemic, gave solid proof to the 'sociality' of the infectious disease. But this is precisely the Achilles tendon of 'biomedical medicine' which relies on 'science' to pin its infectious enemy down in the passive body of a particular patient and is poorly equipped with the 'art' of dealing with the complex bio-psycho-social milieu in which the patient lives and the disease thrives. In this sense, the 'biomedical' health care system in Hong Kong was doomed to run into great difficulties in its combat against SARS epidemic.

Hence, the most valuable lesson the SARS epidemic has given to Hong Kong is to have made clear the serious disjuncture between the 'science' and the 'art' of medicine in the health care system in Hong Kong. In fact, this disjuncture has been ignored by the medical community for a long time, and people have simply taken it for granted that it is the nature of medicine for it to be more scientific than humanistic. This basic dichotomy in turn has given rise to an array of others including curing versus caring, interventional versus preventive, personal versus communal, etc. In other words, the humanistic side of medicine has been allowed to give way to the scientific side. Our claim can be validated by looking at the organizational structure of the health care system in the public sector in Hong Kong under the 'Health, Welfare and Food Bureau' (HWFB). Under this Bureau, the two most important departments directly dealing with health and diseases are Department of Health (DH) and the Hospital Authority (HA) and they are separately organized and operationally independent of each other. DH is responsible for public health, health promotion and dental health, and HA is in charge of treatment of all patients in the public sector by operating 43 hospitals and rehabilitation centres, as well as 59 general outpatient clinics. In 2003, HA employed about 53,000 staff and had an annual budget of HK$29.6 million (US$1=HK$7.8) which was ten times larger than that of DH, providing the best proof that medicine in Hong Kong is based on the individual-based interventional 'biomedical' model and not on the population- and community-based preventive 'bio-psycho-social' model. Furthermore, traditionally there has been little or no communication and coordination between these two departments of health services. Other relevant agencies under the HWFB include the Social Welfare Department, Government Laboratory, Food and Environmental Hygiene Department and Agriculture, Fisheries and Conservation Department and each operates independently of the others. For quite some time, HA has been very proud of the world-class hospitals it operates, confidently believing that the 'science' of medicine alone will triumph over all calamities nature can bring – until SARS hit when it realized too late that the disease can only be conquered by a concerted effort of all the departments within HWFB.

When the government-appointed SARS Expert Committee met in the aftermath of the epidemic, it became aware of the incredible lack of communication between DH and HA by noting that DH learned of the first major SARS outbreak in a HA hospital (Prince of Wales Hospital) from media reports at least one day after the outbreak came to light! In other words, the management in HA, boxed in their scientific rationalizations, perceived the outbreak as an 'in-house' hospital problem to be dealt with by the hospital. Since the outbreak was not understood from a 'bio-psycho-social' perspective, its public health implications were not readily appreciated and it might seem illogical to HA to notify DH of the matter. This prompted the Committee's criticism that 'there was a lack of common understanding from a population-based perspective between DH and HA on how to respond to a communicable disease outbreak of this scale. There was also a lack of full appreciation of the total implications for the wider community at this early stage' (SARS Expert Committee Report 2003, 72). Later on, when DH was involved, there was much confusion in the chain of command and duplication of activities. For example, patient contact tracing was simultaneously being conducted by DH, HA and independent university investigators with the result that patients were inappropriately approached more than once and by more than one agency. Another example was related to issuing personal hygiene guidelines for elderly people living in residential care homes. Many of these elderly people guidelines simultaneously from both DH and HA, and they contained advice of infection control measures that were inconsistent with each other. It is clear that in trying to control a large epidemic in a small and overcrowded place like Hong Kong, a population-based approach is needed and both DH and HA should participate with DH taking the lead. In an attempt to improve collaboration between DH and HA in the future, the Committee recommended that '[I]nfection control and epidemiological experts should be based in every major hospital, working as employees of DH seconded to HA. These individuals will have responsibility for hospital infection control, data collection and reporting, and regular liaison between colleagues in HA and DH' (SARS Expert Committee Report 2003, 108). The Committee also recommended that the government should consider merging the functions of the separate departments under HWFB 'in order to improve the capacity for coordination across the departments, and to facilitate policy-making and commissioning for health protection matters' (SARS Expert Committee Report 2003, 88). The Committee also hinted at the need for change in medical training because the focus of the current curriculum 'is almost exclusively on clinical practice and, in general, health care workers receive inadequate training in infection control and public health' (SARS Expert Committee Report 2003, 140). They are sensible recommendations. But we strongly believe that unless government officials, health care workers and educators in universities, particularly the medical faculties in the two universities, realize that much of the deficiencies in the health care system have their origin in a fundamental misappropriation of the 'biomedical' conception of medicine, and are willing to return to a more person-centered and more community-based 'bio-psycho-social' model, the organizational rearrangements and additions in the training curriculum recommended by the Committee are nothing more than 'band-aid' treatments for a deep and lasting wound. What Hong Kong needs is a change in its world view and mindset about health, disease and medicine and to inculcate the community with a new medical ethos. Until that happens, there can be no meaningful changes in structures, institutions and programmes.

Conclusion

To summarize, the SARS epidemic has demonstrated to the health care profession as well as the public at large that there are two sides to medicine, the science and the art, the technical and the humanistic, the individual and the communal and they are mutually interdependent on each other. We have seen that the 'science' of medicine alone was inadequate to make an effective response to the SARS epidemic, and we suggest that this is due to an ongoing disjuncture between the two inseparable aspects of medicine. During the SARS outbreak, the disjuncture manifested itself at all levels of the community between health care agencies, public and private sector HCPs, patients and HCPs, SARS and non-SARS patients, and people who were affected and unaffected by SARS, leaving extensive and deep gaping wounds in a variety of relationships that sustain the community. Having paid a costly lesson, the health care community and the general public in Hong Kong have learned that the health and illness of individual persons can only be adequately managed by the concerted effort and cooperation of the whole community, and people have been awakened to the fact that the 'science' and 'art' are both indispensable for it to accomplish its mission.

References

Au, S.Y. (2004) 'Why Elderly People did Worse in SARS', *Hong Kong SARS Forum, Hospital Authority, Hong Kong*, 8–11 May 2004. Available at (www.hkgs.org.hk/SSIE.html) accessed 13 January 2007.

Charlene, A. and Galarneau, C.A. (2002) 'Health Care As a Community Good', *Hastings Center Report*, 33–40.

Chui, A.K.K., Rao, A.R.N., Chan, H.L.Y. and Hui, A.Y. (2004) 'Impact of Severe Acute Respiratory Syndrome on Liver Transplantation Service', *Transplantation Proceedings*, 36: 2302–303.

Dai, D., Chan, J. and Woo, J. (2007) 'The Silent SARS Shedder in Elders: A Hypothesis', *Hong Kong SARS Forum, Hospital Authority, Hong Kong*, 8–11 May 2004. Available at (www.hkgs.org.hk/SSIE.html) accessed 13 January 2007.

Davis, M.C. and Kumar, C.R. (2003) 'The Scars of SARS – Balancing Human Rights and Public Health Concerns', *Hong Kong Lawyer*, (www.hk-lawyer.com) accessed 21 March 2007.

Fowler, R.A., Guest, C.B., Lapinsky, S.E. and Sibbald. W.J. (2004) 'Transmission of Severe Acute Respiratory Syndrome During Intubation and Mechanical Ventilation', *Am J Respir Crit Care Med*, 169: 1198–202.

Gostin, L.O. (2002) 'Law and Ethics in a Public Health Emergency', *Hastings Center Report*, 9–11.

Hui, E.C. (2002) *At the Beginning of Life: Dilemmas in Theological Bioethics* (Downers Grove, Illinois: IVP Press).

Hui, E.C. (2005) 'Doctors as Fiduciaries: Do Medical Professionals have the Right Not to Treat?', *Poiesis & Praxis*, 3: 256–76.

Koh, D. (2003) 'SARS: Health Care Work can be Hazardous to Health', *Occupational Medicine*, 53: 241–3.

Kong, T.T., Dai, D.L.K., Leung, M.F. and Au, S.Y. (2003) 'Severe Acute Respiratory Syndrome (SARS) in Elders', *JAGS*, 51: 1182.

Lau, J.T., Leung, P.C., Wong, E.L. and Fong, C. (2005a) 'The Use of an Herbal Formula by Hospital Care Workers During the Severe Acute Respiratory Syndrome Epidemic in Hong Kong to Prevent Severe Acute Respiratory Syndrome Transmission, Relieve Influenza-related Symptoms, and Improve Quality of Life: A Prospective Cohort Study', *J Altern Complement Med*, 11(1): 49–55.

Lau, T.F., Leung, P.C., Wong, E.L. and Fong, C. (2005b) 'Using Herbal Medicine as a Means of Prevention Experience During the Sars Crisis', *Am J Chin Med*, 33(3): 345–56.

Lee, S.H. (2003) 'The SARS Epidemic in Hong Kong: What Lessons have we Learned', *Journal of the Royal Society of Medicine*, 96: 374–8.

Lee, S.H., Chan, L.Y.Y., Chau, A.M.Y., Kwok, K.P.S. and Kleinman, A. (2005) 'The Experience of Sars-related Stigma at Amoy Gardens', *Social Science & Medicine*, 61: 2038–46.

Man, C.Y., Yeung, R.S., Chung, J.Y. and Cameron, P.A. (2003) 'Impact of SARS on an Emergency Department in Hong Kong' , *Emerg Med (Fremantle)* 15(5–6): 418–22.

SARS Expert Committee Report (2003)

Tse, M.M., Pun, S.P. and Benzie, I.F. (2003) 'Experiencing SARS: Perspectives Of The Elderly Residents And Health Care Professionals In A Hong Kong Nursing Home', *Geriatr Nurs*, 24(5): 266–9.

Veatch, R.M., Gaylin, W. and Steinbock, B. (1996) 'Can the Moral Commons Survive Autonomy', Hastings Center Report, 26: 41–7.

Chapter 5
A Proposal Based on 'The Tragedy of the Commons': A Museum of Bioprospecting, Intellectual Property Rights and the Public Domain[1]

Joseph Henry Vogel

Introduction

'The Tragedy of the Commons' by Garrett Hardin (1968) is one of the most cited articles in all of science. Having taught the tragedy in its distilled version for many years, I have only recently reread the original article. I am startled to find that the text holds important and overlooked lessons for access to genetic resources and fair and equitable benefit-sharing (ABS). I will take a few quotes, shamelessly out of context, and apply them to ABS. What emerges is a proposal for a 'Museum of Bioprospecting, Intellectual Property Rights and the Public Domain' that is wholly consistent with both the letter and spirit in which Hardin penned his *oeuvre*. Admittedly, the spirit of 'The Tragedy' is Malthusian which is also consistent with the grim reality of the mass extinction crisis.

'*It is our considered professional judgment that this dilemma has no technical solution*' (italics in the original, Wiesner and York, quoted by Hardin 1968, 250). The quote within the quote is from two American physicists who were contemplating the arms race at the height of the Cold War; it is the opening salvo of Hardin's argument. In hindsight, the quote is ironic because economists have long cited 'The Tragedy of the Commons' as *the technical solution* to the problem of 'open access'. Almost mechanically, economists perceive the tragedy in:

---

1 English translation of 'Una propuesta basada en "La tragedia de los comunes": Un museo de bioprospección, de los derechos de propiedad intelectual y del conocimiento público,' which originally appeared in Spanish in *Revista de Ciencias Sociales*, núm 16, invierno 2007, 118–35. Support provided by The Institutional Research Fund (FIPI) of The Office of the Dean of Graduate Studies and Research (DEGI) of The University of Puerto Rico-Río Piedras.

1. Global warming, thereby justifying the permit trading Clean Development Mechanism of The Kyoto Protocol to the Framework Convention on Climate Change (i.e., 'enclosure of the atmosphere commons');
2. Collapsing fisheries beyond the 200 nautical miles limit of national waters, thereby justifying the enforcement of the United Nations Convention on the Law of the Seas (i.e., 'regulation of the ocean commons'); and
3. Mass extinction, thereby justifying a Special Protocol to the Convention on Biological Diversity (CBD) to establish a biodiversity cartel (i.e., 'enclosure of the genetic commons').

A careful rereading of 'The Tragedy' leads me to believe that Hardin, if he were alive, would probably be neither impressed nor flattered. Enclosure (#1 and #3) or regulation (#2) is only the necessary condition for a solution; neither is sufficient (Hardin 1968). Hardin recognized that denial would thwart any acceptance of the technical solution and felt '[e]ducation can counter the natural tendency to do the wrong thing, but the inexorable succession of generations requires that the basis for this knowledge be constantly refreshed' (Hardin 1968, 255). In other words, the solution must include continuing education. Flipping a few pages to the penultimate sentence of 'The Tragedy', Hardin mentions again 'the role of education' (Hardin 1968, 263) which, he had hoped, would enable '… mutual coercion, mutually agreed upon by the majority of the people affected' (Hardin 1968, 261).

Hardin's identification of a class of problems which 'cannot be solved in a technical way' is especially relevant today (Hardin 1968, 251). The US does not ratify the aforementioned treaties over the global commons, not because the government does not understand the technical solution, but because various non-technical aspects bedevil that solution. Paradoxically, those non-technical aspects lend themselves to technical analysis. Primary among them is the presence of (1) powerful and concentrated interests who stand to lose from the technical solution and (2) weak and atomistic beneficiaries who do not stand to gain *sufficiently* to justify battle with those who will lose. In the first of our examples above, *vis-à-vis*, global warming, those losing interests literally occupy the US presidency.

Has 'education counter[ed] the natural tendency to do the wrong thing[?]' Unfortunately, no; what Hardin did not foresee in 1968 is the extent to which powerful and concentrated interests would (mis)shape public opinion. Expanding our previous example, the major TV channels in the US provided live coverage of the five hurricanes that lashed Florida in 2004 but did not connect any of the dots with global warming (Shellenberger and Nordhaus 2004). Hardin would probably not have despaired; he always drummed into the reader that everything has its limits. At some point, a threshold of evidence is passed and the emperor is naked for all to see. For the US, that threshold seems to have been Hurricane Katrina which struck the Gulf Coast in late August 2005. The performance of George W. Bush was televised in *real time* and prompted his own press secretary, Scott McClellan, to implore the American public 'not to play the blame game' (Krugman 2005). But it was too late. A limit had been passed. On 15 September,

Bush accepted limited responsibility and promised to rebuild the stricken area but *without* giving up any of his cherished tax cuts (*New York Times* 2005).

In the spirit of Hardin, one can say that The Federal Emergency Management Agency (FEMA) and George W. Bush were just the proximate causes for the artificial disaster caused by Hurricane Katrina. They constitute the explanation for 'how' it happened. The ultimate cause lies with the steadfast denial of a tragedy of the commons long in the making. It is the explanation for 'why' it happened. The rest of the opening quote by Wiesner and York is painfully prescient: 'If the great powers continue to look for solutions in the area of science and technology only, the result will be to worsen the situation' (Hardin 1968, 250). '*Quis custodiet ipsos custodies*? – "Who will watch the watchers themselves?"' (Hardin 1968, 257).

The mere existence of a convention on biological diversity is evidence that a critical mass of governments has perceived the problem of mass extinction and decided to do something about it. Because the drafters could not agree on what they would do, they immortalized their differences in a wishy-washy language that was faxed out of Africa (United Nations Environment Programme Headquarters) to Brazil, just hours before the inauguration of the Earth Summit in 1992. Interpretations over the technical and non-technical issues of the text were left to the future Conferences of the Parties (COPs). Outstanding among those issues would be ABS.

Who's complaining? The COP is a perk for bored bureaucrats who like international travel and can pocket some of their *per diems*; it is a veritable bonanza for consultants who advise those bureaucrats. So, it is understandable, albeit not forgivable, that official participants now foresee that an international regime over ABS will take another ten years of negotiation (GRAIN 2005). Obviously, the system is being milked but perhaps milking is not the best metaphor – it implies some expenditure of work – ask any farmer or try it yourself. To capture the true essence of ABS discussion, I would prefer the Cuban metaphor: bottles. Bureaucrats and consultants sit like bottles waiting to be filled. One can only hope that taxpayers will finally begin to complain. Again, Hardin is uncannily relevant:

> At the present time, in liberal quarters, something like a taboo acts to inhibit criticism of the United Nations. There is a feeling that the United Nations is 'our last and best hope,' that we shouldn't find fault with it; we shouldn't play into the hands of the archconservatives. However, let us not forget what Robert Louis Stevenson said: 'The truth that is suppressed by friends is the readiest weapon of the enemy' (Hardin 1968, 258).

> [W]e need to re-examine our individual freedoms to see which ones are defensible … Individuals locked into the logic of the commons are free only to bring on universal ruin; once they see the necessity of mutual coercion, they become free to pursue other goals (Hardin 1968, 263).

Although I have explicitly argued for a cartel over genetic resources and associated knowledge since 1995 (Vogel 1995, 1997, 1999, 2000 and 2004), only in 2005 has cartelization been *seriously* discussed in international forums. Why such resistance? I suspect it owes much to history. Colonialism has been a protracted trauma for many countries and still is in places like Puerto Rico which, incidentally, suffers the highest lifetime prevalence of schizophrenia in the world (Goldner et al. 2002). One need not be a political scientist or a psychiatrist to understand why 'sovereignty' is a sacred cow in the CBD. Emotions stir when nationalists hear that 'States have sovereign rights over their own biological resources' (the preamble of the Convention on Biological Diversity).

From the cold lens of economic theory, sovereignty boomeranged. The CBD enabled neighboring states to compete with one another in the consummation of Material Transfer Agreements (MTAs) over common genetic resources and associated knowledge. These agreements are also known as bilateral contracts in contrast to a multilateral accord that would set (minimum) limits on benefits. In a White Paper on the successful uses of biodiversity, commissioned for the 1996 Summit of the Americas, I predicted that no state would get much of anything from such bioprospecting (see section, 'The Impossibility of a Successful Case Without a Cartel', Vogel 1997). This has been borne out, time and again, in the royalty rates offered in MTAs, typically one half of one per cent (Peña-Neira et al. 2002). My prediction was neither brilliant nor lucky. One hundred and fifty years of microeconomic theory have established that the competitive price of any good will be driven down to the marginal cost of its production. For genetic resources, that price is the cost of collecting a few kilos of dry leaves, somewhere between $50 and $200 (Laird 1993). The only reason why royalty rates are not even lower than one half of one per cent is due to the transaction costs of negotiating those MTAs.

Observing the general revulsion to MTAs, I now predict that it will not be long before 'biofraud' displaces 'biopiracy' in popular speech. In our age of mass extinction, it is no longer morally acceptable to access genetic resources for free or for a token amount. The evolution of such values was foreseen in 'The Tragedy' when Hardin writes '*[t]he morality of an act is a function of the state of the system at the time it is performed*' (italics in original, Hardin 1968, 256). Unfortunately, that sentence is almost mathematical in its conciseness. Unpacking it is necessary and has finally come, some 40 years later, in the best-selling *Collapse* by Jared Diamond (2005). After compiling 400 pages of case studies, Diamond concludes: 'The modern world provides us with abundant secular examples of admirable values to which we cling under conditions where those values no longer make sense … [p]erhaps a crux of success or failure as a society is to know which core values to hold on to, and which ones to discard and replace with new values, when times change' (Diamond 2005, 432–3).

I would assert that a core value that needs to be discarded is the freedom to negotiate access bilaterally. Again, this is my value judgement based on my understanding of the tragedy of the commons as well as my own personal trajectory; let us assume it is not yours. Value judgements must be vetted which is a value judgement in and of itself. Alan Bloom, the American philosopher championed by conservatives, tells us why: 'the intellectual, who attempts to influence … ends up in the power of the would-be influenced' (Sleeper 2005). Bloom cherished openness and saw the educator as *provocateur* for debate. At the opposite end of the political spectrum is Paulo Freire, the Brazilian philosopher, openly Marxist, who claimed that neutrality was illusory – either one is with the oppressed or with the oppressor (Freire 1970). Synthesizing Bloom and Freire, one could declare oneself with biodiversity conservation *á la* Freire yet provoke debate on ABS *á la* Bloom. The synthesis means that the ballyhooed principle of 'Prior Informed Consent' in the CBD must begin with the public at large. Are citizens sufficiently informed about bioprospecting, intellectual property and the public domain to accept, say, the Bonn Guidelines? I am sure they are not.

Think Locally, Act Globally! A Network of Museums Dedicated to Bioprospecting, Intellectual Property Rights and the Public Domain

Any analogy is only insightful to the extent of equivalence in the things compared. For example, let us tweak the following passage from 'The Tragedy' and then put between parentheses Hardin's original words followed by a colon and other words more appropriate to ABS:

> Ruin is the destination toward which all [men: states] rush, each pursuing [his: its'] own best interest in a society that believes in the [freedom: sovereignty] of [the commons: its genetic resources]. [Freedom: Sovereignty] in [a commons: negotiating access bilaterally] brings ruin to all (Hardin 1968, 254).

The analogy yields a practical conclusion: 'fair and equitable benefit-sharing' and 'sovereignty over genetic resources' are irreconcilable; to promote the conservation of biodiversity through ABS, national governments will have to give up their hard won right to negotiate access bilaterally. Others will disagree and their disagreement does not necessarily mean that they are the lackeys of industry. Indeed, many of my critics are visceral opponents to the whole notion of private property. They would prefer to replace sovereignty, not with a cartel, but with the pre-CBD doctrine of 'The Common Heritage of Mankind', for instance, open access.

Hardin saw the salubrious nature of such debate. 'After reaching what seems to be an unavoidable conclusion, one must endeavor to shuck off one's commitment and examine the conclusion as an unfriendly opponent would. Changing places, can one see another possibility?' (Hardin 1973, 206). If I were my own critic, I would refuse the analogy of 'Ruin is the destination ...' Are the things compared really equivalent? In 'The Tragedy', Hardin was referring to tangibles such as a cow pasture; genetic resources belong to a class of goods that are intangible such as intellectual property. The cost of excluding access to intangibles is orders of magnitude greater than divvying up a pasture with barbed wire. We all know that lawyers are outrageously expensive and that patent lawyers are the most expensive of the outrageously expensive. As my own opponent, I would argue that licences for intellectual property thwart research and development (R&D) and give way to a 'tragedy of the anti-commons' (Heller and Eisenberg 1998). Even worse, I would pipe in, opportunists are motivated to 'bio-squat' whole genomes from the comfort of their computer terminals (Oldham 2005). Changing places and resuming my original role as advocate of the biodiversity cartel, I would now rejoin 'true, true, true' but the transactions costs are surmountable (Vogel 1994, 2000, 2005 and 2008).

To whom should governments listen? Advocates of bilateral bioprospecting? Advocates of the public domain? Or some hypothetically schizophrenic professor in Puerto Rico? In an InterAmerican Development Bank monograph, Clifford Russell and Philip Powell noted wryly:

> … policy makers in a developing country will have someone on their side almost no matter what they decide to do. Instead of the infamous two-handed economists, they are presented with a veritable Asian god with six, eight, or a dozen arms from which they must choose one applicable to their particular problem setting (Russell and Powell 1996, 27).

I return to Hardin's quote of Wiesner and York that 'this dilemma has no technical solution'. My simple proposal is to create a network of museums dedicated to the *controversy* over bioprospecting, intellectual property rights, and the public domain. Should we continue with bilateral bioprospecting? Set up a biodiversity cartel? Or restore 'The Common Heritage of Mankind?' Before political leaders can act globally in the CBD forum, their constituents must have thought locally about the alternatives. With enough reflection and debate, the right answer will emerge. After all, that is how democracy is supposed to work.

The early critics to 'The Tragedy of the Commons' would have vociferously disagreed, not so much with the logic of my argument but with its assumptions. For example, Beryl Crowe would have challenged the assumption of a common value system through which agreement on ABS could emerge. A diversity of values would seem to frustrate any bargaining and compromise as distinct groups 'set the stage for either confrontation or surrender ...' (Crowe 1969, 1105). The CBD disproves that criticism by its very existence. For all its operational flaws, the CBD does express a shared value across the 190 ratified countries, *vis-à-vis*, a commitment to conservation. Likewise, time has also proven wrong Crowe's dismissal of Hardin's assumption that 'coercive force' exists or can be effectively administered. The treaty over Trade Related Intellectual Property Rights (TRIPs), ratified approximately one year *after* the CBD, is effectively administered through the World Trade Organization (WTO). Proof of its coercive force lies in decisions which run contrary to the very US interests which spearheaded TRIPs (e.g., the 2001 Doha Declaration on TRIPs and Public Health which circumvents patent rights for better access to life saving drugs).

A more cogent criticism against the museum would be on practical grounds. The devil is always in the details. A museum is not just an abstraction; it is also bricks and mortar. If we build a museum, will anyone come? Hardin gives us a clue in *Exploring New Ethics for Survival: The Voyage of the Spaceship Beagle*: '[t]o be effective, education has to be tied to the culture; that means that education must vary from country to country, and from culture to culture' (Hardin 1973, 197). The fact that the public across socio-economic and geographic divides reveres traditional knowledge is an excellent indicator that demand exists. Despite a countervailing culture of disparagement by the medical establishment, people still want to be engaged in this issue. To the extent that the exhibits designed in any one country are culturally relevant in others, the exhibits could travel thereby affording network economies.

Any network must have a node. Where should *that* be? The pros and cons of candidate sites must be carefully weighed by those who will finance the initiative. To 'counter the natural tendency to do the wrong thing', we must keep in mind that our ultimate goal is to 'act globally' through the CBD. Although I am obviously biased, I believe that a remarkably strong case can be made for selecting the US Commonwealth of Puerto Rico. The case rests on a combination of facts unique to Puerto Rico:

1. The US Senate has not ratified the CBD which means that genetic resources in Puerto Rico, like those in the rest of the US, are 'open access'; US citizens in the 50 federated states do not yet perceive the value of 'mutual coercion, mutually agreed upon' with respect to biodiversity conservation;
2. Some 1.3 million tourists disembark in old San Juan each year and the majority are US citizens; there is no museum of a scientific nature in the immediate environs;
3. The US is a world headquarters for biotech R&D and Puerto Rico is the US headquarters for its manufacture; within Puerto Rico, government efforts are ongoing to create 'clusters' that will integrate research and development from the academic, industrial, and public sectors;
4. The University of Puerto Rico is a comprehensive research institution as classified by the Carnegie Endowment; across its 11 campuses, all themes related to 'bioprospecting, intellectual property rights, and the public domain' are covered by expert faculty;
5. The island boasts pristine natural reserves within easy access to the capital city, is bilingual (Spanish/English), and serves as an airport hub for the Caribbean; and
6. Non-profit institutions in Puerto Rico can enjoy the 501(c)(3) status of the US Treasury Department thereby permitting private foundations or individuals in the US to donate and claim tax exemption.

Conclusion

Twenty-five years after *Science* published 'The Tragedy of the Commons', Hardin would comment 'the weightiest mistake in my synthesizing paper was the omission of the modifying adjective "unmanaged"'(Hardin 1998, 683). In other words, Hardin would not change the contents of 'The Tragedy' one iota. He would have just changed the title to avoid a fallacy of equivocation between 'open access' and what Elinor Ostrum calls 'common pool resources' (1990). Although such steadfastness may infuriate Hardin's critics, I share his sentiment and, not surprisingly, find his conclusion to 'The Tragedy' apropos. Hardin writes in the opening sentence of the concluding remarks '... the [unmanaged] commons if justifiable at all, is justifiable only under conditions of low-population density' (Hardin 1968, 262). The analogy holds perfectly with ABS. Again, through some word substitutions: 'The Common Heritage of Mankind' (*de facto* or *de jure*), if justifiable at all, is justifiable only under conditions where extinction is at the natural rate.

Hardin cautioned not to underestimate the difficulties of interdisciplinary analysis even though 'The Tragedy' was his very first attempt at such analysis. 'The more specialities we try to stitch together, the greater are our opportunities to make mistakes – and the more numerous are our willing critics' (Hardin 1998, 683). The advice is sobering for my proposal. A 'Museum of Bioprospecting, Intellectual Property Rights, and the Public Domain' must stitch together, *inter alia*, specialists in architecture, anthropology, biotechnology, economics, education, law, museology, political science, regional development, taxonomy and web design. The saving grace is that, short of nuclear war, the stakes could not be higher.

Proposals need money and to our list of specialists we must also add the professional schmoozer. The money of a government surplus or that of a well heeled philanthropist could make a huge difference in the future natural history of the planet. Given the scope of the proposal, I could go on and on, but in deference to the memory of Hardin I will not. Hardin's *oeuvre* was exactly 6,474 words (a mere five pages in length). Living well within that limit (4,353 words), I will close with another one of Hardin's gems:

> As nearly as I can make out, automatic rejection of proposed reforms is based on one of two unconscious assumptions: (i) that the status quo is perfect; or (ii) that the choice we face is between reform and no action; if the proposed reform is imperfect, we presumably should take no action at all, while we wait for a perfect proposal. But we can never do nothing. That which we have done for thousands of years is also action. It also produces evil (Hardin 1968, 262).

References

Crowe, B. (1969) 'The Tragedy of the Commons Revisited', *Science,* 166: 1103–107.

Diamond, J. (2005) *Collapse* (New York: Penguin).

Freire, P. (1970) *Pedagogy of the Oppressed* (New York: Continuum).

Goldner, E., Hsu, L., Waraich, P. and Somers, J. (2002) 'Prevalence and Incidence Studies of Schizophrenic Disorders: A Systematic Review of the Literature', *The Canadian Journal of Psychiatry*, 47: 833–43.

GRAIN (2005) 'Restituting the benefits from biodiversity: A perspective on the CBD regime on access and benefit-sharing' (www.grain.org/seedling/?id=327).

Hardin, G. (1968) 'The Tragedy of the Commons', *Science*, 162: 1243–8 in G. Hardin (1973) *Exploring New Ethics for Survival: The Voyage of the Spaceship Beagle* (Maryland: Penguin) 250–64.

Hardin, G. (1973) *Exploring New Ethics for Survival: The Voyage of the Spaceship Beagle* (Maryland: Penguin).

Hardin, G. (1998) 'Essays on Science and Society: Extensions of "The Tragedy of the Commons"', *Science*, 280, 5364: 682–3.

Heller, M. and Eisenberg, R. (1998) 'Can Patents Deter Innovation? The Anticommons in Biomedical Research', *Science*, 280: 698–701.

Krugman, P. (2005) 'Point Those Fingers', *The New York Times*, 9 September (www.nytimes.com).

Laird, S. (1993) 'Contracting for Biodiversity Prospecting' in W. Reid et al. (eds) *Biodiversity Prospecting* (USA: World Resource Institute) 99–130.

New York Times (2005) 'Editorial: Mr. Bush in New Orleans', 16 September (www.nytimes.com).

Oldham, P. (2005) 'Global Status and Trends in Intellectual Property Claims: Genomics, Proteomics and Biotechnology', Submission to the Executive Secretary of the Convention on Biological Diversity. Available at UNEP/CBD/WG-ABS/3/INF/4.

Ostrom, E. (1990) *Governing the Commons* (New York: Cambridge University Press).

Peña-Neira, S., Dieperink, C. and Addink, G. (2002) 'Equitably sharing benefits from the utilization of natural genetic resources: the Brazilian interpretation of the Convention on Biological Diversity', Draft article presented at the 6th Conference of the Parties to the Convention on Biological Diversity, The Hague, Netherlands, 19 April.

Posey, D. (1999) *Cultural and Spiritual Values of Biodiversity* (London: United Nations Environment Programme).

Reid, W. et al. (eds) (1993) *Biodiversity Prospecting* (USA: World Resource Institute).

Russell, C.S. and Powell, P.T. (1996) 'Choosing Environmental Policy Tools: Theoretical Cautions and Practical Considerations', Washington, DC, no.

Env-102, InterAmerican Development Bank, Social Programs and Sustainable Development Department, Environment Division.

Shellenberger, M. and Nordhaus, T. (2004) *Death of Environmentalism: Global Warming Politics in a Post-Environmental World* (www.thebreakthrough.org/images/Death_of_Environmentalism.pdf).

Sleeper, J. (2005) 'Allan Bloom and the Conservative Mind', *The New York Times Book Review,* 4 September, 27.

Vogel, J. (1994) *Genes for Sale* (New York: Oxford University Press).

Vogel, J. (1995) 'A Market Alternative to the Valuation of Biodiversity: The Example of Ecuador', *Association of Systematics Collection Newsletter*, October, 66–70.

Vogel, J. (1997) 'The Successful Use Of Economic Instruments To Foster Sustainable Use Of Biodiversity: Six Case Studies From Latin America And The Caribbean', White Paper commissioned by the Biodiversity Support Program on behalf of the Inter-American Commission on Biodiversity and Sustainable Development in preparation for the Summit of the Americas on Sustainable Development, Santa Cruz de la Sierra, Bolivia. *Biopolicy Journal*, 2, (PY97005) (www.bdt.org/bioline/py).

Vogel, J. (1999) 'The Convention on Biological Diversity and Equitable Benefit-sharing: An Economic Analysis' in D. Posey, *Cultural and Spiritual Values of Biodiversity* (London: United Nations Environment Programme) 530–31.

Vogel, J. (ed.) (2000) *El cártel de la biodiversidad* (Quito: CARE).

Vogel, J. (2004) 'Nada en bioprospección tiene sentido excepto a la luz de la economía', *Revista Iberoamericana de Economía Ecológica*, Joseph Henry Vogel, *REDIBEC*, no. 1, October. (www.redibec.org/archivos/revista/revista5_3.htm).

Vogel, J. (2007) 'Reflecting Financial and other Incentives of the TMOIFGR: The Biodiversity Cartel', in M. Ruiz and I. Lapeña (eds) *A Moving Target: Genetic Resources and Options for Tracking and Monitoring their International Flows* (Gland, Switzerland: IUCN) 49-76, available at http://data.iucn.org/dbtw-wpd/edocs/EPLP-067-3.pdf.

Wiesner, J. and York, H. (1964) 'National Security and the Nuclear Test Ban', *Scientific American*, 211: 4, 27–35.

Chapter 6

Law, Ethics and Wildlife Disease: An Australian Perspective

Hamish McCallum

Introduction

The last few years have witnessed a burgeoning interest in wildlife disease (McCallum and Dobson 1995; Daszak et al. 2000; Cleaveland et al. 2002). The major role that infectious diseases have played in the history of human civilization is well known (Diamond 1997). Until recently, however, diseases were not considered to be important in the ecology of wild populations even though the impact of diseases in crowded conditions of intensive agriculture and livestock husbandry is also well known. The paradox owes to the simplistic maxim that 'a well adapted parasite does not harm its host' (May and Anderson 1990). Diseases are now being recognized as important drivers of the population dynamics of wild populations (Hudson et al. 2002) and have direct and indirect impacts on human well-being, raising a host of critical legal and ethical issues which can be divided into four categories.

First, the majority of emerging infectious diseases of humans arise from wildlife reservoirs (Bengis et al. 2004). A reservoir is one or more species which maintains a disease and on which the disease usually has a limited effect. HIV AIDS emerged at some point in the last 50 years from SIV, a virus endemic in chimpanzees in Africa. SARS emerged in Asia in the period 2002–2003 from a wildlife reservoir, although the exact identity of the reservoir species remains uncertain (Weiss and McLean 2004). Avian influenza, as its name suggests, has its reservoirs amongst a range of bird species.

Second, diseases of livestock can be extraordinarily significant economically. The direct cost of the recent foot and mouth epidemic in the United Kingdom has been estimated at 3 billion pounds (Haydon et al. 2004). Many of these livestock diseases, as with human diseases, have reservoirs in wildlife. For example, bovine tuberculosis is a significant problem in the dairy industry in both the United Kingdom and in New Zealand. In the United Kingdom, badgers are thought to have a significant role as a reservoir. Attempts to control the infection via culling of badger populations create conflicts between wildlife conservation and agriculture (Macdonald et al. 2006). In New Zealand, the introduced Australian brushtail possums are reservoirs for bovine tuberculosis (Barlow 1991). In many cases, however, it is unclear whether livestock or domestic animal populations are acting as reservoirs of infection that impact wildlife populations or whether the reverse is the case (Alexander and Appel 1994).

Third, diseases of wildlife may be critically important for biodiversity conservation. One example is the chytrid fungus that appears to be responsible for wide-scale declines and many extinctions of frogs in otherwise pristine rainforest environments, particularly in Australia and Central America (Berger et al. 1998). A second example is the Tasmanian Devil facial tumour disease that is currently threatening the survival of the largest remaining marsupial carnivore (Hawkins et al. 2006; McCallum and Jones 2006; McCallum et al. 2007).

Fourth, wildlife diseases are being used and are proposed as control agents for over abundant pest species. So far, control has been attempted through introduction into a new area of pathogens found naturally somewhere else in the particular pest species or its close relatives. The most well known and successful example is the introduction of myxomatosis into rabbits in Australia and Europe in the 1950s (Fenner and Fantini 1999). Myxomatosis was a relatively benign pathogen of a related species in South America, but was extraordinarily pathogenic to European rabbits when first introduced to wild populations. More recently, there have been proposals to genetically engineer parasites or pathogens for release as control agents (Tyndale-Biscoe 1994a; McCallum 1996). In Australia, such genetically engineered control agents have been proposed for mice and rabbits. In New Zealand, attempts are being made to genetically engineer a parasitic nematode worm to control brushtail possum populations (Gilna et al. 2005).

Each of the four categories raises a different set of legal and ethical issues. There is a common theme in several that relates to quarantine or movement controls, which need to be weighed against the increasing tendency towards 'globalization' and free trade. Categories one to three have a common theme of emerging disease. Novel emerging diseases have become a particularly serious problem recently, which is partially due to globalization and increased trade. The process of 'pathogen pollution' (Lafferty and Gerber 2002; Anderson et al. 2004), by which pathogens are transferred from an area in which they are endemic into new areas in which the native species have had no evolutionary exposure, has been identified as a major factor in disease emergence. Human encroachment on natural ecosystems, including fragmentation and habitat destruction has brought species and pathogens into close contact in ways that have not occurred before, with the resulting potential for disease emergence (McCallum 2008). Finally, global climate change is causing range shifts of host species, increases of abundance of disease vectors and changes in disease biology, all of which may cause disease emergence (Kovats et al. 2001; Anderson et al. 2004; Haines et al. 2006).

Wildlife and Emerging Infectious Diseases of Humans

At least 70 per cent of emerging infectious diseases of humans have arisen from wildlife reservoirs (Bengis et al. 2004) and are termed zoonotic diseases. For some such diseases (e.g., HIV AIDS) the transition from animals to a human infection occurred sometime ago and, thereafter, the disease maintained itself within the human population. While there are clearly major legal and ethical issues associated with such diseases, they do not directly relate to the wildlife that were the original source of infection and remain beyond the scope of this particular chapter. Others, such as Ebola, are capable of short human to human transmission chains but the threat to human populations arises from repeated transmission from wildlife reservoirs (Leendertz et al. 2006). Some zoonotic diseases (e.g., rabies) extremely rarely transmit from human to human and the threat to human populations relies entirely on animal to human transmission.

Control of the impact of zoonotic diseases that are dependent on ongoing transmission from animals to humans can be accomplished by control of the disease within the wildlife reservoir or by limitation of transmission from animals to humans. Both of these options carry significant legal and ethical implications. Control of disease within wildlife populations may involve culling or vaccination. Culling clearly has the potential to create conflicts between legislation designed for wildlife conservation and that associated with public health. Although vaccination of free-ranging wildlife populations is technically difficult, it has nevertheless been accomplished with considerable success against rabies in both Europe and North America (Rupprecht et al. 2004). The vaccine, however, is a genetically engineered pox virus (Paoletti 1996), which raises legal and ethical issues associated with the release of genetically modified organisms. In the case of rabies, the public health consequences of an epidemic are so major, with a case fatality rate in humans of virtually 100 per cent, that these considerations do not appear to have inhibited the use of the vaccine. More generally, substantial amounts of any bait delivered vaccine will inevitably be consumed by non-target species, which must be considered whenever vaccination of a wildlife population is attempted.

Limitation of transmission from animals to humans may include restrictions on transborder or interregional movement of potentially infected animals, strategies to limit interactions between humans and potentially infected wildlife or vaccination of the human population, which again raises legal and ethical questions associated with each situation.

Wildlife and Diseases of Domestic Stock

Many of the issues associated with zoonotic disease apply equally to emerging diseases of domestic stock arising from wildlife reservoirs. In particular, the same strategies of control within the wildlife populations are relevant, as are policies concerned with restriction of movement of potentially infected wildlife. However, two key differences are evident.

The first difference is knowledge of the direction of the spillover. Is the spillover occurring from the wildlife to the domestic stock or vice versa? This is particularly the case when the same or closely related species are in both domestic and free-ranging populations. For example, salmon aquaculture has significant problems associated with 'fish lice', which are parasitic crustaceans that can reach very high population densities in the crowded conditions of fish farms (Krkosek et al. 2006). While fish farm managers may assert that wild salmon are the source of fish lice infections, it is becoming increasingly clear that the fish farms effectively amplify the level of infection to such an extent that the survival of wild salmon stocks is compromised. In Canada, this has raised substantial issues under wildlife conservation legislation.

The second difference is the strategy of intensive culling of foci of infection. In the veterinary literature, it is called 'stamping out' and constitutes perhaps the major strategy used to control emergent disease events (Ferguson et al. 2001). Obviously, such a strategy is ethically unacceptable in human populations. When it is applied to livestock populations, it raises a variety of legal and ethical issues associated with compulsion to report disease events, enforcement of destruction of stock and compensation for the destruction.

Wildlife Disease and Biodiversity Conservation

It is becoming increasingly clear that emergent infectious diseases pose substantial threats to many endangered species. The principal legal instrument for biodiversity conservation in Australia is the Environment Protection and Biodiversity Conservation Act (1999), usually cited by its acronym, the EPBC Act. In addition to identification and listing of threatened species and threatened ecological communities, the Act provides for recognition of 'key threatening processes' and, where it is found appropriate and feasible, reduction of the influence of these processes through the threat abatement plans. Key threatening processes are described as follows:

3. A process is a *threatening process* if it threatens, or may threaten, the survival, abundance or evolutionary development of a native species or ecological community.
4. A threatening process is eligible to be treated as a key threatening process if:
   a it could cause a native species or an ecological community to become eligible for listing in any category, other than conservation dependent; or
   b it could cause a listed threatened species or a listed threatened ecological community to become eligible to be listed in another category representing a higher degree of endangerment; or
   c it adversely affects two or more listed threatened species (other than conservation dependent species) or two or more listed threatened ecological communities.

Infectious diseases of wildlife could clearly satisfy these criteria and, of the 16 key threatening processes listed since the act was passed, two refer explicitly to infectious disease of wildlife: 'Psittacine Circoviral (beak and feather) disease affecting endangered psittacine species', listed in April 2001 and 'Infection of amphibians with chytrid fungus resulting in chytridiomycosis', listed in July 2002.

Once a process has been accepted as a key threatening process, the Minister must decide within 90 days whether a threat abatement plan is the most 'feasible, effective and efficient way to abate the process'. Thereafter, a plan must be developed within two years. Threat abatement plans had been prepared for both the above disease-related threatening processes. The Australian National Audit Office (2007) has recently strongly criticized the implementation of the EPBC Act, particularly with respect to inadequate procedures to ensure implementation of plans and inadequate resourcing.

The current epidemic of an infectious cancer (Tasmanian Devil facial tumour disease) threatening the Tasmanian Devil raises a range of ethical and legal issues (McCallum and Jones 2006). The disease has spread, since its first discovery in 1996, over most of the range of the Devil, causing population declines of up to 90 per cent (Hawkins et al. 2006; McCallum et al. 2007) and leading to real concerns of the extinction of this largest surviving marsupial carnivore. In the absence of any vaccine or treatment available to be used on wild animals, management options are limited (Jones et al. 2007). They include culling of infected animals and isolation of disease-free animals in places, such as offshore islands, where the animals can be protected from disease.

The island translocation option is currently the only strategy for which there is a high level of confidence in its likely success (McCallum and Jones 2006). Introduction of generalist predators to offshore islands has frequently produced substantial conservation problems (Courchamp et al. 2003), although in all such cases the prey species affected have had no evolutionary exposure to the particular predator (especially cats) (Salo et al. 2007). The islands being proposed for Tasmanian Devil translocation hold no prey species that do not coexist with Devils on the main island of Tasmania. Nevertheless, the proposal has raised some concerns, particularly as IUCN guidelines suggest extreme caution in introducing species to any area outside their natural range (IUCN 1987).

Translocating Tasmanian Devils to offshore islands invokes the Australian Environment Protection and Biodiversity Conservation Act (1999) and raises some interesting legal dilemmas. The Act requires an environmental risk assessment to be taken for any action that may negatively impact on threatened species or communities, or a range of listed marine or migratory species. All offshore islands of Tasmania that potentially might be suitable for Devils hold a range of such species. The clear presumption of the Act is that 'actions' have potential negative consequences for biodiversity. How the Act should most appropriately be applied when the proposed action is being undertaken for a biodiversity benefit to one species, with potentially negative implications for some other species is uncertain.

Are all endangered species equivalent in terms of conservation value? In my opinion, an action is justifiable from a diversity conservation point of view if its benefit to biodiversity conservation of one species exceeds the risk to other species. In the case of the Tasmanian Devil, failure to establish disease-free populations has an unacceptable risk of leading to extinction of species in the wild. Unless there was a demonstrable risk of extinction of some other threatened species as a result of Devil introduction to an island, then the action would be justifiable.

A further limitation of the Act is that it is solely concerned with assessing the risk of actions to biodiversity. It does not assess the risk of failure to act. This distinction, of course, has strong parallels with the distinction between 'sins of omission' and the more serious 'sins of commission', as drawn by Aquinas (see the English Dominican Province translation of *The Summa Theologica*, 1920). Whether mediaeval theology should be used as a guide to twenty-first-century biodiversity conservation is doubtful.

Infectious Disease as a Control Strategy for Pest Wildlife

Two distinct issues are at play. First, existing pathogens introduced into new environments fall under legislation regulating biological control agents, viz. The Biological Control Act (1984), which, *inter alia*, limits the ability of damages to be claimed for effects of declared biological control agents on other enterprises. For example, the plant *Echium plantagineum* is known as 'Paterson's curse' to graziers because it is toxic to cattle. The same plant is known as 'Salvation Jane' to beekeepers in parts of South Australia because it produces excellent honey. Beekeepers attempted (ultimately unsuccessfully) to restrict the introduction of a biological control agent on the basis that it would affect their livelihood (Huwer et al. 2005). One could similarly imagine that the aquarium trade might seek to prevent the introduction of a disease that was highly pathogenic to European carp, which are a serious pest in Australian Inland waterways, on the basis that the disease might also affect goldfish which are closely related carp species. If such a pathogen were to be found and it was declared a biological control agent under Australian legislation, such a claim for damages could not succeed. Existing pathogens might also raise concerns under animal welfare legislation. It is certainly the case that diseases, such as myxomatosis and rabbit haemorrhagic disease, produce quite significant suffering in the individual they affect.

Genetically modified pathogens raise all these issues together with substantial additional concerns. In Australia and New Zealand, large-scale research programmes have been undertaken into the development of genetically engineered pathogens capable of sterilizing their hosts. In Australia, such agents have been investigated for the control of rabbits, house mice and European foxes (Tyndale-Biscoe 1994a, 1994b; McCallum 1996; Cowan and McCallum 1997). In New Zealand, the principal target is the Australian brushtail possum (Gilna et al. 2005). This technology has been advocated as being more acceptable ethically than lethal control (Oogjes 1997; Morris and Weaver 2003). However, it involves a range of ethical and legal considerations. Release of GMOs into the environment is closely regulated in almost all jurisdictions. In Australia, regulation is via the Office of the Gene Technology Regulator. It is likely that there would be particular concerns raised about genetically engineered mammalian pathogens. In addition, there is a range of international conventions and protocols associated with the release of genetically modified organisms. The Cartegena Protocol to the Rio Convention on biodiversity has the objective of 'ensuring an adequate level of protection in the field of safe transfer handling and use of living modified organisms resulting from modern biotechnology that may have adverse effects on the conservation and sustainable use of biological diversity ... specifically focusing on transboundary movements'. This would clearly apply to any genetically modified control agent for pest wildlife, particularly as wildlife that are regarded as pests in one country may be viewed as important components of biodiversity in other countries (Angulo and Cooke 2002, Gilna et al. 2005). At the time of writing this article, Australia had yet to sign or ratify the protocol, although New Zealand has done so.

Conclusion

Wildlife disease is an important issue for human health, economic well-being and biodiversity conservation. Management of wildlife disease raises serious ethical and legal issues that have not been widely recognized. Recent trends in globalization, climate change and biotechnology mean that these issues will become increasingly significant.

References

Biological Control Act (1984) In Commonwealth of Australia.

Alexander, K.A. and Appel, M.J.G. (1994) African wild dogs (Lycaon pictus) endangered by a canine distemper epizootic among domestic dogs near the Masai Mara National Reserve, Kenya. *Journal of Wildlife Diseases*, 30: 481–5.

Anderson, P.K., Cunningham, A.A., Patel, N.G., Morales, F.J., Epstein, P.R. and Daszak, P. (2004) Emerging infectious diseases of plants: pathogen pollution, climate change and agrotechnology drivers. *Trends in Ecology and Evolution*, 19: 535–44.

Angulo, E. and Cooke, B. (2002) First synthesize new viruses then regulate their release? The case of the wild rabbit. *Molecular Ecology*, 11: 2703–709.

Australian National Audit Office (2007) The Conservation and Protection of National Threatened Species and Ecological Communities Audit Report 2006–2007, no. 31.

Barlow, N.D. (1991) Control of endemic bovine Tb in New Zealand possum populations: Results from a simple model. *Journal of Applied Ecology*, 28: 794–809.

Bengis, R.H., Leighton, F.A., Fischer, J.R., Artois, M., Morner, T. and Tate, C.M. (2004) The role of wildlife in emerging and re-emerging zoonoses. *Revue Scientifique Et Technique De L Office International Des Epizooties*, 23: 497–511.

Berger, L., Speare, R., Daszak, P., Green, D.E., Cunningham, A.A., Goggin, C.L., Slocombe, R., Ragan, M.A., Hyatt, A.D., McDonald, K.R., Hines, H.B., Lips, K.R., Marantelli, G. and Parkes, H. (1998) Chytridiomycosis causes amphibian mortality associated with population declines in the rain forests of Australia and Central America. *Proc. Natl. Acad. Sci.* USA, 95: 9031–6.

Cleaveland, S., Hess, G.R., Dobson, A.P., Laurenson, M.K., McCallum, H.I., Roberts, M.G. and Woodroffe, R. (2002) 'The role of pathogens in biological conservation', pp. 139–50 in P.J. Hudson, A. Rizzoli, B. Grenfell and H. Heesterbeck (eds). *The Ecology of Wildlife Diseases*. (Oxford: Oxford University Press).

Courchamp, F., Chapuis, J.L. and Pascal, M. (2003) Mammal invaders on islands: impact, control and control impact. *Biological Reviews*, 78: 347–83.

Cowan, D. and McCallum, H. (1997) Discussion session: Is fertility control an option? *Reproduction Fertility and Development*, 9: 61–4.

Daszak, P., Cunningham, A.A. and Hyatt, A.D. (2000) Emerging infectious diseases of wildlife – threats to biodiversity and human health. *Science*, 287: 443–9.

Diamond, J.M. (1997) *Guns, Germs and Steel: The Fates of Human Societies* (London: Jonathan Cape).

Fenner, F. and Fantini, B. (1999) *Biological Control of Vertebrate Pests: The History of Myxomatosis; An Experiment in Evolution*. (Wallingford (UK) and New York (US): CABI Publishing).

Ferguson, N.M., Donnelly, C.A. and Anderson, R.M. (2001) Transmission intensity and impact of control policies on the foot and mouth epidemic in Great Britain. *Nature*, 413: 542–8.

Gilna, B., Lindenmayer, D.B. and Viggers, K.L. (2005) Dangers of New Zealand possum biocontrol research to endogenous Australian fauna. *Conservation Biology*, 19: 2030–32.

Haines, A., Kovats, R.S., Campbell-Lendrum, D. and Corvalan, C. (2006) Climate change and human health: Impacts, vulnerability and public health. *Public Health*, 120: 585–96.

Hawkins, C.E., Baars, C., Hesterman, H., Hocking, G.J., Jones, M.E., Lazenby, B., Mann, D., Mooney, N., Pemberton, D., Pyecroft, S., Restani, M. and Wiersma, J. (2006) Emerging disease and population decline of an island endemic, the Tasmanian Devil, Sarcophilus harrisii. *Biological Conservation*, 131: 307–24.

Haydon, D.T., Kao, R.R. and Kitching, R.P. (2004) The UK foot and mouth disease outbreak – the aftermath. *Nature Reviews Microbiology*, 2: 675–80.

Hudson, P.J., Rizzoli, A., Grenfell, B.T., Heesterbeck, H. and Dobson, A.P. (eds) (2002) *The Ecology of Wildlife Diseases* (Oxford University Press).

Huwer, R.K., Briese, D.T., Dowling, P.M., Kemp, D.R., Lonsdale, W.M., Michalk, D.L., Neave, M.J., Sheppard, A.W. and Woodburn, T.L. (2005) Can an integrated management approach provide a basis for long-term prevention of weed dominance in Australian pasture systems? *Weed Research*, 45: 175–92.

IUCN (1987) Position statement on translocation of living organisms. IUCN, Gland.

Jones, M., Jarman, P., Lees, C., Hesterman, H., Hamede, R., Mooney, N., Mann, D., Pukk, C., Bergfeld, J. and McCallum, H. (2007) Conservation management of Tasmanian Devils in the context of an emerging, extinction-threatening disease: Devil Facial Tumor Disease, *EcoHealth.*

Kovats, R.S., Campbell-Lendrum, D.H., McMichael, A.J., Woodward, A. and Cox, J.S. (2001) Early effects of climate change: Do they include changes in vector-borne disease? *Philosophical Transactions of the Royal Society of London Series B-Biological Sciences*, 356: 1057–68.

Krkosek, M., Lewis, M.A., Morton, A., Frazer, L.N. and Volpe, J.P. (2006) Epizootics of wild fish induced by farm fish. *PNAS*, 103: 15506–510.

Lafferty, K.D. and Gerber, L.R. (2002) Good medicine for conservation biology: The intersection of epidemiology and conservation theory. *Conservation Biology*, 16: 593–604.

Leendertz, F.H., Pauli, G., Maetz-Rensing, K., Boardman, W., Nunn, C., Ellerbrok, H., Jensen, S.A., Junglen, S. and Christophe, B. (2006) Pathogens as drivers of population declines: The importance of systematic monitoring in great apes and other threatened mammals. *Biological Conservation*, 131: 325–37.

Macdonald, D.W., Riordan, P. and Mathews, F. (2006) Biological hurdles to the control of TB in cattle: A test of two hypotheses concerning wildlife to explain the failure of control. *Biological Conservation*, 131: 268–86.

May, R.M. and Anderson, R.M. (1990) Parasite-host co-evolution. *Parasitology* 100: S89–S101.

McCallum, H. (1996) Immunocontraception for wildlife population control. *Trends in Ecology and Evolution*, 11: 491–3.

McCallum, H. (2008) 'Landscape structure, disturbance and disease dynamics' in V. Eviner, F. Keesing and R. Ostfeld (eds). *Ecology of Infectious Diseases: Interactions Between Diseases and Ecosystems* (Princeton: University Press).

McCallum, H. and Dobson, A.P. (1995) Detecting disease and parasite threats to endangered species and ecosystems. *Trends in Ecology and Evolution*, 10: 190–94.

McCallum, H. and Jones, M. (2006) To Lose Both Would Look Like Carelessness: Tasmanian Devil Facial Tumour Disease. *PLoS Biology*, 4: 1671–4.

McCallum, H., Tompkins, D.M., Jones, M., Lachish, S., Marvanek, S., Lazenby, B., Hocking, G., Wiersma, J. and Hawkins, C. (2007) Distribution and impacts of Tasmanian Devil facial tumor disease. *EcoHealth.*

Morris, M.C. and Weaver, S.A. (2003) Minimizing harm in possum control operations and experiments in New Zealand. *Journal of Agricultural and Environmental Ethics*, 16: 367–85.

Oogjes, G. (1997) Ethical aspects and dilemmas of fertility control of unwanted wildlife: an animal welfarist's perspective. *Reproduction Fertility and Development*, 9: 163–8.

Paoletti, E. (1996) Applications of pox virus vectors to vaccination: An update. *PNAS*, 93: 11349–53.

Rupprecht, C.E., Hanlon, C.A. and Slate, D. (2004) Oral vaccination of wildlife against rabies: Opportunities and challenges in prevention and control, pp. 173–84 in A. Schudel and M. Lombard (eds). *Control of Infectious Animal Diseases by Vaccination* (Basel: Karger).

Salo, P., Korpimäki, E., Banks, P.B., Nordström, M. and Dickman, C.R. (2007) Alien predators are more dangerous than native predators to prey populations. *Proceedings of the Royal Society of London B: Biological Sciences*, 274: 1237–43.

St Thomas Aquinas (1920) *The Summa Theologica*, translated by Fathers of the English Dominican Province, (www.newadvent.org/summa/3079.htm) accessed 26 May 2007.

Tyndale-Biscoe, C.H. (1994a) Virus-vectored immunocontraception of feral mammals. *Reproduction Fertility and Development*, 6: 281–7.

Tyndale-Biscoe, C.H. (1994b) The CRC for biological control of vertebrate pest populations: fertility control of wildlife for conservation. *Pacific Conservation Biology*, 1: 160–62.

Weiss, R.A. and McLean, A.R. (2004) What have we learnt from SARS? *Philosophical Transactions of the Royal Society of London B: Biological Sciences*, 359: 1137–40.

Chapter 7
Environmental Risk, Environmental Liability and the Regulation of Biotechnology: Mediating Law and Biology?

Christopher Rodgers

Introduction

Developing a legal response to the emergence of agricultural biotechnology poses a number of unique challenges. The potential interaction of GMOs with natural ecosystems is complex and not yet fully understood. This makes the development of risk management and risk allocation techniques problematic. It also complicates the search for suitable liability rules, that is, rules providing a basis for compensation claims where losses are alleged to flow from GMO releases to the environment. This chapter will limit itself to a consideration of risk management and the potential liabilities for 'environmental' damage attributed to GMOs – that is, biodiversity loss and damage to the wider 'unowned' environment. It will consider the approach to these issues adopted under the aegis of the UN Convention on Biological Diversity in the Cartagena Protocol on Biosafety, and the application of the EC's Environmental Liability Directive of 2004 to GMOs. It has been suggested that the approach to liability and risk offered by the 2004 Directive provides a model for the wider adoption of measures under the Cartagena Protocol on Biosafety. However, this chapter will conclude that the Directive is flawed in important respects and cannot be taken as a model for the wider development of liability regimes in international law.

Risk, Environmental Liability and the Cartagena Protocol

The Cartagena Protocol on Biosafety (the Protocol) was concluded in January 2000 under the terms of the 1992 UN Convention on Biological Diversity, and its focus is squarely on the protection of the natural environment (see generally, Qureshi 2000; Street 2001). Its entry into force was delayed (under Article 37 ibid.) until 90 days after the deposit of the 50th instrument of ratification, acceptance, approval or accession by states or regional economic integration organizations that are parties to the CBD. The 50th ratification took place in June 2003. Much academic discussion has centred on the interrelationship between the Protocol's provisions and the treaties of the World Trade Organisation. Nevertheless, when the European Court of Justice considered the legal basis of the Protocol in Opinion 2/2000 (*Cartagena Protocol*),[1] it concluded that its primary purpose was the protection of biological diversity against the potentially detrimental effects of the transboundary movement of living modified organisms. In the court's view it was not a trade measure intended to promote or regulate international trade *per se*. Consequently the Protocol was ratified by the Community under the EC Treaty basis specific to environmental policy. The Community and the individual EC member states share competence to ratify the Protocol. Both the United Kingdom and the European Union are parties to the Protocol.

The Protocol applies to trade (transboundary movements) in 'Living Modified Organisms' (hereafter 'LMOs'), namely 'any living organism that possesses a novel combination of genetic material obtained through the use of modern biotechnology' (Article 3(g)). Its scope is therefore somewhat narrower than that of the World Trade Organization's Sanitary and Phyto Sanitary (SPS) and Technical Barriers to Trade (TBT) agreements, in that it does not apply to products derived from, or manufactured using, GMOs which no longer contain living genetically altered material in their final form.

The main thrust of the Protocol is to apply a system of informed consent before the introduction of GMOs from one country to another takes place. The Protocol differentiates between:

- LMOs intended for introduction into the environment (for example, genetically modified seeds to be used for the production of GM crops), and
- LMOs that are intended for direct use in food or feed or for processing (for example, GM Soya or tomatoes). These are referred to as 'LMO-FFPs'.

Trade in both types of LMO is subjected by the protocol to the informed consent of the importing state. However, because the potential ecological problems arising from LMOs intended for direct introduction into the environment of the importing state are greater, this type of LMO must be subjected to a more stringent approval process before transboundary shipments can take place. In the case of LMOs for introduction into the environment (e.g., seeds) the Protocol applies the principle of 'Advance Informed Agreement' (AIA). This requires that the importing party carry out risk assessments before the first intentional transboundary movement of the product in question (Article 15(2)). The risk assessment must be carried out in a 'scientifically sound and transparent manner' in accordance with Annex III of the Protocol, and on a case by case basis. In the case of LMO–FFPs on the other hand, a less demanding procedure is applied requiring the importing and exporting states to inform the parties to the Protocol, through the Biosafety Clearing House established for this purpose, of any decision regarding the domestic use of a LMO

1 [2001] ECR 1-000: see also Dashwood, A. (2002) 39 CMLR 353–68.

which may be subject to transboundary shipment for direct use as food, feed or for processing (Article 11).

There are a number of areas where the approach taken by the Cartagena Protocol differs from that adopted in the WTO Agreements. These differences of approach inevitably lead to tensions in the way in which the two sets of treaty provision apply to trade in GMOs, especially in cases where one of the protagonists is not a party to the CBD (for example, the US). The Protocol makes detailed provision for the application of the precautionary principle in relation to trade in GMOs and for risk assessment. It does not, however, contain detailed provision for environmental liability in the event of damage from LMOs emerging – this is an aspect of the Protocol that is under ongoing discussion and development. The proposals for the addition of an environmental liability section to the protocol will be discussed below. Before the liability issues can be explored, however, they must be contextualized against the Protocols principles for risk assessments and risk management.

(a) Risk Assessment Under the Cartagena Protocol

The Cartagena Protocol gives detailed guidelines for the risk assessment to be carried out before a transboundary movement of LMOs is permissible. It does so in much greater detail than the corresponding provision of the SPS Agreement of the WTO, although (like the SPS agreement) the risk assessment must be scientifically sound and transparent, and carried out on a case by case basis. Furthermore, Article 16 specifically addresses issues of risk *management*, an issue on which the SPS agreement gives no specific guidance.

Under Article 15 and Annex III of the Protocol, risk assessment must be undertaken with the objective of identifying and evaluating the possible adverse effects of living modified organisms on the conservation and sustainable use of biological diversity in the likely potential receiving environment, also taking into account risks to human health. This is complemented by provisions in Article 16, which require that signatories to the Protocol establish and maintain appropriate mechanisms, measures and strategies to regulate, manage and control risks identified in the risk assessment provisions of the Protocol associated with the use, handling and transboundary movement of living modified organisms. Measures based on risk assessment must be imposed to the extent necessary to prevent adverse effects of the living modified organism on the conservation and sustainable use of biological diversity within the territory of the Party of import. Parties to the Protocol must also endeavour to ensure that any living modified organism, whether imported or locally developed, has undergone an appropriate period of observation that is commensurate with its life cycle or generation time before it is put to its intended use.

Detailed rules for the execution of risk assessment under the Protocol, on a case by case basis, are laid down in Annex III. Risks associated with living modified organisms, or the products of LMOs (i.e., processed materials that are of living modified organism origin), that contain detectable novel combinations of replicable genetic material obtained through the use of biotechnology, should be considered in the context of the risks posed by the non-modified recipients or parental organisms in the likely potential receiving environment (Annex III para 5). The methodology for applying risk assessment is laid down in Annex III para 8. This requires that the risk assessment be applied using the following steps, and in the following order:

a. An identification of any novel genotypic and phenotypic characteristics associated with the living modified organism that may have adverse effects on biological diversity in the likely potential receiving environment, taking also into account risks to human health;
b. An evaluation of the likelihood of these adverse effects being realized, taking into account the level and kind of exposure of the likely potential receiving environment to the living modified organism;
c. An evaluation of the consequences should these adverse effects be realized;
d. An estimation of the overall risk posed by the living modified organism based on the evaluation of the likelihood and consequences of the identified adverse effects being realized;
e. A recommendation as to whether or not the risks are acceptable or manageable, including, where necessary, identification of strategies to manage these risks; and
f. Where there is uncertainty regarding the level of risk, it may be addressed by requesting further information on the specific issues of concern or by implementing appropriate risk management strategies and/or monitoring the living modified organism in the receiving environment.

Scientific and technical details to consider in each case are identified in Annex III para 9. These include, for example, the biological characteristics of the recipient organism or parental organisms (such as its taxonomic status, common name, origin, centres of origin and centres of genetic diversity, and habitat where the organisms may persist or proliferate), the relevant biological characteristics of the donor organisms, and the characteristics of the vector and its host range. Information on the location, geographical, climatic and ecological characteristics of the likely receiving environment must also be taken into account, including relevant information on its biological diversity.

(b) Application of the Precautionary Principle

Article 10.6 of the Protocol provides that:

> lack of scientific certainty due to insufficient relevant scientific information and knowledge regarding the extent of the potential adverse effect of a living

> modified organism on the conservation and sustainable use of biological diversity in the Party of import … shall not prevent that Party from taking a decision, as appropriate, with regard to the import of the living modified organism in question … in order to avoid or minimise such potential adverse effects.

This expressly permits the application of the precautionary principle in the AIA procedure for the transboundary movement of LMOs. Article 11.8 applies the principle in similar terms to the notification requirement applied to LMO–FFPs. The precautionary principle is also evident in the provisions for risk assessment. Annex III para 6 provides that the lack of scientific knowledge or scientific consensus should not necessarily be interpreted as indicating a particular level of risk, an absence of risk, *or an acceptable risk* (italics added).

In its attitude to the application of precaution, the Protocol's provisions are in stark contrast to those of the SPS Agreement, which is based on scientific rationality principles and only permits derogations on a temporary basis from scientific risk assessment. Any decision to bar imports of GMOs or GM derived products under the SPS agreement can only be justified on the precautionary principle for temporary periods and subject to reassessment within a reasonable time using such scientific knowledge as has been acquired in the intervening period. Furthermore, Article 2 para 4 of the Cartagena Protocol preserves the parties' rights to take action 'that is more protective of the conservation and sustainable use of biological diversity than that called for in this Protocol', provided that any action taken is consistent with the objectives of the Protocol and compliant with other obligations under international law. These provisions would appear to conflict with the corresponding provisions of the SPS agreement in their application to trade in GMOs, and could raise difficult questions of interpretation and application (as to which, see below).

It can be argued than the Biosafety Protocol is based on a 'social rationality' model, in that it allows considerations of socio-economic factors to be taken into account when an importing state is assessing a product's suitability for importation (Smyth et al. 2004, 90–3). Article 26 provides that the Parties can, in reaching a decision on importing LMOs or under their domestic measures implementing the Protocol, take into account, 'consistent with their international obligations, socio-economic considerations arising from the impact of living modified organisms on the conservation and sustainable use of biological diversity, especially with regard to the value of biological diversity to indigenous and local communities'. This raises an important question as to the orientation and objectives of the Biosafety protocol, and introduces an undefined social evaluation element into the process of risk assessment and management. It also differentiates it from the approach to risk assessment taken by the WTO Agreements, which are (by contrast) strongly based on notions of scientific rationality. The Protocol has been criticized, for example, for failing to ensure clearly and adequately that its biosafety provisions (such as risk assessments, risk management, handling, and transparency requirements) are not used in an arbitrary or unjustifiably discriminatory manner, or as disguised restrictions on international trade (Qureshi 2000).

(c) Compatibility with WTO Disciplines

The precise relationship between the Protocol and the WTO agreements is a matter of some uncertainty, as is their status relative to each other in international law. Given the inconsistencies in the approach to trade in GMOs evident in the SPS agreement and the Biosafety Protocol this could become a matter of some importance. Which provides the appropriate forum for the determination of disputes? The Biosafety Protocol is itself ambivalent about its relationship with other instruments of international trade law. Three of its recitals variously: (i) recognize that 'trade and environment agreements should be mutually supportive with a view to achieving sustainable development'; (ii) emphasize that it must not be 'interpreted as implying a change in the rights and obligations of a Party under any existing international agreements'; but also (iii) state the parties' understanding that the recital before mentioned 'is not intended to subordinate this Protocol to other international agreements'.

General principles of law applied to treaty interpretation are unhelpful in resolving the tensions between the two sets of rules. Where different rules exist in different international treaties, the first question to ask is whether the parties to an international dispute are bound by each of the agreements in question – if they are not then the rules that will apply in the resolution of the dispute will be the treaty provisions which they have both ratified and which are therefore legally binding on them. Significantly, the US has ratified neither the Cartagena Protocol nor its parent treaty, the Convention on Biological Diversity. In the case of a dispute arising between the US and EU as to the application of precautionary measures to prevent trade in GMOs, therefore, the former could legitimately point to the fact that it is not a signatory to the Cartagena Protocol and is not therefore bound by its provisions, for example, those allowing a precautionary stance to be taken to GMOs in the absence of clear scientific evidence or risk. It is, however, a signatory to the SPS agreement, as is the EU, and could therefore argue than the SPS Agreement, and its more restricted provisions on the application of the precautionary principle, should be applied.

The relationship between the Protocol and the SPS Agreement was considered – in circumstances arising from the EU moratorium on GM approvals – by the dispute resolution panel report in *EC – Approval and Marketing of Biotechnological Products* (WTO 2006). The complainants in this dispute – the US, Canada and Argentina – had not ratified the Cartagena Protocol, although all were (like the EU itself) parties to the relevant WTO Agreements. The dispute panel indicated that in these circumstances if a member of the WTO was not a party to another international agreement (in this case the Protocol) then that agreement could not be considered relevant to the resolution of a given dispute except as a guide to the interpretation of terms used in the WTO Agreements. The more expansive approach to precaution in the Protocol, which allows socio-economic factors to be taken into account, was not therefore applicable in the dispute between the EU and the three complainants over the *de facto moratorium* on GMO approvals in this case.

Another principle that would apply, where both parties to a dispute are signatories to a treaty, is that in Article 30(3) of the Vienna Convention on the Law of Treaties 1969 viz. that the later in time prevails. This would give primacy to the Cartagena Protocol in disputes involving trade in GMOs, as it was concluded in 2000, six years after the SPS Agreement. This is arbitrary and unsatisfactory, however, and ignores the fact that the WTO Agreements are currently subject to renegotiation in the Doha Round of trade negotiations. It would seem strange were the conclusion of a renegotiated SPS agreement to reverse the choice of applicable law in a subsequent dispute in which the parties were signatories of both treaties. It is perhaps worth noting here that the US has steadfastly refused to open up the scientific basis of the SPS for renegotiation, although this is something for which the EU has pressed consistently. There is as yet no clear guidance as to how these issues can (or will) be resolved in future cases (for a review of the options, see Schoenbaum 2000).

Developing a Liability Regime for the Cartagena Protocol

The role of 'sound science' and the precautionary principle in identifying and managing risk were, therefore, hugely problematic in the negotiation of the Cartagena Protocol. Street notes that there were 18 references to socio-economic considerations in the final negotiating text of the Protocol, which were all bracketed to reflect the lack of agreement on these parts of the text (Street 2001, 254). The final text adopted represented a compromise in which socio-economic considerations can be used to justify decisions based on precaution, but only after the parties have carried out a scientific risk assessment that conforms to the Protocol's requirements and those of the WTO agreements. The closely related question of potential liabilities flowing from GMO releases proved even more vexed. Agreement on a treaty provision governing liability and redress proved impossible. An enabling clause was therefore included in Article 27 of the Protocol authorizing further work to establish a liability mechanism to govern claims for redress flowing from the transboundary movement of LMOs.

An *ad hoc* working group of legal and technical experts was established by the first meeting of the Conference of the Parties. This has met on three subsequent occasions (for the report issued following its third meeting, see UNEP 2007). Although its work is still at a preliminary stage, it has identified a number of key elements that must be included in a liability scheme, and has reviewed a wide range of signatories' legal approaches and practices in relation to environmental liability and their potential application to GMOs. The report, submitted following its third meeting in Curiba, Brazil in March 2006, in particular, identified a number of key issues for further research and discussion. The issues are wide-ranging, and the possible scientific interactions of GMOs with biodiversity are so complex that the task of capturing them in a scheme for liability and redress is likely to prove extremely problematic. For the purposes of the strictly legal analysis offered in this paper the relevant issues can be grouped under the following heads:

1. The application of a limitation period, after the expiry of which claims for redress will be inadmissible;
2. Quantification of alleged losses, for example, to biodiversity;
3. The development of an appropriate insurance mechanism to underpin liability; and
4. *Locus Standi* (standing) to bring claims for redress.

(a) Limitation Periods

Most legal systems apply limitation periods to time-bar claims for redress after a fixed period has elapsed following the occurrence of alleged damage or loss to a potential claimant. Limitation periods can be either relative or absolute: a relative limitation period will bar claims after a fixed period has elapsed following the identification of damage flowing from the act complained of; an absolute limitation period will bar claims after a fixed period as elapsed following the act alleged to have caused the damage, irrespective of when the damage was identified. The application of the principles of limitation of liability to damage flowing from GMO releases is complicated in that the scientific interaction of GMOs with wild plants and the wider environment will emerge over a long period of time, and its impact on biodiversity may not become apparent for a considerable period after the release has taken place. Similarly, the extent of scientific knowledge required to identify and analyse alleged impacts on biodiversity may be inadequate at the time of the GMO release, but may change in the years following.

The European Union's submissions to the Working Group on Liability support the use of both relative and absolute time limits in any regime developed for GMO liabilities (UNEP 2006, 53). It should take into consideration the fact that harmful effects may only manifest themselves after a long period of time, and that damage due to the biological activity of LMOs, or due to the fact that the organisms themselves are living and may reproduce, may only appear after several generations from the (intentional or unintentional) release of the LMO in question. Absolute time limits should be kept distinct from any applicable relative time limit; for instance, the period during which a victim should be allowed to bring a claim after identification of the damage and the person liable. The 2004 EU Environmental Liability Directive applies an absolute time limit, barring claims if more than 30 years has elapsed since the emission or event that is alleged to have given rise to the damage alleged (Article 17, discussed further below). Norway, on the other hand, applies both a relative and absolute limitation period in its general civil law: claims for damages cannot be made more than 20 years after the event alleged to have caused damage has taken place (an absolute bar) or more than three years after discovery of the damage alleged (a relative bar).

Given the complex scientific interactions engaged in possible damage arising from GMO releases, the EU's suggestion of an approach based on both a relative limitation period and an absolute one would seem appropriate. The identification of an appropriate limitation period may, however, prove difficult. Given the extended time frame for the emergence of the full effects of GMO interactions with the natural environment, the inclusion of a relative time limit would appear essential, allowing a claim within a fixed period following the discovery or identification of the damage alleged. A further complicating issue that will arise here, nevertheless, concerns the relevance of changes in scientific knowledge in the years following a GMO release – should identification of the alleged 'damage' be permitted many years later using scientific methods unknown at the time of the release? This issue is further complicated when one considers the application of risk assessment techniques engaged prior to GMO releases, such as those set out in Annex III of the Cartagena Protocol itself. If a GMO is 'safe' to release according to the state of scientific knowledge at the time of release, and has been authorized following a risk assessment carried out according to domestic legal processes that accord with the Protocol, should those responsible for the release not be entitled to a 'state of the art' defence protecting them against future potential liabilities which were not only unforeseen at the time of the release, but were unforeseeable given the (then) state of scientific knowledge? These are the sort of problems to which the unique interaction of law and biology in the regulation of GMO releases gives rise, and which most domestic legal systems do not have to consider in their application of limitation rules to ordinary civil claims. The Norwegian approach might offer a useful model, therefore, but it would have to be substantially modified before it might offer a suitable model for redress for any environmental damage alleged to flow from GMO releases.

(b) Quantifying Environmental Losses

One of the principal weaknesses of civil liability systems in their application to environmental liability is their reliance on monetary valuation and cost benefit analysis as the basis for the remediation of damage. Evaluating loss to the 'unowned' environment is extremely difficult to undertake in these terms, and the environmental losses likely to flow from GMO releases will fall squarely within this category. The primary function of a liability mechanism should be to restore natural resources to their baseline condition before the damage complained of took place. In this respect, the EU's 2004 Environmental Liability Directive provides a useful model for consideration. The Environmental Liability Directive's framework for assessing damages focuses on developing plans to restore damaged natural resources and resource services, rather than assessing the monetary value of the damage to the resource. In other words, the responsible party pays for the cost of implementing the compensatory restoration project, not the monetary value of the interim losses. This has the advantage of making economic valuation techniques less controversial and thereby more acceptable to potential liable parties (Brans 2005). Annex II of the Directive provides for 'primary restoration' damages to be assessed on the basis of measures taken to restore damaged natural resources (and natural resource services) to their baseline condition. Compensatory measures include off site measures, such as creating a replacement habitat elsewhere, where primary restoration is not possible. The person responsible for the damage can be held liable for the cost of restoring the injured natural habitat to baseline condition, compensation for interim loss of resource services during the restoration period, and (in addition) the costs of assessing damages and legal and enforcement costs (Articles 2 and 8 of the Directive).

(c) Insurance Mechanisms

The primary function of a liability mechanism is the allocation of risk. Whether losses (however quantified) are recoverable from the party who carries that risk involves a variety of further issues that, in the special case of GMO liability, would preclude recovery without the establishment of some form of insurance, or of a liability fund appropriated to cover potential claims. Given the long timescale over which interactions with biodiversity will emerge, it is entirely likely that those responsible for their original release may have ceased to trade or gone into liquidation (in the case of limited companies), or may be deceased, untraceable or bankrupt (in the case of an individual). The development of an insurance mechanism appropriate to indemnify against environmental losses flowing from GMO releases is therefore of pivotal importance. The special nature of the problems surrounding the development of GM technology and its interactions with the natural environment also mean, however, that this will be difficult to bring to fruition. Indeed, a paper presented to the first meeting of the Cartagena Protocol Working Group on Liability and Redress suggested that issues relating to insurability were the primary reasons why several important international treaties on Environmental Liability (for example, the Basel Convention on Liability and Compensation and the UNECE Convention on Civil Liability for Damage Caused During Carriage of Dangerous Goods) have not yet entered into force (UNEP 2005).

A key problem in developing an insurance mechanism for GMO-related liabilities is that it could only indemnify claimants in monetary terms. It follows that the only risks that would be insurable are those that are generally accepted and about which there is consensus as to the value of the damaged entity and the way the loss can be compensated. If liability were based on a restoration model of the kind found in the EU Environmental Liability Directive, for example, the insurable risk would be that of having to fund restoration work to the satisfaction of the public authorities, where natural habitats had been damaged as a result of a GMO release to the environment for which the insured was responsible. Although this model, as noted above, makes it easier to gain consensus on the valuation of 'damage', it is still unsuitable as a basis for the development of an insurance mechanism – partly because the cost of executing possible remediation work will remain unquantifiable until damage actually occurs, and partly because the likelihood (risk) of damage will also be difficult to quantify. The likelihood of a consensus emerging is not assisted by the wide disparity in the views of members of the Working Group on Liability. The EU favours the use of voluntary insurance (UNEP 2006, 57), whereas other members of the Group (such as Greenpeace) favour the establishment of an Indemnity Fund with contributions from the biotechnology industry (UNEP 2006, 60–65). Another approach, using the Norwegian Gene Technology Act as its basis, would be to impose an obligation to take financial security for liability as a condition of the approval of a deliberate or contained use of GMOs by the regulator.

(d) Standing and Access to Redress

Should individuals have access to the courts of signatory states of the CBD for redress where damage arising from GMO releases is alleged? Or should a liability model instead limit redress to the public authorities? The issue of standing is usually the preserve of national legal systems. The Working Group has considered the experience of the EC Environmental Liability Directive, however, which offers an example of a different approach. The Directive relies largely on the competent public authorities to implement its liability scheme, and does not enable legal or natural persons affected by environmental damage to sue polluters directly. However, it provides natural and legal persons, in certain prescribed circumstances, with a right to require the competent authority to act according to the obligations set under the Directive and to challenge through a review procedure the competent authority's decisions, acts or failures to act (UNEP 2006, 75).

Risk Assessment and the Regulatory Approval Framework in the EU

It will be clear from the above discussion that agreement on a liability mechanism under the Cartagena Protocol is some way off. Equally clear is the fact that the existing legislation on GMO releases in the EU provides one of the clearest examples not only of the development of a regulatory model for the application of scientific risk assessment prior to releases into the environment, but also of a fully developed mechanism for mediating alleged liabilities arising from GM cropping. In the second part of this chapter we will, therefore, examine the extent to which these offer a sound model for wider adoption under the aegis of the Protocol.

Within the EU the 'environmental' impacts of GM cropping are primarily dealt with by European environmental legislation. The 1990 Directive on Deliberate Releases into the Environment of Genetically Modified Organisms (Directive 1990/220/EC) required the member states to establish technocratic authorization processes before permitting the release of GMOs. A revised text of the Deliberate Releases Directive was adopted in 2001 (Directive 2001/18/EC). This strengthened the scientific risk assessment procedures in order to require the 'direct, indirect, immediate and delayed' effects of a GMO release to be taken into account before it can be authorized. In summary, the Directive requires the carrying out of field trials under licence ('Part B' authorizations for experimental releases), and prohibits the subsequent marketing of a genetically modified crop or seed without a second authorization – a so-called 'Part C authorization' – that permits commercial releases. Under the 2001 Directive market authorizations have to be reviewed and renewed every ten years.

The approach adopted in the EC Deliberate Releases Directive is strongly premised on the application of the 'precautionary principle' of European environmental law. Article 174 (2) of the EC Treaty states that, 'Community policy on the environment shall … be based on the precautionary principle and on the principles that preventive action should be taken, that environmental damage should as a priority be rectified at source and that the polluter should pay.' The European Commission published a Communication in 2000 giving guidance to the member states on the application of the principle. This states 'where there are threats of serious or irreversible damage, lack of full scientific certainty shall not be used as a reason for postponing cost-effective measures to prevent environmental degradation' (CEC 2000a). The approach adopted within the regulatory context of EC environmental law utilizes the precautionary principle primarily as a risk management tool. Identifying an acceptable level of scientific risk of environmental damage is a political matter for the member states. In *Pfizer v European Commission*, (2002) the European Court of Justice ruled that the precautionary principle can be invoked to justify legislative action wherever there is more than a hypothetical risk of damage, even if the risk that exists cannot be fully demonstrated by available scientific means. Clearly, this gives wide latitude for the application of precaution in approving (or not approving) GMO releases.

By way of an example of the manner in which these legislative requirements have been introduced by the member sates, an administrative consent procedure was established in the United Kingdom by the Environmental Protection Act 1990. Sections 108–112 of the 1990 Act require that the release of a GMO into the environment cannot be lawfully undertaken without the consent of the Secretary of State, who must be satisfied that it is 'safe'. As a consequence, new varieties of GM seed can only be marketed after trial plantings have taken place under a Part B licence that involve a release to the environment in controlled conditions, and following official listing on the register of national seed varieties.

Expert scientific advice on the safety of releases is provided to the United Kingdom's Department of the Environment Food and Rural Affairs (hereafter referred to as DEFRA) by a specialist scientific body, the Advisory Committee on Releases to the Environment (hereafter ACRE). The ACRE plays a key role in the administrative consent apparatus. It reviews all applications for the release of GMOs to the environment (i.e., both Part B and Part C consents) and advises the relevant ministers as to the potential risks to human health and the wider environment arising from them. It has developed a number of Guidance Notes to assist applicants and define the parameters within which it exercises its advisory role in the regulatory process. Of particular importance is ACRE Guidance Note 12 on environmental risk assessment (DEFRA 2001), and ACRE Guidance Note 16 on Best Practice in the Design of Post Market Monitoring Plans (DEFRA 2004). The ACRE Guidance on post market monitoring plans is potentially very important in any consideration of environmental liability flowing from GM releases. The Guidance Note's articulation of what the regulator will expect in terms of the ongoing monitoring of the impact of GM crops will be relevant, for example, to determine whether cross-pollination of nearby organic crops is reasonably foreseeable (a key factor in establishing liability in private law), and may inform a court's view of the behaviour of the parties in a lawsuit. The Guidance operationalizes the requirement in the 2001 Deliberate Releases Directive for ongoing scientific monitoring of GM releases following the grant of a Part C licence for commercial release to the market. Annex III to Directive 2001/18/EC requires applicants for GM authorizations to supply information which includes not only a risk assessment of the possible impacts on human health and the environment of the release requested, but also a detailed post marketing monitoring plan to monitor emerging effects following the grant of market authorization. Data generated by the monitoring process will be important in the process for the ten-yearly review of GM licences now required under the revised Directive.

The basis for the application of scientific risk assessment under these procedures is largely outside the remit of judicial review through the courts. This is clearly illustrated by the only case in which this issue has arisen in the United Kingdom, *R v Secretary of State for the Environment ex parte Watson* [1999]. The court of appeal was asked to declare invalid an approval granted by the minister to the National Institute for Agricultural Botany for field trials of GM maize at a site in Devon. The claimant, an organic sweetcorn producer, based his action in judicial review alleging the decision to grant a licence for trail plantings for the GM crop was *ultra vires* and void. The action was unsuccessful. This case is important because it illustrates, first, the courts' unwillingness to question the risk assessment undertaken by the regulator. The Environmental Risk Assessment carried out by ACRE indicated that in optimal climatic conditions the maximum contamination of the defendant's sweetcorn crop that could be expected if the crops were planted 200m apart was one kernel in a thousand. The two crops were in fact planted 2 km apart. As a result, in ACRE's view the danger of cross-contamination was so small as to be statistically insignificant. The court refused to interfere with the scientific basis for this assessment, and held that the minister was acting reasonably in following its advice. The courts will not impugn a risk assessment other than on the normal grounds of judicial review – for example, where it is based on irrelevant considerations, or is 'Wednesbury unreasonable' (i.e., is such that no reasonable body could have arrived at the decision on the basis of the evidence before them). That was not the case here.

Second, the court made a number of comments *obiter dicta* on the likely outcome of the plaintiff's claim had it been framed instead as a nuisance action. In the course of a short judgement dismissing the claim, Buxton L.J. commented that the applicant's case 'sounded like one of private nuisance' and should have been pleaded as such, as the claim was ultimately aimed at restricting the NIAB's right to use its property for an otherwise legitimate purpose. He also indicated, however, that the court would have also been unsympathetic to a claim framed in this alternative manner. The court characterized organic farming as a 'hypersensitive' land use and, therefore, as unprotected in the law of nuisance. The decision therefore graphically illustrates the difficulties likely to be faced by a claimant seeking to establish liability for alleged GM 'contamination' in the private nuisance. There are, for example, difficult problems of causation, and in establishing that the cross-fertilization of a non-GM crop is either property damage in the required sense, or is causing an unreasonable interference with the neighbour's land use. These demonstrate very clearly the potential importance of a public liability regime if redress is to be made available for alleged losses suffered by organic and non-GM farmers as a result of the introduction of GM agriculture. In this regard, much reliance has been placed on the potential of the 2004 EC Environmental Liability Directive to offers redress for environmental damage flowing from GM releases.

The 2004 EC Environmental Liability Directive

Scientific risk assessment is an integral feature of the GMO authorization process, even though the terms on which this is done may be controversial and contested in some quarters. Where, despite the risk assessment carried out prior to the grant of a licence for release, damage to any of the environmental media (land, water, air) or to biodiversity is threatened following a GMO release, a public liability mechanism is provided for in the EC's Environmental Liability Directive of 2004 (Directive 2004/35/EC of the European Parliament and of the Council). This applies for the remediation of 'environmental damage' and 'biodiversity damage' – but not for economic loss, other commercial losses or property damage.

Most legal systems, in both the Roman law tradition and the common law family, fail to provide adequate provision in their private law for civil liability for 'environmental' damage (for a review, see ICEAC 2005). The European Commission's initiative to rectify this lacuna in relation to the civil law of the various member states of the EU originated in a hastily prepared Green Paper issued in 1993, which reviewed the civil liability regimes in the various member states and suggested the Europe-wide establishment of a strict liability regime for damage resulting from pollution, for instance, one in which the establishment of liability would not require proof of fault (typically negligence) on the part of the polluter. When the subsequent White Paper on Environmental Liability was issued by the Commission in 2000 (CEC 2000b), the proposals had moved away from establishing a strict liability regime located within the private law of the member states, and had moved instead towards imposing a public liability mechanism that is one that operated through the member states' administrative direction and regulatory cost recovery mechanisms to identify and allocate responsibility for environmental damage. This was intended to ensure that those who threaten or cause environmental damage should bear the cost of preventing and repairing that damage.

The White Paper expressly noted the desire of several member states to ensure that legislation should address the issue of environmental damage caused by the release of GMOs. This commitment was taken forward in the Directive on Environmental Liability, which was adopted in 2004. When the Commission's final proposal for a Directive on Environmental Liability were first published in 2002 (CEC 2002) they proved to be rather more limited than initially proposed (for criticism, see Jones 2002; Lee 2002). In the form eventually adopted, the Directive is one of a composite package of measures intended for GMOs. Its adoption was an integral part of the deal struck by member states to secure the revision to the Deliberate Releases Directive that was finally agreed in 2001. Agreement between the European Commission and the European Parliament on the adoption in 2001 of a strengthened Deliberate Release Directive was only reached in the EU Conciliation Committee on condition that environmental liability for GMOs be addressed within a set timescale. The provisions on GMOs subsequently included in the Environmental Liability Directive delivered that undertaking.

The liability regime under the Directive applies to two different categories of damage – 'environmental damage' to which a strict liability regime is applied, and biodiversity damage to which a fault-based regime can be applied (Article 3.1 of Directive 2004/35/EC). Both are defined with some precision and in scientific terms. 'Environmental damage' has three possible components: it means first, damage to protected species and natural habitats; second, water damage that significantly and adversely affects the ecological, chemical and/or quantitative status or ecological potential of the waters concerned; and third, land damage, meaning any land contamination which creates a significant risk of human health being adversely affected as a result of the direct or indirect introduction in on or under the land of substances, preparations or microorganisms (Article 2.1). Damage is defined to mean a measurable adverse change in a natural resource or measurable impairment of a natural resource service (Article 2.2).

The Directive is based squarely on an administrative liability model, requiring the member states to establish administrative mechanisms for identifying and remediating environmental damage where it occurs, and cost recovery mechanisms to ensure that the financial cost of rectifying damaged is recovered from those responsible for causing it and that remediation takes place at the polluter's expense. This implements 'the polluter pays' principle in EC law, and reflects a policy approach focused on 'internalizing' the environmental costs generated by the polluter's production methods. This approach is implemented by provisions in Annex III, which requires the member states to ensure that operators whose activities fall within the categories there listed must bear the cost of taking action to prevent or to clean-up such environmental damage as they threaten or cause, irrespective of fault. Member states are required to establish strict liability regimes as regards administrative direction to prevent harm (Article 5), and regarding remedial action to reimburse costs incurred by public bodies in remedial action (Article 6). As regards biodiversity damage, liability extends to all operators (not just those carrying out Annex III activities) to bear the costs of protecting and repairing legally protected wildlife sites (Article 3.1 (b)). As far as GMOs are concerned, the Directive encompasses environmental damage resulting from both the contained use of GMOs (including transport) and from the deliberate release of GMOs to the environment in accordance with the authorization procedures under Directive 2001/18/EC. These are both occupational activities listed in Annex III, and will engage strict liability under Article 3 of the Directive (Annex III paras. 11 and 12).

Despite this, the 2004 Directive has several limitations that will impair its utility as a mechanism for (i) determining issues of liability arising from GMO releases to the environment and (ii) providing for redress and restoration of the environment. In the first place the Directive is not retrospective (Article 19). It must have been implemented by the member states by 30 April 2007, and does not apply to any emission event or incident that took place before that date. It also applies an absolute (and not a relative) limitation period for the application of liability and cost recovery. Accordingly, the Directive does not apply to any damage if more than 30 years has elapsed since the emission, event or incident that resulted in the damage that has occurred (Article 17). The emergence of damage arising from the introduction of GMOs to the environment will potentially have a very long time frame, and this is especially the case with damage to biodiversity. The replacement of wild non-GM weed species with volunteers or outcrosses from GM plant varieties may, for example, take considerably longer than 30 years to emerge, and the environmental impacts may not be discernable for many years. As has already been noted above, this problem has been identified as a major concern by the Intergovernmental Committee for the Cartagena Protocol on Biosafety charged with producing an international regime for liability and redress (Smyth et al. 2004, 94–5). The limitation model used in the Environmental Liability Directive is similar to that used in the international treaties reviewed by the Intergovernmental Committee for the Cartagena Protocol (and criticized by Smyth et al. 2004 in their application to GMOs).

The application of an *absolute* (rather than a relative) limitation period, could also give rise to a number of additional problems. Proving the necessary causal link between a particular GMO release and its genetic affects on biodiversity after a period of (say) 20 to 30 years will in practice be impossible, even if the limitation period has not expired. A related problem for the purposes of establishing causality will be the necessity of identifying the 'emission, event or incident' (the terms used in Article 17) by which the GMO was released. This will be necessary for the purposes of calculating when the 30-year limitation period starts to run. Because the limitation period is an absolute one, it will run from the date of the GMO release – not from the date when the damage became apparent, as would be the case if a relative limitation bar (such as that applied in Norway to civil liability claims, discussed above) were to apply. In the case of GMO releases, the cross-pollination of wild weed species with commercial GM plant varieties will take place continuously over a period of time as a consequence of seasonal cross-pollination. It may be impossible to establish a single 'emission, event or incident' as the causative factor leading to environmental damage.

The Directive's scope is also comparatively narrow as to the *types of damage* to which it may potentially apply. It does not apply to damage to the person or goods. Neither does it apply to property damage, unless it falls within the narrow definition of 'land damage' comprised within the wider definition of environmental damage used in the Directive, that is it creates a significant risk to human health (Article 2.1 (c)). Most important of all, however, is the very limited scope of its application in the case of biodiversity damage. As regards biodiversity, liability only extends under Article 2.3 to damage to the conservation status of natural habitats and protected species that are *either* protected under the EC Wild Birds Directive of 1979 (Council Directive 79/409/EEC) or the EC Habitats and Species Directive of 1992 (Council Directive 92/43/EC), *or* for which areas for protection or conservation have been designated under the national legislation of the member state: see Article 2.1 (2) and (18) (definitions of 'biodiversity' and of 'environmental damage').

In basing protection exclusively on protected habitats and species, the Directive eschewed the approach in the Convention on Biological Diversity, which defines biodiversity in much wider terms. It was felt that introducing notions of variability in living organisms as an attribute of defining damage would raise difficult *questions* as to how such damage would be quantified and what would be the threshold of damage entailing liability (CEC 2002, 17). Nevertheless, an approach based primarily on protecting wildlife habitats in national and European designated sites would impose a severe geographical restriction on the scope of liability. When the Natura 2000 network of protected European wildlife sites envisaged under the 1992 Habitats Directive is fully established, it is anticipated that it will extend to no more than 10 per cent of the geographical land mass of the European Union. Perhaps more important, most protected habitats will be in wilderness areas (for example, upland or wetland habitats) far from sites where GM cropping is likely to be envisaged.

The potential scope of the liability mechanism is further limited by the restrictive definition of biodiversity 'damage' in the Environmental Liability Directive itself. Bioiodiversity damage is defined so as to exclude adverse effects which result from an act which was expressly authorized by the relevant authorities in accordance with provisions implementing the regime for the management of special areas of conservation under the Habitats Directive, or in accordance with provisions of national law having an equivalent effect in relation to habitats or species. In the context of the relevant regulatory regime in the United Kingdom, for example, important habitats and species are given protection through the designation of

Sites of Special Scientific Interest (SSSI) under the Wildlife and Countryside Act 1981 (as amended). The owner or occupier of a site thus designated cannot carry out an operation notified to him in the site notification as likely to damage the conservation interest – unless he has the permission of the regulator. The granting of operational consent under Section 28E of the 1981 Act for an operation likely to damage the conservation interest of an SSSI (such as ploughing and planting a field with GM maize) will therefore preclude liability arising under the Directive, even if biodiversity damage is caused by it.

The Directive also includes a number of exceptions to liability, several of which are potentially important in respect of liability for GMOs. It establishes a 'state of the art' defence that provides that no liability will accrue for damage arising from emissions or activities that were not considered harmful according to the state of scientific knowledge at the time when the emission was released or the activity took place (Article 8.4). The exact scope of this defence is uncertain, but it has the potential to exclude a wide range of liability in cases involving GMOs – not least because the release will have been sanctioned following an environmental risk assessment which (presumably) will have been based on the most up to date scientific evidence available at the time (see Lee 2003). The Directive also includes a compliance defence, providing that no liability will accrue for damage caused by 'an emission or event expressly authorised by … an authorisation conferred by or given under applicable national laws and regulations' (Article 8.4(a)). This defence would preclude liability from arising in cases where GMO releases have been authorized under national legislation introduced to implement Directive 2001/18/EC. Neither defence can apply where the operator is negligent. The state of the art and compliance defences are not mandatory, and their potential to limit the scope of the Directive in relation to GMOs will depend upon how many member states opt to include them in their implementing legislation.

Conclusion

It was noted above that the problems identified by the Working Group on Liability and Redress established under the Cartagena Protocol fell under four broad headings: the application of limitation periods, quantification of losses, the development of an insurance mechanism, and *Locus Standi* to bring claims in the courts. To what extent does the Environmental Liability Directive offer solutions to these problems and provide a possible model for wider adoption under the aegis of the Cartagena Protocol?

The obvious conclusion from the discussion of the Directive's limitations presented here is that it is unlikely to have a significant effect on damage resulting from GMOs. Of the four problem areas identified by the Working Group on Liability, the only area in which the Directive offers a radical approach meriting further study is in relation to the quantification of damage. As noted above, the Directive's approach to protecting the 'unowned' environment is based on developing plans for the restoration of damaged natural resources and resource services, and on the application of the polluter pays principle to internalize environment remediation costs. This has the merit of avoiding difficult issues of placing a monetary valuation on damage to environmental resources and biodiversity. Its approach to the other problems of GMO liability and risk assessment are more limited. The member states are not required to impose compulsory insurance requirements, although the Directive does exhort them to investigate appropriate insurance mechanisms with a view to developing a coherent insurance market in environmental liability. This is a project to which the European Commission intends to return in the near future. And, as noted above, the imposition of an absolute limitation bar will lead to particular problems in relation to identifying GMO-related damage and imposing liability, even in cases which are clearly within the remit of the Directive. The use of a combined approach would be more appropriate in cases in which GMO releases are implicated, involving the use of an absolute bar, coupled with a relative limitation period barring actions within a fixed time following the identification of 'damage' flowing from a GMO release.

The Directive will undoubtedly impose more stringent safeguards in wildlife sites designated for protection under the EC's Habitats and Wild Birds Directives, as member states will be required to apply strict liability for biodiversity damage that results from the release of GMOs to the environment. The territorial limits placed upon the scope of the proposed liability, however, mean that its practical impact may be minimal. In focusing exclusively on the Natura 2000 network of protected wildlife habitats and protected species it ignores wider farmland biodiversity, which will remain unprotected against the long term consequences of the introduction of GM cropping. Perhaps most important of all, however, are its restrictions on standing to bring claims. The payment of compensation to individuals for environmental damage is expressly prohibited under the terms of Article 3.3 of the Directive. As a public liability regime, it confers no jurisdiction whatever on private individuals or NGOs to bring claims for environmental damage. It does, however, give NGOs and individuals a right to press the regulator to take action, and member states must provide them with the right to challenge the basis of the regulators decision either in a court or other independent tribunal. This concession is unlikely to prove of major benefit, however, given the courts' reluctance to interfere with decisions based on risk assessment in the regulatory approval process for GMOs, as clearly demonstrated in the *ex parte Watson* decision. Whatever the merits of its approach to cost recovery as a basis for liability, therefore, the Directive remains a flawed model for the resolution of the many complex and difficult liability issues to which the commercialization of GM agriculture are likely to give rise.

References

Brans, E.H.P. (2005) 'Liability for Damage to Public Natural Resources', *Environmental Law Review*, 7: 90–109.

Cartagena Protocol on Biosafety (1992) The protocol to the Convention on Biological Diversity (CBD) *International Legal Materials* 31: 818.

CEC (2000a) *Communication on the Precautionary Principle*, 2000 COM 1 Final.

CEC (2000b) *White Paper on Environmental Liability*, 2000 COM 66 Final.

CEC (2002) *Proposal for a Directive on Environmental Liability*, 2002 COM 17 Final.

DEFRA (2001) *Guidance on the Assessment of the Impact on Wider Biodiversity from Proposed Cultivation of GM Crops* (ACRE Guidance Note 12).

DEFRA (2002) The Criteria used by ACRE to gauge harm when giving advice on the risks of releasing genetically modified organisms to the environment, available at (www.defra.gov.uk/environment/acre/harm/pdf/acre_harm_report_.pdf).

DEFRA (2004) *Guidance on Best Practice in the Design of Post Market Monitoring Plans*, ACRE Guidance note 16.

International Court of Environmental Arbitration and Conciliation (ICEAC) (2005) 'Consultative Opinion on Liability of Public and Private Actors for Genetic Contamination of Non-GM Crops', *Environmental Law Review*, 7: 253–72.

Jones, B. (2002) 'European Commission: Proposal for a Framework Directive on Environmental Liability', *Environmental Law and Management*, 14: 5–10.

Lee, M. (2002) 'Tort, Regulation and Environmental Liability', *Legal Studies*, 22: 33–52.

Lee, M. (2003) 'Regulatory Solutions for GMOs in Europe: the Problem of Liability', *Journal of Environmental Law and Policy*, 12: 311.

Qureshi, A.H. (2000) 'The Cartagena Protocol on Biosafety and the WTO – Coexistence or Incoherence?', *International and Comparative Law Quarterly*, 49: 835.

Schoenbaum, T.J. (2000) 'International Trade in Living Modified Organisms: the New Regimes', *International and Comparative Law Quarterly*, 49: 856.

Smyth, Phillips, Kerr and Khachatourians (2004) *Regulating the Liabilities of Agricultural Biotechnology* (CABI Publishing).

Street, P. (2001) 'Trading in Risk: the Biosafety Protocol, GMOs and the World Trade Organisation', *Environmental Law Review*, 3: 247.

UNEP (2005) Report of the Working Group on Liability and Redress, 'Status of Third party Liability Treaties and an Analysis of Difficulties facing Their Entry into force', *UNEP/CBD/BS/WG-L&R/1/INF/3*.

UNEP (2006) Report of the Working Group on Liability and Redress, March 2006 'Channelling of Liability', *UNEP/CBD/BS/COP-MOP/3/10*.

UNEP (2007) Report of the Working Group on Liability and Redress in the Context of the Cartagena Protocol on Biosafety on its Third Meeting, March 2007, *UNEP/CBD/BS/WG-L&R/3/3*.

WTO (2006) 'EC – Approval and Marketing of Biotechnological Products', *WT/DS291/INTERIM; WT/DS292/INTERIM; WT/DS293/INTERIM*.

Chapter 8

Legitimizing Regulatory Decision-Making about Genetically Modified Organisms under the *Gene Technology Act 2000* (Cth)

Charles Lawson and Richard Hindmarsh

Introduction

As a measure of the collective concern about the high social costs from restrictions on competition (together with the inefficiencies in the market from less than optimal allocation of resources), Australia has undertaken an extensive review of its regulations and government actions to remove anti-competitive arrangements that cannot be justified to achieve an identifiable benefit or 'public interest'.[1] In the first steps along this path the Hilmer Committee undertook a broad ranging policy review of the restrictions on competition in Australia and proposed a number of reforms directed at removing barriers to competition with the aim of benefiting consumers, promoting business competition, fostering innovation and making the Australian economy more flexible, thereby 'improving its capacity to respond to external shocks and changing market opportunities' (Independent Committee of Inquiry into Competition Policy in Australia 1993, xvi). The Hilmer Committee Report recommended that '[a] mechanism to promote reform of regulation that unjustifiably restricts competition form a central plank of a national competition policy' (Independent Committee of Inquiry into Competition Policy in Australia 1993, 211) and then recommended all Australian governments abide by a series of principles, including that:

> There should be no regulatory restrictions on competition unless clearly demonstrated to be in the public interest … Proposals for new regulation that

1 This process may be traced back to the establishment of a *National Competition Policy* following the Independent Committee of Inquiry into Competition Policy in Australia 1993 report, the enactment of provisions following the Government response to that report (*Competition Policy Reform Act 1995* (Cth)) and formal agreement of a *National Competition Policy* between the Commonwealth, States and Territories (see National Competition Council 1998); Commonwealth Parliament 1991, 1761; details about the stewarding of the *National Competition Policy* agreement are reviewed in Harman 1996, 208–17.

> have the potential to restrict competition should include evidence that the competitive effects of the regulation have been considered; that the benefits of the proposed restriction outweigh the likely costs; and that the restriction is no more restrictive than necessary in the public interest … All existing regulation that imposes a significant restriction on competition should be subject to regular review to determine [that the restriction on competition is] clearly demonstrated [to be in the] public interest (Independent Committee of Inquiry into Competition Policy in Australia 1993, 212).

Following the Hilmer Committee Report, a number of measures were initiated to put the report's broader recommendations into effect.[2] These included amendments to the *Trade Practices Act 1974* (Cth) and *Prices Surveillance Act 1983* (Cth),[3] three inter-governmental agreements (including the *Competition Principles Agreement*), and related reforms to the electricity, gas, water and road transport industries (National Competition Council 1998). A significant part of the *Competition Principles Agreement*, for the purposes of this chapter, was that governments around Australia review the anti-competitive effects of their existing legislation (*Competition Principles Agreement* cl 5(3)) and ensure those proposals for new legislation that restricts competition be consistent with the 'guiding principle' (*Competition Principles Agreement* cl 5(5)):

> … that legislation (including Acts, enactments, Ordinances or regulations) should not restrict competition unless it can be demonstrated[4] that:
>
> (a) the benefits of the restriction to the community as a whole outweigh the costs; and

---

2 For a review of the key measures and operation of the National Competition Policy: Deighton-Smith 2001.

3 See *Competition Policy Reform Act 1995* (Cth); see also the Commonwealth Parliament 1995, 2793–801; corresponding legislative amendments were also to be introduced in the various states and territories.

4 The construction of the *Competition Principles Agreement* cl 5(1) relies on the term 'demonstrated' in setting out the standard to be achieved in applying the 'guiding principle' in reviewing existing legislation and proposed legislation that restricts competition, while the *Competition Principles Agreement* cl 5(5) expressly requires 'evidence' that proposed legislation restricting competition is consistent with the 'guiding principle'. While this might be construed as a lower standard for reviewing existing legislation, the preferable construction is evidence demonstrating that the guiding principle has been satisfied. That is, 'legislation that restricts competition must be accompanied by evidence that the benefits of the restriction to the community as a whole outweigh the costs, and that the objectives can only be achieved by restricting competition': Productivity Commission 2003, 7; see also National Competition Council 2002, 1.

(b) the objectives of the legislation can only be achieved by restricting competition (*Competition Principles Agreement* cl 5(1)).

A timetable for reviewing legislation was agreed in 1996 (Council of Australian Governments 1995, 7).[5] The approach to conducting and the content of these legislation reviews under the *Competition Principles Agreement* is primarily addressed in the Terms of Reference, although there may be additional considerations (*Competition Principles Agreement* cl 5(9)), mandatory procedures (Office of Regulation Review 1998, A1) and guidance from other sources (Centre for International Economics 1999). Essentially, the objective in conducting the legislation reviews is to assess whether the arrangements restrict competition, whether the benefits to the community as a whole outweigh the costs (including the broader assessment of the 'public interest'), that it can clearly be demonstrated that the benefits exceed the costs and whether the same objectives can be achieved by other better means (Centre for International Economics 1999, 7). Further, the regulation in force should be both 'efficient', in terms of 'minimizing compliance and other costs imposed on the community' and 'effective' in 'addressing an identified problem' (Productivity Commission 2003, 1). Unfortunately, and despite nearly five years of operation, the *Gene Technology Act 2000* (Cth) (the GT Act) has not been subjected to a *Competition Principles Agreement* review, albeit some aspects of the legislative scheme have been subjected to some analysis (Productivity Commission 2004, 72).[6]

The second element of the *Competition Principles Agreement* is its application to proposals for new legislation. The approach adopted by the Australian Government when proposing new legislation is to undertake public consultation with those affected and assess the possible restrictions on competition. The Office of Regulation Review (ORR) (now the Office of Best Practice Regulation) is the Australian Government's 'regulation watchdog' with the charter that '[w]hilst maintaining an economy-wide perspective, the ORR is to focus its efforts on regulations which restrict competition' (Office of Regulation Review 1998, A11). As part of its task reviewing Regulatory Impact Statements (RIS) prepared for new legislation,[7] the ORR recognizes that 'restrictions on competition have been

5 This timetable was extended to 30 June 2002 (Council of Australian Governments 2000, 5), and presumably has now been extended again: Council of Australian Governments 2004, 2006.

6 The recent review of the *Gene Technology Act 2000* (Cth) (the GT Act) by an independent panel appointed by Gene Technology Ministerial Council did not consider the *Competition Principles Agreement* as part of its terms of reference: Independent Panel Reviewing the Gene Technology Act 2006, 67–76.

7 A RIS has seven key elements – the problem or issues which give rise to the need for action, the desired objective(s), the options (regulatory and/or non-regulatory) that may constitute viable means for achieving the desired objective(s), an assessment of the impact (costs and benefits) on consumers, business, government and the community of each option,

singled out for special attention in RISs' (Office of Regulation Review 1998, A3).[8] The key objective of the RIS is:

> Preparation of a [RIS] is a critical feature of the regulation making process, primarily because doing so formalises and evidences the steps that should be taken in policy formulation. It helps to ensure that options to address a perceived policy problem are canvassed in a systematic, objective and transparent manner, with options ranked according to their net economic and social benefits. The RIS embodies this analytical process (Office of Regulation Review 1998, A11).

The RIS for the GT Act was addressed in the presentation of the legislation before Parliament and sets out in some detail the justifications for the GT Act (see generally Explanatory Memorandum 2000). The GT Act formally regulates dealings with certain organisms that have been modified through 'gene technology':[9] genetically modified (GM) organisms (GMOs).[10] The GT Act was considered necessary because 'GMOs and GM products present a range of possible health and environmental risks to the community' (Explanatory Memorandum 2000, 12). The key concern appears to have been that consumers and the community lacked the relevant knowledge and information to be able to assess those risks:[11]

---

a consultation statement, a recommended option, and a strategy to implement and review the preferred option: Office of Regulation Review 1998, A2.

8 Although noting that the ORR's charter is broader than merely considering competition restrictions and extends to the costs and benefits to business (and small business in particular): Productivity Commission 2003, 73.

9 Where 'gene technology' means 'any technique for the modification of genes or other genetic material, but does not include: (a) sexual reproduction; (b) homologous recombination; or (c) any other technique specified in the regulations for the purposes of this paragraph': GT Act s 10.

10 GT Act s 10 defines 'GMO' to mean a 'genetically modified organism', which in turn, is defined to mean: '(a) an organism that has been modified by gene technology; (b) an organism that has inherited particular traits from an organism (the initial organism), being traits that occurred in the initial organism because of gene technology; (c) anything declared by the regulations to be a genetically modified organism, or that belongs to a class of things declared by the regulations to be genetically modified organisms; but does not include: (d) a human being, if the human being is covered by para (a) only because the human being has undergone somatic cell gene therapy; or (e) an organism declared by the regulations not to be a genetically modified organism, or that belongs to a class of organisms declared by the regulations not to be genetically modified organisms'. The *Gene Technology Regulations 2001* (Cth) (the GT Regulations) do not presently declare anything to be a GMO for the purposes of para (c), although GT Reguation 5 does declare a number of organisms set out in sch 1 as being not GMOs for the purposes of para (e) of the GMO definition.

11 Although this sentiment was not reflected in the second reading speech: Commonwealth Parliament 2000a, 18105–106.

> While the level of knowledge about possible risks is growing in the community, there remains inadequate information available to the community and consumers … Individuals may also have difficulty in assessing and processing available information to help them make informed choices about what levels of possible risk they consider to be acceptable to their health and safety … [T]here are possible risks to public health and the environment that may not be properly taken into account by either the industry involved with GMOs or GM products, or the consumers, or users of GMOs or GM products … There are difficulties in relying upon industry to provide the necessary information and make appropriate risk assessment and management decisions (Explanatory Memorandum 2000, 12).[12]

On this basis there was considered to be 'a case for government intervention to assess and manage the risks and to provide information to consumers and the community' (Explanatory Memorandum 2000, 12). Perhaps most significantly, however, the pre-existing voluntary scheme[13] was considered to lack 'credibility in meeting the broad concerns of the community about the risks posed by not having in place, sufficient mechanisms to ensure adequate openness and transparency in its risk assessment and management roles, nor sufficient enforcement capabilities' with a consequence that might 'harm the ability of industry to market GMOs and GM products assessed as safe' (Explanatory Memorandum 2000, 13). Then in assessing the costs and benefits of a regulatory scheme,[14] the benefit for the community that outweighed any costs was:

> Assurances that all GMOs used in Australia have been comprehensively assessed by an independent Regulator as being safe in terms of the health of people and the impact on the environment. Public confidence in the regulation of GMOs also has positive downstream effects for industry, manifesting in increased consumer acceptance of GMOs assessed to be safe (Explanatory Memorandum 2000, 42).

In other words, the GT Act's purpose was to promote the quality (or legitimacy) of GMOs (and GM products) through a governmental institution making an independent risk assessment about the likely risks posed by GMOs

---

12 Noting that: 'because, in an objective aggregate sense, it may not be in their [industries'] best interests to draw the possibility of risk to the attention of prospective consumers and the community generally. Equally, consumers might discount the usefulness of industry provided information on that basis': Explanatory Memorandum 2000, 12.

13 For a review of the early developments eventually leading to the GT Act: Independent Panel Reviewing the Gene Technology Act 2006, 21–5.

14 This was the founding principle articulated in the Independent Committee of Inquiry into Competition Policy in Australia 1993, 206–208 and the subsequent codification of this principle in the *Competition Principles Agreement* binding the Commonwealth, States and Territories to facilitate effective competition to promote economic efficiency and benefits for consumers (*Competition Principles Agreement* cl 5(1)), as part of the *National Competition Policy*: National Competition Council 1998.

(Commonwealth Parliament 2000a, 18104; see also Hain et al. 2002, 165). The intended consequence was to promote commercial transactions in GMOs and GM products as safe for consumers and the broader community.[15] Put another way, the purpose of the GT Act was to address the problems of asymmetric information, with the GT Act establishing an independent institution that might provide the necessary reassurances on community concerns about the health and safety, and environmental effects of GMOs (and GM products). It is therefore appropriate to assess the operation and implementation of the GT Act according to this framework, and the imperative that the GT Act was *only* justified as a regulatory measure to address the market failure for an institutional assurance about the quality (human health and safety and the environment) of GMOs and GM products.

The contention of this chapter is that the GT Act in its current structure and its current implementation is failing to provide the kinds of assurances necessary to address the asymmetric information in the markets for GMOs (Part 2). As a consequence, consumers may be reluctant to conclude a bargain because of their uncertain information about the quality of goods (information asymmetry), but might be assured by an institution that provides some quality standard, contributing positively to market efficiency and promoting economic welfare.[16] Applying information asymmetry considerations to GMOs assumes that consumers (and the community) may be uncertain about the quality of GMOs, and in particular their possible detrimental health and safety and environmental consequences.[17] A further assumption is that through regulatory intervention under the GT Act to regulate some GMOs, consumers (and the broader community) can be provided with the necessary health and safety and environmental assurances to conclude bargains involving GMOs.[18] While it is accepted that these assumptions are open to question and that there are other factors in determining consumer choices,[19] the purpose of this chapter is to illustrate that a strict liability scheme (Part 3) and more rigorous decision-making under the GT Act (Part 4) is possible and that it is consistent with the purpose of dealing with the market failure of information asymmetry that the GT Act was intended to address. The chapter concludes that introducing a strict liability scheme and addressing the existing flaws in decision-making about releasing GMOs into the environment are necessary to establish public trust and promote the market for valuable GMOs (and GM products) (Part 5).

---

15 There is a considerable literature on this issue: Newell 2002, 5–7.

16 For the classical statement of this concept: Akerlof 1970; for a recent statement in the context of consumer protection policy: Hadfield et al. 1998.

17 Noting that GT Act s 3 provides that '[t]he object of this Act is to protect the health and safety of people, and to protect the environment, by identifying risks posed by or as a result of gene technology, and by managing those risks through regulating certain dealings with GMOs'.

18 See James and Burton 2003 and the references therein.

19 For example, price discounting might be a significant factor in consumer preferences for some GMOs: James and Burton 2003.

Information Asymmetry Theory

The significant advance in the economics of information asymmetry was the recognition that the information available to purchasers in a market for goods and services about those goods and services was important in ensuring quality and the ongoing viability of the market.[20] The traditional conception of the problem and its solution is usually illustrated by the market for new and used cars, primarily 'for its concreteness and the ease in understanding rather than for its importance or realism' (Akerlof 1970, 489). According to this conception, the quality of a new or used car may be difficult for a purchaser to assess, there being some probability that the car is either of satisfactory quality (good quality) or unsatisfactory quality (bad quality or a lemon) (Akerlof 1970, 489). However, the seller is more likely to be aware of the quality, and because the purchaser does not have this information, the seller will be able to sell the unsatisfactory quality cars at a price at or approaching that of satisfactory quality cars (Akerlof 1970, 489). The consequence is that purchasers, unable to tell the difference between satisfactory quality and unsatisfactory quality, will drive down the price paying less for satisfactory quality as they are concerned about paying too much for unsatisfactory quality, with the consequence of ever decreasing market price, market quality and market size (Akerlof 1970, 488).

The information asymmetry between the seller and the purchaser can be addressed, at least in part, through an institution that provides some kind of guarantee about the quality (Akerlof 1970, 499–500). For example, licensing doctors, lawyers and barbers provides some form of independent assessment about basic quality standards and an assurance about a level of proficiency necessary to have obtained the licence (Akerlof 1970, 500). Thus, governmental intervention in the market may also be desirable to increase the welfare of all parties in the market through providing some form of quality assurance for purchasers (Akerlof 1970, 488). The expected consequence of governmental intervention will be to maintain the price and quality and also avoid the decline in market size (and perhaps even market extinction) (Akerlof 1970, 488).

Applying information asymmetry conceptions to GMOs and GMO regulation might be characterized as:

a. The potential purchasers of GMOs might be uncertain about the 'quality' of the GMO, being uncertain about the possible detrimental health and safety effects of GMOs on people (whether valid or not), and the possible detrimental effects of GMOs on the environment (whether valid or not).

20 There is an extensive literature on the application of information asymmetry theory, the foundation author considering insurance, the employment of minorities, the costs of dishonesty, and credit markets in under-developed countries: Akerlof 1970, 492–9; for another examination of the theory as it might apply to GMOs: Donat 2003, 437–9.

b. The differences between non-GMOs and GMOs are not readily discernable by potential purchasers (in the absence of clear and meaningful labelling), so that:
   i. Purchasers are faced with the potential risks of detrimental health and safety effects from GMOs (such as allergenic reactions, and so on).
   ii. Purchasers might be promoting detrimental environmental effects from GMOs by providing a market for GMOs that have detrimental consequences for the environment (such as contamination, weediness, and so on).
c. The producers and marketers (including the supply chain handlers) of GMOs may not recognize, or may discount, a purchaser's concerns (whether valid or not) about the possible health and safety and environmental effects.
d. Governmental intervention through regulating GMOs provides an independent assurance for purchasers about the likely health and safety effects and effects on the environment through an assessment of risk, and imposing of penalties that operate to ameliorate a purchaser's concerns about the possible health and safety and environmental effects.
e. Without governmental intervention, information asymmetry theory suggests that:
   i. The prices of GMOs (and possibly non-GMOs equivalents) will decline as sceptical purchasers are unwilling to pay for satisfactory quality (that is non-GMOs and GMOs with *no* detrimental health and safety and environmental effects) when they can not distinguish them from unsatisfactory quality (that is GMOs with detrimental health and safety and environmental effects).
   ii. The quality of GMOs will decline as producers and marketers (including the supply chain handlers) do not have the price premium signals to favour satisfactory quality that purchasers might otherwise desire from unsatisfactory quality.
   iii. The size of the market for GMOs will reduce and possibly extinguish as GMOs with increasingly detrimental health and safety and environmental effects (whether valid or not) are placed onto the market.

Strict Liability

Among the legal liability regimes strict liability is one of the ways of imposing liability for damage and internalizing the costs of an activity.[21] Strict liability provides a means of compensating third parties that suffer damage in the future by including those likely future costs in the price of the GMO (internalizes the

21 Other statutory and common law liability schemes (such as negligence laws, and so on) may also apply, although their application to internalize the costs of damage is by no means certain: Lee and Burrell 2002, 529–35; Rogers 2002, 3–6.

costs), as well as providing an incentive for producers and marketers (including the supply chain handlers) to avoid or minimize those likely risks and prospects of future damage.[22] Thus, strict liability may reinforce the existing institutional arrangements by assuring purchasers that with the prospect of bearing all the costs of liability, producers and marketers (including the supply chain handlers) of GMOs will *only* bring quality products to market. Without a reassuring legal liability regime in some form, information asymmetry theory suggests that purchasers will pay a lower price for GMOs as they take on the burden of the risk or prospect of damage (some of it non-financial), and further reduce the quality and size of the market.

This section of the chapter, under the following headings, examines '*The GT Act's prohibitory scheme and its reach*' and identifies '*The "gaps" in the existing liability regime*', followed by a discussion about the potential to address this concern with '*Conclusions about strict liability schemes*'. The purpose of this analysis is to illustrate that if the GT Act's purpose was to address the quality of GMOs and promote a market for GMOs, then providing the independent institution with the appropriate guarantee about the quality is essential to maintaining and promoting the future quality of GMOs (and GM products).

The GT Act's Prohibitory Scheme and Its Reach

Essentially the GT Act prohibits all 'dealings with' GMOs (GT Act s 10)[23] unless they are allowed, either because they satisfy defined criteria (GT Act s 78)[24] or they are licenced by the Gene Technology Regulator (the Regulator) under the GT Act (see GT Act part 5). The allowable dealings are those dealings that are exempt from licensing (GT Act ss 32(1) and 32(4) and *Gene Technology Regulations 2001* (Cth) (GT Regulations) r 6), a notifiable low risk dealing (GT Act ss 32(1) and 76 and GT Regulations rr 12 and 13), a licenced dealing (GT Act s 32(1) and part 5 and GT Regulations rr 7–11), a dealing on the GMO Register (GT Act s 32(1) and s 76), or a dealing with an organism, or class of organisms, declared to be outside the definition of a GMO (GT Act s 10 and GT Regulations r 5). However, in considering information asymmetries and liability arrangements the

22 There is an extensive economic literature on this issue: Polinsky 1980; Shavell 1980.

23 GT Act s 10 defines 'deal with, in relation to a GMO, means the following: (a) conduct experiments with the GMO; (b) make, develop, produce or manufacture the GMO; (c) breed the GMO; (d) propagate the GMO; (e) use the GMO in the course of manufacture of a thing that is not the GMO; (f) grow, raise or culture the GMO; and (g) import the GMO; and includes the possession, supply, use, transport or disposal of the GMO for the purposes of, or in the course of, a dealing mentioned in any of paras (a) to (g)'.

24 Noting that GT Act s 78 (declared to be a GMO) and GT Regulations r 5 (organisms that are not genetically modified organisms), 6 (dealings exempt from licensing) and 12 and 13 (notifiable low-risk dealings).

GT Act makes an important distinction between those GMOs outside the GT Act's prohibitory scheme and those within the GT Act's prohibitory scheme, the GT Act *only* applying to the latter.

GMOs outside the prohibitory scheme The GT Act does not deal with an organism, or class of organisms, declared to be outside the definition of a GMO (GT Act s 10 and GT Regulations r 5). This is potentially a large class and could capture some significant dealings, noting that the Regulator may have no knowledge of such dealings as they are outside the scope of the GT Act's obligations. For example, 'an organism mentioned in Schedule 1 is not a genetically modified organism' (GT Regulations r 5), that includes: '[a] mutant organism in which the mutational event did not involve the introduction of any foreign nucleic acid (that is, non-homologous DNA, usually from another species)' (GT Regulations schedule 1 part 1 (item 1)). This will include a GMO that has been subjected to any form of mutation that does 'not involve the introduction of any foreign nucleic acid', such as chemical, radiation, and so on, mutation and potentially extend to genetic modification with its own nucleic acid (such as the introduction of multiple gene copies) and possible even homologous DNA from the same species.[25]

Further, the potential class of organisms excluded from being GMOs for the purposes of the GT Act may be expanded by the definition of the term 'gene technology' (see GT Act s 10 and GT Regulations r 4). Under the current arrangements this 'does not include' organisms that are modified through the techniques of 'sexual reproduction' (GT Act s 10 (para (a) of the definition of 'gene technology')), 'homologous recombination' (GT Act s 10 (para (b) of the definition of 'gene technology')) and 'somatic cell nuclear transfer if the transfer does not involve genetically modified material' (GT Regulations r 4).

GMOs within the prohibitory scheme For those GMOs within the scope of the GT Act, the GT Act does not seek to avoid *all* risks posed by GMOs, but rather to identify and evaluate risks (hazards) and manage them, acknowledging that a certain amount of risk is acceptable (Explanatory Memorandum 2000, 39). The assessment of risk is built into the regulatory framework imposed by the GT Act that classifies different dealings according to their perceived risks (GT Act s 32(1)),[26] and consideration of a 'checklist' of possible hazards (GT Act

25 Another example is the exemption from licensing of '[a] plant formed by: (a) embryo rescue; (b) in vitro fertilisation; (c) zygote implantation; or (d) protoplast fusion': GT Regulations schedule 1 part 1 (item 5). This could include a plant that was 'modified by gene technology' and as a final step relied on the technique of embryo rescue or protoplast fusion, thereupon ceasing to be a GMO for the purposes of the Act.

26 GT Act s 32(1) providing for exempt from licensing dealings (ss 32(1) and 32(4) and GT Regulations rr 6–11); notifiable low-risk dealings (s 32(1) and part 6 div 2 and rr 12–13); licenced dealings (s 32(1) and part 5 and rr 7–11); dealings with GMOs on the Register of GMOs (ss 32(1) and 76); or dealings with an organism, or class of organisms,

ss 49(2) and 51(1) and GT Regulations r 10).[27] For the dealings not requiring a licence, the risks are considered to be 'negligible' or 'not present any significant risks' (Explanatory Memorandum 2000, 22). For the licenced dealings (so-called Dealings Not involving Intentional Release (DNIR) (GT Act part 5 div 3) and Dealings involving Intentional Release (DIR) (GT Act part 5 div 4) of the GMO into the environment) a methodology for identifying, evaluating and managing risks according to a *Risk Analysis Framework* is applied (OGTR 2005a):

> Risk assessment involves identifying sources of harm, and assessing the likelihood that harm will occur and the consequences if it does occur. Risk management refers to evaluating which risks require management and selecting and implementing the plans or actions that may be taken to ensure that those risks are controlled. Risk communication involves an interactive dialogue between stakeholders and risk assessors and risk managers (OGTR 2005a, 5).

The GT Act then proscribes various offences for the prohibited dealings (GT Act ss 32–37),[28] with the elements of the offence being detailed in the *Criminal Code Act 1995* (Cth) (GT Act s 8(1)).[29] This essentially distinguishes between 'physical elements' and 'fault elements' (*Criminal Code Act 1995* (Cth) sch).[30] An offence, consisting of physical elements and fault elements (*Criminal Code Act 1995* (Cth) sch (s 3.1(1))), is established by proving[31] 'the existence of such physical elements as are, under the law creating the offence, relevant to establishing guilt' (*Criminal Code Act 1995* (Cth) sch (s 3.2(a))), and 'in respect of each such physical element for which a fault element is required, one of the fault elements for the physical element' (*Criminal Code Act 1995* (Cth) sch (s 3.2(b))). The elements of the prohibited dealing offences and maximum penalties are:

---

declared to be outside the definition of a GMO (s 10 and r sch 1 pt 1); other formal statutory elements of the regulatory scheme for GMOs (and GM products) include the *Agricultural and Veterinary Chemicals Code Act 1994* (Cth) and the *Therapeutic Goods Act 1989* (Cth); there is, however, a 'mass' of non-legal rules, codes, circulars, practice notes, international conventions and ethical codes: Black 1998, 621.

27 Noting that other risks may also be identified through the consultation process (ss 50, 52 and 56), and in considering the application and preparing the risk assessment according; Hayes 2004, 32.

28 Except the Crown (s 6(2)) and noting that there is provision for no doubling-up of liabilities (s 18) and conduct by directors, employees and agents (s 188).

29 *Criminal Code Act 1995* (Cth) sch (ch 2) sets out the general principles of criminal responsibility with effect on and after 15 December 2001 (s 2.2).

30 *Criminal Code Act 1995* (Cth) sch (s 4.1): '[a] physical element of an offence may be: (a) conduct; (b) a result of conduct; or (c) a circumstance in which conduct, or a result of conduct, occurs' (s 4.1(1)), and sch (s 5.1); '[a] fault element for a particular physical element may be intention, knowledge, recklessness or negligence' (s 5.1(1)).

31 *Criminal Code Act 1995* (Cth) sch requires that the prosecution prove the existence of the matter (s 13.1(1)) beyond reasonable doubt (s 13.2(1)).

a. Dealing with a GMO without a licence – A person 'is guilty of an offence' (GT Act s 32(1)) if they deal with a GMO covered by the GT Act and either 'knows' or 'is reckless as to whether or not the dealing' is not exempt from licensing (GT Act s 32(1)(d)), not a notifiable low-risk dealing (GT Act s 32(1)(c)), not authorized by a GMO licence (GT Act s 32(1)(b)), and not on the GMO Register (GT Act s 32(1)(e)). The maximum penalties for an 'aggravated offence' (GT Act s 38)[32] are 'imprisonment for 5 years or 2,000 penalty units' (GT Act s 32(2)(a))[33] and in other cases 'imprisonment for 2 years or 500 penalty units' (GT Act s 32(2)(b)).
b. Breaching conditions of a GMO licence – A person 'is guilty of an offence' (GT Act ss 34(1) and (2)) if they hold a GMO licence (GT Act s 34(1)) or they are 'covered by a GMO licence' (GT Act s 34(2)),[34] and 'intentionally takes an action or omits to take an action' (GT Act ss 34(1)(a) and (2)(a)), and either 'knows' or 'is reckless as to whether or not the action or omission contravenes the licence' (GT Act ss 34(1)(b) and (2)(b)). The maximum penalties for an 'aggravated offence' (GT Act s 38) are 'imprisonment for 5 years or 2,000 penalty units' (GT Act s 34(3)(a)) and in other cases 'imprisonment for 2 years or 500 penalty units' (GT Act s 34(3)(b)), with there being a separate offence for 'each day (including the day of a conviction for the offence or any later day) on which the person is guilty of the offence' (GT Act s 34(4)).
c. Breaching conditions on GMO Register – A person 'is guilty of an offence' (GT Act s 36(1)) if they deal with a GMO on the GMO Register (GT Act s 36(1)(b)) 'knowing that it is a GMO' (GT Act s 36(1)(a)) and the dealing contravenes a condition specified in the GMO Register (GT Act s 36(1)(c)). The maximum penalty is '50 penalty units' (GT Act s 36(1)).
d. Dealing with a notifiable low-risk dealing not according to the GT Regulations – A person 'is guilty of an offence' (GT Act s 37(1)) if they deal with a notifiable low-risk dealing GMO (GT Act s 37(1)(b)) 'knowing' that it is a GMO (GT Act s 37(1)(a)) and the dealing is 'not undertaken in accordance with the Regulations' (GT Act s 37(1)(c)). The maximum penalty is '50 penalty units' (GT Act s 37(1)).

In addition to these offences, the GT Act also proscribes limited strict liability offences (GT Act ss 33, 35, 36(2) and 37(2)). The *Criminal Code Act 1995* (Cth)

32 Where 'the commission of the offence causes significant damage, or is likely to cause significant damage, to the health and safety of people or to the environment' (s 38(1)).

33 Noting that 'penalty units' are defined in the *Crimes Act 1914* (Cth) s 4AA(1) where 'penalty unit means $110'.

34 An additional requirement is that the person 'has knowledge of the conditions of the licence' (s 34(2)(c)).

sets out that where there is an offence of strict liability (*Criminal Code Act 1995* (Cth) sch (ss 6.1(1) and (2))), then 'there are no fault elements' for either 'any of the physical elements of the offence' (*Criminal Code Act 1995* (Cth) sch (s 6.1(1)(a))) or 'that physical element' (*Criminal Code Act 1995* (Cth) sch (s 6.1(2)(a))). The 'defence of mistake of fact'[35] is available (*Criminal Code Act 1995* (Cth) sch (ss 6.1(1)(b) and 6.1(2)(b))) together with 'any other defence' (*Criminal Code Act 1995* (Cth) sch (s 6.1(3))). Essentially the strict liability offences are:

a. Dealing with a GMO without a licence – A person 'is guilty of an offence' (GT Act s 33(1)) if they deal with a GMO and they are 'not authorised by a GMO licence' (GT Act s 33(1)(b)), 'the dealing is not a notifiable low-risk dealing' (GT Act s 33(1)(c)), 'the dealing is not an exempt [from licensing] dealing' (GT Act s 33(1)(d)), and 'the dealing is not included on the GMO Register' (GT Act s 33(1)(e)). The maximum penalties for an 'aggravated offence' (GT Act s 38) is '200 penalty units' (GT Act s 33(3)(a)) and in other cases '50 penalty units' (GT Act s 33(3)(b)).
b. Breaching conditions of a GMO licence – A person 'is guilty of an offence' (GT Act s 35(1) and (2)) if they hold a GMO licence (GT Act s 35(1)) or they are 'covered by a GMO licence' (GT Act s 35(2)),[36] and 'takes an action or omits to take an action' (GT Act ss 35(1)(a) and (2)(a)) and the 'action or omission contravenes the licence' (GT Act ss 35(1)(b) and (2)(b)). The maximum penalties for an 'aggravated offence' (GT Act s 38) is '200 penalty units' (GT Act s 35(4)(a)) and in other cases '50 penalty units' (GT Act s 35(4)(b)).
c. Breaching conditions on GMO Register – A person 'is guilty of an offence' (GT Act s 36(1)) if they deal with a GMO on the GMO Register and the dealing contravenes a condition specified in the GMO Register (GT Act s 36(2)). The maximum penalty is '50 penalty units' (GT Act s 36(1)).
d. Dealing with a notifiable low-risk dealing not according to the GT Regulations – A person 'is guilty of an offence' (GT Act s 37(1)) if they deal with a notifiable low-risk dealing GMO and the dealing is 'not undertaken in accordance with the Regulations' (GT Act s 37(2)). The maximum penalty is '50 penalty units' (GT Act s 37(1)).

The GT Act also provides the Regulator with express power to 'give directions' to a current licence holder or to a person covered by a current licence where the Regulator 'believes on reasonable grounds' that the licence holder or person

35 Being the defence that '(a) at or before the time of the conduct constituting the physical element, the person considered whether or not facts existed, and is under a mistaken but reasonable belief about those facts; and (b) had those facts existed, the conduct would not have constituted an offence': *Criminal Code Act 1995* (Cth) sch (s 9.2(1)).

36 An additional requirement is that the person 'has knowledge of the conditions of the licence' (s 32(2)(c)).

covered by the licence is 'not complying with this GT Act or the regulations in respect of a thing' (GT Act ss 146(1)(a) and (2)(a)) and that the exercise of the power is necessary 'in order to protect the health and safety of people or to protect the environment' (GT Act ss 146(1)(b) and (2)(b)). However, the directions are limited to 'requiring the person, within the time specified in the notice, to take such steps in relation to the thing as are reasonable in the circumstances for the person to comply with this GT Act or the regulations' (GT Act ss 146(1) and (2)). Failure by the licence holder or person covered by the licence to comply with the directions is an offence (GT Act s 146(3)),[37] and the Regulator may arrange for the steps specified in the notice to be taken (GT Act s 146(4)) and recover an amount equal to the cost as a debt due to the Commonwealth (GT Act s 146(5)). Significantly, the directions power was expressly intended to deal with containment:

> This provision effectively enables a 'clean-up' or remediation to be undertaken, either by the Regulator or via the direction of the Regulator, where, for example, a condition of licence has been breached resulting in the accidental release of a GMO, and there is a need to re-contain the GMO (Explanatory Memorandum 2000, 90).

Further offences arise under the GT Act where a current licence holder fails to comply with directions given by the Regulator (GT Act ss 53(4) and 146(3)), a person unlawfully discloses 'confidential commercial information' (GT Act s 187(1)) or another person unlawfully discloses 'confidential commercial information' knowing it is 'confidential commercial information' (GT Act s 187(2)), submission of false or misleading information or documents (GT Act s 192), interference with dealings with GMOs (GT Act s 192A), refuse or fail to answer a question about the import or export of goods (GT Act s 164(4)), the return of identity cards (GT Act s 151), and the application and use of warrants (GT Act ss 175(1) and (2)).

The Regulator may also suspend or cancel a current licence by notice in writing given to the holder of a GMO licence, if she 'believes on reasonable grounds that the licence holder, or a person covered by the licence, has committed an offence against this GT Act or the regulations' (GT Act s 68(b)). In these circumstances any dealing with a GMO will be prohibited because it is 'not authorized by a GMO licence' (GT Act ss 32(1)(b), 33(1)(b) and 60).

The significance of the GT Act's prohibitory approach is that it reaches *all* GMOs, including those non-GMOs defined to be GMOs for the purposes of the GT Act (GT Act s 10 (para (c))) but excluding those GMOs defined not to be

37 The maximum penalties for an 'aggravated offence' is '2000 penalty units' and in other cases '500 penalty units', although the *Crimes Act 1914* (Cth) s 4K (dealing with continuing and multiple offences) does not apply so this is not a daily offence committed until the requirement is complied with (s 146(6)).

GMOs for the purposes of the GT Act (GT Act (para (e)) and GT Regulations r 5), and then provides:

a. A blanket assessment of 'negligible' or 'no significant' risk for exempt from licensing dealings, notifiable low-risk dealings and dealings on the GMO Register.
b. A tailored risk assessment for those dealings requiring a licence (so-called Dealings Not involving Intentional Release (DNIR) and Dealings involving Intentional Release (DIR) of the GMO into the environment).

Importantly, the Regulator applying the GT Act makes *no* claims that dealings with GMOs pose no risks. Inherent in the GT Act as a regulatory scheme is that it accepts that some identified and some unidentified risks may occur. As a consequence, some loss or damage might be expected, albeit that the Regulator may be minimizing or moderating such an eventuality.

The 'Gaps' in the Liability Arrangements

The GT Act addresses some issues of liability by providing for criminal sanction for breach of the GT Act (GT Act ss 32(1), 33(1), 33(2), 34(1), 34(2), 35(1), 35(2), 36(1), 36(2) and 37), and gives the Regulator some powers to require that a problem be rectified when the legislation has been breached (GT Act s 146). However, the GT Act makes no comprehensive provision for a statutory right of action for a remedy for those affected by economic, health or environmental loss or damage resulting from GMOs. Further the loss or damage is not affected by whether the dealing is either authorized by the GT Act or not authorized by, and breaches the GT Act. In other words, the GT Act may minimize the likely risks posed by GMOs by identifying some risks and seeking to minimize their impact through appropriate management, but the GT Act *does not* establish a cause of action for any third parties affected by economic, health or environmental loss or damage resulting from GMOs.[38] The recourse in these circumstances would be through the common law and other existing statutory schemes (see also Department of Agriculture, Fisheries and Forestry 2003, 6–14):

> Specific legislation relating to liability for the risks posed by gene technology does not exist, nor has liability been tested in the courts. Common law provides a means for redressing problems arising from GMOs. Remedies might also be sought through environmental protection and pollution control legislation,

38 Notably, the Australian Government asserts the view that '[l]iability for environmental damage (such as loss of biodiversity) and personal injury (e.g., allergenicity, toxicity) has been excluded as a regulatory system has been implemented to avoid such dangers and thus the risk to those in the agricultural community is minimal': Department of Agriculture, Fisheries and Forestry 2003, 1.

> and legislation relating to wild animals and abnormally dangerous activities. Liability in relation to food would be caught under the Trade Practices Act (House of Representative Standing Committee on Primary Industries and Regional Services 2000, 159).

As a consequence of this approach, there remain 'gaps' in the GT Act's liability scheme:

a. The GT Act's prohibitions against exempt from licensing dealings (GT Act s 32(1) and s 32(4) and GT Regulations r 6), notifiable low-risk dealing (GT Act s 32(1) and part 6 div 2 and GT Regulations part 3 div 2), licensed dealings (GT Act s 32(1) and part 5 and GT Regulations rr 7–11), and dealings on the GMO Register (GT Act s 32(1) and s 76), relate to 'physical elements' (*Criminal Code Act 1995* (Cth) sch (s 4.1)) and 'fault elements' (*Criminal Code Act 1995* (Cth) sch (s 5.1)) of the statutory offence. Any amounts paid as a penalty will be 'public money' for the purposes of the *Financial Management and Accountability Act 1997* (Cth) and form part of the Consolidated Revenue Fund.[39] Further, amounts recovered from the licence holder, or a person covered by a GMO licence, by the Regulator from 'clean-up', remediation, and so on, to comply with the GT Act (GT Act ss 146(1) and (2)), is merely the amount to repay an amount expended by the Regulator (see GT Act s 146(5)). These prohibitions:
   i. *Do not* address the loss, damage or injury as a result of the conduct that is prohibited, or for amounts to be paid to those suffering loss, damage or injury as a result of the offence.
   ii. *Do not* address activities that are not identified as a risk (hazard) that can be managed in authorizing the dealing at the time it is assessed by the Regulator. As an inherently risky product GMOs, and identified and unidentified risks and the prohibitions, only relate to the conditions and other limits placed on them as a result of known risks to the Regulator. Thus, risks unknown to the Regulator, but potentially known to the person dealing with the GMO,[40] that eventuate are not prohibited.

---

39 *Financial Management and Accountability Act 1997* (Cth) s 5 provides 'public money' means '(a) money in the custody or under the control of the Commonwealth; or (b) money in the custody or under the control of any person acting for or on behalf of the Commonwealth in respect of the custody or control of the money; including such money that is held on trust for, or otherwise for the benefit of, a person other than the Commonwealth': see also *Financial Management and Accountability Act 1997* (Cth) part 3; *Financial Management and Accountability Regulations 1997* (Cth) part 6; *Financial Management and Accountability Orders 2005* (Cth) part 3.

40 Noting that GT Act s 192 a person must not, in an application or complying with the Act, give or produce false or misleading information or document, subject to a criminal sanction for the offence; there is not, however, any positive requirement to give or produce

   iii. *Do not* address organisms, or classes of organisms, that are declared to be outside the definition of a GMO (GT Act s 10 and GT Regulations r 5).
b. The Regulator has the power to require 'clean-up', remediation, and so on, as part of the general power to require compliance with the GT Act during the period of a licence (GT Act ss 146(1) and (2)). However, this power:
   i. *Only* extends to the current licence holder, or a person covered by the licence, and so will not apply to an expired, suspended, surrendered or cancelled licence (GT Act s 60).
   ii. *Only* deals with contamination where the licence holder or a person covered by the licence is not complying with the GT Act, and will not address contamination that has been sanctioned by the GT Act. For example, a contamination event that has been assessed as a reasonable risk.
   iii. *Only* addresses the licence holder, or a person covered by the licence, and does not address any dealing with a GMO declared not to the GMOs for the purposes of the GT Act (GT Act s 10 (para (e))), exempt from licensing dealing (GT Regulations r 6) or notifiable low-risk dealings, or other persons covered by any of these dealings.
   iv. *Only* addresses 'such steps in relation to the thing as are reasonable in the circumstances for the licence holder [or the person covered by a GMO licence] to comply with this GT Act or the regulations' (GT Act ss 146(1) and (2)).
   v. *Only*, where the licence holder or a person covered by the licence does not comply with the Regulator's direction, liability for a one-off penalty of up to a maximum of '2,000 penalty units' ($220,000) (GT Act ss 146(3) and (6); see also *Crimes Act 1914* (Cth) s 4AA(1)).

The directions power expressly *does not* require the licence holder, or a person covered by the licence, to address the loss, damage or injury caused to a third person or the public good.

c. Where a person suffers loss or damage resulting from GMOs the GT Act *does not* establish a cause of action, instead leaving the person to find recourse through a range of statutory and common law liability arrangements. While these arrangements may provide an adequate and effective resolution, in some circumstances they may not. For example, the determination of liability for simple common law negligence only addresses the loss or damage resulting from GMOs if the GMO producers and marketers (including the supply chain handlers) meet or exceed the legal standard of care (defined by the court), and if this standard is not met the injurer's liability for the loss or damage is zero. In the case of a statutory

information or documents that is known to the person and might materially affect the application or compliance with the Act.

> liability scheme the injurer will only be liable if the particular elements of the statutory scheme have been satisfied. Consumers (and the community) will be unsure whether their particular circumstances will necessarily be protected against loss or damage, the assessment only being possible after the event.

Conclusions About Strict Liability

This chapter assumed that consumers (and the community) might be uncertain about the quality of GMOs (and GM products), and that regulatory intervention under the GT Act might provide consumers and the broader community with the necessary health and safety and environmental assurances to conclude bargains involving GMOs and GM products. The analysis in this chapter suggests that the GT Act was implemented, at least in part, to address the information asymmetry faced by consumers and the community to the introduction of GMOs. The expectation from imposing regulation on some dealings with GMOs was that the benefits from assurances that GMOs had been independently and comprehensively assessed as safe for health and the environment would be consumer and the community confidence, and a positive downstream effect for industry manifest as acceptance of GMOs as safe (Explanatory Memorandum 2000, 42).

The response in the GT Act was to create a separate and independent institution in the Regulator capable of providing an assessment about the likely risks with the power to control various uses of some GMOs in a way that minimized the potential loss or damage. Included in this scheme are criminal sanctions (including strict liability) for some conduct and a power for the regulator to clean-up or remediate some contaminations. However, the analysis in this chapter also suggests that significant 'gaps' exist in the statutory liability scheme, leaving other common law and statutory schemes to provide an uncertain remedy for any economic, health and safety or environmental loss or damage resulting from GMOs.

Importantly, the Regulator in applying the GT Act makes *no* claims that dealings with GMOs pose no risks. Further, in applying the GT Act and assessing risk under the *Risk Analysis Framework*, the Regulator relies on a standard of substantial equivalence and familiarity to the non-GMO parental organism:

> The Regulator can only consider risk posed by or as a result of gene technology. Therefore risks posed by a particular GMO need to be considered in the context of the risks posed by the unmodified parental organism in the receiving environment. For DIRs this might be considered by examining whether the GMO would cause an adverse outcome over and above that which would occur if the status quo were maintained, that is, if the GMO was not deployed in the environment. For DNIRs the contained facilities prevent exposure to the environment although the potential for unintended release must be considered (OGTR 2005a, 31).

The effect of applying this standard of substantial equivalence and familiarity is to avoid a detailed assessment of GMOs by recognizing only those risks posed by the 'novel' GMO, while at the same time promoting biotechnology as an innovative and competitive technology and downplaying potential environmental hazards (Barrett and Abergel 2000).[41] For example, in assessing the risks of releasing GM canola into the environment the Regulator 'considered' that 'the risks to human health and safety, or to the Australian environment, from the commercial release of any of Bayer's seven GM canola lines are no greater than those posed by non-GM canola that is they are as safe as conventional canola' (Bayer 2003, 10; see also Lawson 2002). As a consequence, the Regulator's decisions might be interpreted as making no legitimate claims about the health and environmental safety of the products (Millstone et al. 1999).

This means that GMOs (and GM products) do pose risks and that some of those risks may eventuate possibly causing loss or damage to third persons and the public good. In considering information asymmetries and how these apply to consumers (and the community) in a way that overcomes the uncertainty about the quality of GMOs, the 'gaps' are likely to undermine the consumer's (and the community's) acceptance of the assurances that the GT Act does provide an adequate assurance. Thus, the question is not whether GMOs pose a novel threat that the current liability arrangements can satisfy,[42] but rather, whether consumers (and the community) would be better assured by a different liability arrangement. It is in this context that a statutory scheme of strict liability for any economic, health or environmental loss or damage resulting from GMOs is one possible solution.

Essentially, the argument is that the producers and marketers (including the supply chain handlers) of GMOs are best placed to know and be aware of the potential and scope of the possible risks of GMOs and their consequences. Without this information consumers (and the community) are unlikely to conclude bargains with GMOs because they are uncertain about the potential health and safety, and environmental consequences. With a more robust assurance through a strict liability scheme about the health and environmental safety of GMOs, consumers (and the community) might be provided with more confidence about the quality of GMOs and so conclude more bargains involving GMOs and GM products.

Further, the costs of providing the best information should be internalized by the producers and marketers (including the supply chain handlers), rather than externalized to the broader community and unfortunate individual consumers. One way to achieve this is through a statutory strict liability scheme that avoids the uncertainties about liability from reliance on the common law and existing statutory

41 Although the merits of 'substantial equivalence' remain hotly contested, compare for examples, Miller 1999; Millstone et al. 1999; see generally McGarity 2002.

42 This appears to have been the principal conclusion of various reviews: Department of Agriculture, Fisheries and Forestry 2003, 2–6 and the references therein.

schemes.[43] Where producers and marketers (including the supply chain handlers) know that they will be strictly liable for any loss or damage, they will factor these costs (and risks of being exposed to those costs) into their considerations about producing and marketing GMOs and GM products. Perhaps significantly, without such an effective incentive to disclose the best information to consumers, to the community and to the Regulator under the GT Act, individual producers and marketers (including the supply chain handlers) of GMOs will favour poorer quality goods (some with risks of adverse health and safety, and environmental outcomes) with a consequential reduction in the size of the market that will follow (Akerlof 1970, 488).

While a comprehensive strict liability scheme under the GT Act is only one possible solution, this chapter shows that it is consistent with the GT Act's purpose of addressing the information asymmetry market failure. The benefit of a strict liability scheme will be to address the existing 'gaps' in the GT Act's liability arrangements and reinforce the Regulator's assurances about the quality of GMOs and GM products for the benefit of consumers and the community.

Decision-Making Rigour

Without a reassuring determination under the GT Act, information asymmetry theory suggests that purchasers will pay a lower price for GMOs as they take on the burden of the risk or prospect of damage (some of it non-financial), and further reduce the quality and size of the market. The GT Act was intended, according to our analysis, to provide the institutional assurance that GMOs will not harm the health and safety of humans or the environment. The rigour of the decision-making is therefore central to providing the necessary assurance about the quality of GMOs that will address the information asymmetry concerns.

The GT Act does not seek to avoid *all* risks posed by GMOs (or GM products), but rather to identify and evaluate risks (hazards) and manage them, acknowledging that a certain amount of risk is acceptable. In addition to the assessments built-in to the GT Act (GT Act s 32(1)),[44] and the 'checklist' of possible hazards (GT

43 Notably, a strict liability scheme was rejected by the Statutory Review of the Gene Technology Act as: '[o]n balance, the Review concluded that a strict liability regime should not be introduced into the Act', although the asymmetric information issues were not addressed: Independent Panel Reviewing the Gene Technology Act 2006, 38–9.

44 GT Act s 32(1) providing for exempt from licensing dealings (ss 32(1) and 32(4) and GT Regulations rr 6–11); notifiable low-risk dealings (s 32(1) and part 6 div 2 and rr 12–13); licenced dealings (s 32(1) and part 5 and rr 7–11); dealings with GMOs on the Register of GMOs (ss 32(1) and 76); or dealings with an organism, or class of organisms, declared to be outside the definition of a GMO (s 10 and r sch 1 part 1); other formal statutory elements of the regulatory scheme for GMOs (and GM products) include the *Agricultural and Veterinary Chemicals Code Act 1994* (Cth) and the *Therapeutic Goods Act*

Act ss 49(2) and 51(1) and GT Regulations r 10),[45] a methodology is applied for identifying, evaluating and managing risks according to a *Risk Analysis Framework* (OGTR 2002a).[46] Other risks may also be identified through the consultation process required by the GT Act (GT Act ss 50, 52 and 56), and in considering the application and preparing the risk assessment according to the GT Act (OGTR 2002a, 19–20 and 28–67; see also Hayes 2004, 32).

The term 'risk' is not defined in the GT Act,[47] although for the purposes of the *Risk Analysis Framework* the term has been applied 'both separately and together' as the 'probability (likelihood) of an event and consequence (the impact of the event when it happens)' (OGTR 2002a, 12 and 70). This takes into account 'the level of hazard of the agent', and 'the level of exposure of the receptor (human, animal, plant, etc.)' (OGTR 2002a, 12 and 70). While there is no universally acceptable or applicable process or procedure for conducting risk assessments with a multitude of possible techniques and methods,[48] common to any risk assessment[49] is an individual's conception of the worth of a particular activity that requires some kind of protection (such as a human fatality or an ecological harm like an unexpected biodiversity loss) (Lawson 2002, 200–201). In addition, the risk posed by the proposed activity is considered to be acceptable (Lawson 2002, 201). Both these involve questions about the reasons for that opinion and

---

1989 (Cth); there is, however, a 'mass' of non-legal rules, codes, circulars, practice notes, international conventions and ethical codes: Black 1998, 621.

45 Noting that other risks may also be identified through the consultation process (ss 50, 52 and 56), and in considering the application and preparing the risk assessment: Hayes 2004, 32.

46 Notably a new framework was implemented in 2005 after the Bayer 2003 decision that included 'risk communication' as a central element of 'risk analysis', being 'risk analysis = risk assessment + risk management + risk communication', although the basic risk assessment methodology remained essentially the same with pejorative changes that promoted 'risk communication'.

47 Noting that there is an ongoing controversy about 'What is risk?' with the presently dominant conception that 'risk' involves some form of 'danger'; for an overview of the different emphases and nuances: Botterill and Mazur 2004, 1–2.

48 For a recent overview of 'best practice' ecological risk assessment for GMOs: Hayes 2004, 8–30; see generally Hayes 1997.

49 The term 'risk assessment' is, however, defined in the Marrakesh Agreement Establishing the World Trade Organization [1995] ATS 8, Annex 1A (Agreement on the Application of Sanitary and Phytosanitary Measures), to which Australia is a member state, to mean '[t]he evaluation of the likelihood of entry, establishment or spread of a pest or disease within the territory of an importing Member according to the sanitary or phytosanitary measures which might be applied, and of the associated potential biological and economic consequences; or the evaluation of the potential for adverse effects on human or animal health arising from the presence of additives, contaminants, toxins or disease-causing organisms in food, beverages or feedstuffs' (Annex A): see also Peel 2004.

perception, and values about the weight of opinion or perception.[50] The interplay of psychological, social and political factors influences this risk opinion and perception (see generally Pildes and Sunstein 1995, 33–43; Slovic 1999 and the references therein; Botterill and Mazur 2004, 3–7), with the consequence that experts and lay people may disagree about risk (Slovic 1999, 697). It is these value judgments that are central to the GT Act's scheme. This is because once it is accepted that adverse events are possible, a decision under the GT Act to allow a dealing with a GMO (or GM product) is, in effect, a decision that any damage as a result of an adverse event is objectively acceptable.[51] The regulatory problem here is comprised of two aspects. First, that a consensus on what is objectively acceptable risk is the foundation of legitimacy. Second, that difference of opinion and perception in assessing risk have the potential to undermine that legitimacy, especially where the 'science' founding the decision is uncertain and the values and preferences supporting a decision have not been disclosed.

This chapter challenges the openness and transparency of the decisions about risk under the GT Act. It does this by assessing the recent licence granted to Bayer CropScience Pty Ltd (Bayer) for the general or commercial release into the environment of herbicide tolerant hybrid system canola (Bayer 2003), that had previously been licenced to Aventis CropScience Pty Ltd (Aventis) for limited or field trial release into the environment (Aventis 2002). The general or commercial release of GMOs into the environment under the GT Act contrasts with other forms of intentional release into the environment (such as limited or field releases) in that these general or commercial releases involve minimal control (OGTR 2003, 91). Further, general or commercial releases follow prior limited releases into the environment 'under strict conditions' (OGTR 2003, 92). The decision to licence a general or commercial release is thus likely to be based on the most comprehensive 'science', including all the relevant data gathered during earlier licensed limited releases (OGTR 2003, 92). In these circumstances the decision to licence a general or commercial release of a GMO into the environment under the GT Act might be expected to illustrate the requirements for objectively acceptable risks assessed under the GT Act. The contribution of our study is to illustrate the paucity of evidence about the GMO under consideration and the consequences of this for making decisions to licence the release of GMOs into the environment under the GT Act.

---

50 See, for examples, Black 1998, 621–2 (conceptualizations of the 'problem'); Burgmann 1999, 127–9 (human frailties in the judgement of risk); Hayes 2004, 25–6 (the place of new technology).

51 Essentially an assessment that the technology's consequences are acceptable and that the aims of the technology are acceptable: Jasanoff 2003 and the references therein; see also Newell 2002, 3 and the references therein pointing out the potential conflict between regulation for the benefit of the public and regulation for commercial interests where governments are both protector of the public interest and promoter of biotechnology.

This part of the chapter briefly outlines the GT Act's regulatory scheme and the methodology for assessing risk (heading *Overview of the regulatory scheme and risk methodology*). This includes the formal requirements of the GT Act and the policy documents supporting a decision to either refuse a licence or issue a licence, and the conditions attached to that licence according to the risk assessment applying the *Risk Analysis Framework*. This is followed by a detailed description of the GMO construction and the key elements of the risk assessment and risk management plan for the limited (field trial) release of Aventis' GM canola and the subsequent general or commercial release of Bayer's GM canola (heading *The GM canola under consideration*). This is necessary as the Regulator's assessment *does not* identify and address each component of the materials introduced to the GMO (Bayer 2003, 37–52). It then provides an analysis of the data and information relied on in reaching a conclusion about the risks posed by the general or commercial release of the GMOs. The significance of this detail is to show the complexity of the GMO construction and the breadth of analysis required to assess the likely risks and consequences of individual and composite components of the GMOs. This analysis also illustrates the paucity of direct quantitative data and information available to support the risk assessment. The following discussion argues that the social construction of both the 'science' underpinning the risk assessment and the concept of 'risk' itself belie value judgments about the opinion or perception of risk that undermine the GT Act's objective of a credible assurance (openness and transparency) about the safety of GMOs (and GM products) (heading *Discussion*). This arguably undermines the legitimacy of GMOs (and GM products) and thus also undermines the policy of objective of the GT Act in promoting commercial transactions in GMOs (and GM products). A deeper analysis of the Bayer licence decision further highlights the sorts of contentions that are likely to undermine that legitimacy.

Overview of the Regulatory Scheme and Risk Methodology

The GT Act provides a detailed regulatory scheme with a number of formal requirements. These formal requirements are then complemented by a *Risk Analysis Framework* setting out a methodology for assessing risks. The following sections overview the formal requirements of the GT Act and the methodology set out in the *Risk Analysis Framework*.

Formal requirements The focus of the GT Act is to 'protect the health and safety of people, and to protect the environment, by identifying risks posed by or as a result of gene technology, and by managing those risks through regulating certain dealings with GMOs' (GT Act s 3; Explanatory Memorandum 2000, 13). The GT Act's scheme, administered by the Gene Technology Regulator (the Regulator),[52]

52 The Regulator is a statutory office holder appointed by the Governor General (s 118(1)) and assisted by persons engaged under the *Public Service Act 1999* (Cth) and made

prohibits all 'dealings with' GMOs (GT Act part 3),[53] unless the dealings are exempt (GT Act ss 32(1) and 32(4) and GT Regulations part 3 div 1), notifiable low risk dealings (GT Act s 32(1) and part 6 div 2 and GT Regulations part 3 div 2), licenced (GT Act s 32(1) and part 5 and GT Regulations rr 7–11), on the Register of GMOs (GT Act ss 32(1) and 76), or dealings with an organism, or class of organisms, declared to be outside the definition of a GMO (GT Act s 10 and GT Regulations sch 1 part 1). For licenced dealings where the GMO is to be intentionally released into the environment (GT Act part 5 div 4),[54] the Regulator considers the characteristics and effects of the genetic modification to the organism (GT Act s 49(2)), and assesses the risks posed by the proposed dealings with the GMO (GT Act s 50(1)). There are minimum requirements for preparing a risk assessment and risk management plan (GT Act ss 51(1) and 51(2)). A risk assessment requires a consideration, over the short and long term (GT Regulations r 10(2)), of a number of aspects. These include the properties of the organism, the effect (or expected effect) of the genetic modification, limits on the dissemination or persistence of the GMO (or its genetic material), or the spread or persistence of the GMO (GT Act s 49(2)). In addition the extent or scale of the proposed dealing, the impact of the dealing on the health and safety of people, the potential of the GMO to be harmful to other organisms, adversely affect ecosystems, transfer genetic materials, spread and persist in the environment, have a selective advantage, or be toxic, allergenic or pathogenic and various (GT Act s 51(1) and GT Regulations r 10). The identified risks must be manageable

---

available for the purpose by the Secretary of the Department of Health and Ageing (s 133): Department of Finance and Administration 2004, 254; notably, the Regulator has set out a service charter of the Office of the Gene Technology Regulator articulating its 'values' as being 'the Australian Public Service Values and Code of Conduct in all aspects of its business. In addition, we value: Professionalism; through integrity, objectivity, excellence, commitment, and consistency. Accountability; through open and transparent processes. Achievement; through effective, efficient and flexible work practices which are focused on delivering timely outcomes. Respect for each other and our stakeholders; through open and effective communication and quality service': Office of the Gene Technology Regulator 2005b, 3.

53 GT Act s 10 defines 'deal with, in relation to a GMO, means the following: (a) conduct experiments with the GMO; (b) make, develop, produce or manufacture the GMO; (c) breed the GMO; (d) propagate the GMO; (e) use the GMO in the course of manufacture of a thing that is not the GMO; (f) grow, raise or culture the GMO; and (g) import the GMO; and includes the possession, supply, use, transport or disposal of the GMO for the purposes of, or in the course of, a dealing mentioned in any of paras (a) to (g)'.

54 Noting that s 10 defines 'environment' to include 'ecosystems and their constituent parts', 'natural and physical resources' and 'the qualities and characteristics of locations, places and areas', s 11 provides 'a dealing with a GMO involves the *intentional release of the GMO into the environment* if the GMO is intentionally released into the open environment, whether or not it is released with provision for limiting the dissemination or persistence of the GMO or its genetic material in the environment'.

based on a risk management plan that considers ways to manage the risks, and based on advice from competent agencies (GT Act s 51(1) and GT Regulations r 10). Further, in making a licence application, some information is prescribed by the GT Regulations (GT Act s 40(2)(a) and GT Regulations r 7(1)(b)), including comprehensive information about the GMO, the dealing, the risks and the risk management (GT Regulations sch 4 part 2).

For the purposes of the GT Act, a risk assessment is the process of evaluating the adverse events that might occur, or may be occurring, to the health and safety of people or the environment, if a proposed dealing is undertaken (GT Act ss 3 and 4). For both the risk assessment and risk management plan, the Regulator is required to seek advice about matters relevant to the preparation of the risk assessment and risk management plan from the states,[55] the Gene Technology Technical Advisory Committee, prescribed Commonwealth agencies,[56] the Environment Minister and any local council the Regulator considers appropriate (GT Act s 50(3)). After preparing the risk assessment and risk management plan, the Regulator is required to publish a notice and seek written submissions from the public, and again seek the advice of the states, the Gene Technology Technical Advisory Committee, prescribed Commonwealth agencies, the Environment Minister and any local council the Regulator considers appropriate (GT Act s 52). The Regulator is also empowered to take other 'appropriate' actions, including holding public hearings, in order to determine the licence application (GT Act s 53).[57] In making a decision whether the risks posed by the dealing can be 'managed in such a way as to protect the health and safety of people and the environment' (GT Act s 56(1)), and so to issue a licence (with or without conditions) (GT Act part 5 div 6), or refuse to issue a licence (GT Act s 55), the Regulator 'must have regard to' a number of policy measures. These include the risk assessment (GT Act s 56(2)(a)) and risk management plan (GT Act s 56(2)(b)), any submissions received about the risk assessment and risk management plan (GT Act s 56(2)(c)) and any policy guidelines issued by the Ministerial Council relating to risks and ways to manage risks (GT Act ss 23 and 56(2)(d)).[58] The Regulator's decision is also required to be consistent with any policy principles issued by the Ministerial Council (GT Act ss

55 This includes the Australian Capital Territory and the Northern Territory: GT Act s 10.

56 Prescribed by the GT Regulations r 9 to be the Australian New Zealand Food Standards; the Australian Quarantine Inspection Service; the National Health and Medical Research Council; the National Industrial Chemicals Notification and Assessment scheme; the National Registration Authority; and the Therapeutic Goods Administration.

57 Noting that the GT Act s 51(1) clarifies that the Regulator is not confined to considering submissions and advice and may take into account other information, including relevant independent research.

58 There are presently no policy guidelines in force.

21 and 57(1)),[59] and the Regulator must be satisfied that the licence applicant is a 'suitable person to hold a licence' (GT Act ss 57(2) and 58).[60]

Risk assessment and risk management methodology The Office of the Gene Technology Regulator has issued guidelines (the *Risk Analysis Framework*) about how the Regulator, assisted by the staff of the Office of the Gene Technology Regulator, will assess risks (OGTR 2002a, 1). Applying the *Risk Analysis Framework* is intended to provide 'a transparent and consistent risk analysis process' (OGTR 2002a, 2), and lead to a 'science-based conclusion' about risks and their management so that '[e]ither risk will be too great to permit the dealing to proceed, or the risk will be manageable through imposed licence conditions, or there will be no risk that requires management' (OGTR 2002a, 17). The assessments being made need to appear as 'an assessment of the likelihood of the hazard occurring and, if it does, the likely consequences of that occurrence' (OGTR 2002a, 9). A potentially significant limitation imposed by the Regulator on every risk assessment is that the *Risk Analysis Framework* is applied in the context of the '[r]isks posed by GMOs will be considered in the context of the risks posed by the non-modified parental organisms in the receiving environment' (OGTR 2002a, 16).[61]

For the intentional release of GMOs into the environment, the *Risk Analysis Framework* involves steps of hazard identification,[62] risk assessment,[63] risk

---

59 The only policy principle in force is the *Gene Technology (Recognition of Designated Areas) Principle 2003* requiring the Gene Technology Regulator to recognize a states' rights to designate under State law special areas that are for either GM or non-GM crops for marketing purposes: McGrath 2003, 36–7; Trantor 2003, 256–8; Ludlow 2004, 18–20.

60 Notably, in general or commercial release applications, '[i]nformation gained from the field trials (and information about the suitability of the applicant based on their conduct of the trials) would be used by the Regulator as part of his/her assessment of any subsequent application for commercial release of the GMO': OGTR 2003, 92.

61 This is the 'doctrine of substantial equivalence' that does not have unanimous support as a base line for an objective method of assessing risk: see for supportive review McHughen 2000, 137–9.

62 'Hazard' meaning 'the capacity of a GMO to produce a particular type of adverse health or environmental effect, directly or indirectly; or an event, sequence of events or combination of circumstances that could potentially have adverse consequences': OGTR 2002a, 12 and 70.

63 'Risk assessment' means 'the process of estimating the potential impact of a hazard on a specified human population or the environment under a specific set of conditions within an identified timeframe': OGTR 2002a, 12 and 70.

management[64] and risk communication,[65] together with consultative steps[66] (OGTR 2002a, 8–14). The Regulator's standard approaches to risk assessment is to consider each identified hazard, to assess 'the magnitude of the consequence if the hazardous event does occur, and the likelihood (in terms of frequency or probability) of the occurrence of each of the hazards noting, where appropriate, that these may differ from region to region or under different circumstances' (OGTR 2002a, 20). The Regulator appears to favour quantitative data and information (OGTR 2002a, 21–2). If this is not available other methods are used, or may be used as well as quantitative approaches. These include 'expert opinion from committees/groups of experts or from individual experts', 'information on potential hazards provided through public consultation', 'published material on analogous situations' and 'risk assessments or information/advice from other regulatory agencies' (OGTR 2002a, 22). This assessment is then conducted within 'parameters', including:

a. 'The risk assessment will be transparent, objective and scientifically based. It is purely based on risk, not on a balance of risk and benefit' (OGTR 2002a, 15).
b. 'When examining risks to the health and safety of people and the environment, risks and potential risks to all living organisms and relevant ecosystems will be considered, for both long and short term effects' (OGTR 2002a, 15).
c. 'Where there are threats of serious or irreversible environmental damage, the lack of full scientific certainty should not be used as a reason for postponing cost effective measures to prevent environmental degradation' (OGTR 2002a, 15).
d. 'If data are unavailable or incomplete, the significance of that absence or incompleteness in undertaking an evaluation of the risks of a proposal to the health and safety of people or the environment will be considered and, if the Regulator considers that the lack of data creates a level of risk that is not manageable, a licence may not be granted' (OGTR 2002a, 16).
e. 'Risks posed by GMOs will be considered in the context of the risks posed by the non-modified parental organisms in the receiving environment. For example, the identified characteristics flowing from the genetic changes to the GMO and its use, which have the potential to cause adverse effects may

64 'Risk management' means 'the process of evaluating alternative actions, selecting options and implementing them in response to risk assessments': OGTR 2002a, 12 and 70.

65 'Risk communication' means 'ensuring that: an open and transparent process of identification of risks associated with (in this case) gene technology and GMOs has been rigorously followed, and; the community is adequately informed about what these risks are and how they are being managed; and public confidence in the regulatory system is maximised': OGTR 2002a, 13 and 70.

66 See OGTR 2002a, 8–14.

> be compared to those presented by the non-modified organism from which it is derived and its use under corresponding situations' (OGTR 2002a, 16).

Significantly, the Regulator accepts that:

> If data are unavailable or incomplete, the significance of that absence or incompleteness in undertaking an evaluation of the risks of a proposal to the health and safety of people or the environment will be considered and, if the Regulator considers that the lack of data creates a level of risk that is not manageable, a licence may not be granted (Office of the Gene Technology Regulator 2002a, 16).

Further, the Regulator accepts that, '[w]here the level of risk is uncertain, but the consequences of the risk being realized would be significant, one might adopt conservative professional judgment in implementing management strategies' (OGTR 2002a, 20). The Regulator contemplates that the uncertainty might be addressed with 'sensitivity analysis' to gain 'a better "feel" for the impact or importance of the assumptions made' (OGTR 2002a, 21).

The Regulator is *only* required by the GT Act to make a decision to either issue, or refuse to issue, the licence (GT Act s 55), and this decision need only be disclosed to the applicant in writing (GT Act s 59). The Regulator's decision to refuse to issue, or issue the licence subject to conditions, is a 'reviewable decision' for the purposes of the GT Act (GT Act s 179), with standing for administrative review expressly limited (GT Act s 183),[67] although judicial review is probably widened to include a state (including the Australian Capital Territory and the Northern Territory) initiated review (GT Act s 183A).[68] The GT Act only requires the Regulator to make copies of the application and prepared risk assessment and risk management plan available to the public (GT Act s 54) (excluding any confidential commercial information) (GT Act s 54(2)(a) and part 12 div 3), or in order to seek advice (GT Act s 52(3)) or invite submissions (GT Act s 52(2)(c)). The Regulator is not required to disclose any updated risk assessment and risk management plan that takes into account any further advice, and any written submissions upon which the Regulator finally relies. Further, some information provided in the application and during the risk assessment process may be characterized as information about 'relevant convictions' and restricted (GT Act ss 54(2)(b) and 58).

Significantly, in the present matter about the Bayer GM canola application, 'some detailed technical information on precise gene constructs and molecular characterization data' supplied in the application and during the risk assessment

---

67 The term 'eligible person' is confined by s 179 to the applicant for the licence and the licence holder.

68 Although there remains the original jurisdiction of the Federal Court under the *Federal Court Act 1976* (Cth) ss 22 and 23.

process was declared 'confidential commercial information' and access to that information restricted (Bayer 2003, 37).[69] Without the determinative risk assessment and risk management plan and this other information,[70] any analysis of the Regulator's methods and analysis are thus speculative. As a result, we confine the following discussion to the prepared risk assessment and risk management plan and other publicly available documents. While these documents may not be definitive, they provide some insight into the matters the Regulator takes into consideration in determining a risk assessment and risk management plan before issuing a general or commercial release licence.

The GM Canola Under Consideration

The GT Act contemplates that each application for a licence to release a GMO into the environment requires a complete consideration of the risks, and how might they be managed (GT Act ss 48–67; see also OGTR 2003, 90–92). Earlier licences for limited or controlled releases into the environment might be expected to provide useful and directly relevant information as they apply the same processes and requirements (OGTR 2003, 91). This is because 'the Regulator's assessment processes, and conditions applied to the licence, will differ' for the general or commercial releases (OGTR 2003, 91). Further:

> … it is expected that before applying to the Regulator to commercially release a GMO throughout Australia (or in certain regions of Australia), the GMO will have been previously licenced by the Regulator as a field trial under strict conditions. The results of the field trials will be used by the Regulator as part of his/her assessment of whether it is safe for the GMO to be more generally commercially released in Australia (OGTR 2003, 92).

This Part sets out the key elements of the risk assessment and risk management plan for the general or commercial release of Bayer's GM canola and the earlier limited release of Aventis' GM canola. We then examine in detail the decision of the Regulator to licence the general or commercial release of Bayer's GM canola.

69 Notably the Regulator asserts that 'this declaration in no way limited the thorough risk assessment of the individual GMOs': Bayer 2003, 37.

70 Note, however, that the Regulator has previously stated that the risk assessment and risk management plan, and summary information, will be made publicly available: Cotton Seed Distributors Ltd 2001, 68.

The Bayer's GM canola Bayer lodged an application for the general or commercial release of 'seven similar' 'lines'[71] of GM canola[72] in seeking a licence to release the GMOs 'in all canola growing regions of Australia[73] and continued product development and research programs' (Bayer 2003, 16). The licence was granted on 25 July 2003 for the 'GMOs'[74] being GM canola 'containing the transformation event[s]' T45, Topas 19/2, MS1, MS8, RF1, RF2 and RF3 (Bayer 2003, 143–4), and 'InVigor[75] hybrid canola (hybrids of canola containing transformation event MS8 and canola containing transformation event RF3)' (Bayer 2003, 143), and permitting 'all dealings with the GMOs' (Bayer 2003, 139).[76]

The canola (*Brassica napus*), an exotic plant in Australia (see generally, OGTR 2002b), were all modified to incorporate tolerance to the herbicide glufosinate ammonium (either the *pat* or *bar* genes) (Bayer 2003, 16–17 and 38–9).[77] Some 'lines' also included a hybrid breeding system (either the *barnase* or *barstar* genes) (Bayer 2003, 16–17 and 38–9),[78] and some included an antibiotic resistance marker (the *nptII* gene) (Bayer 2003, 16–17 and 38–9).[79] Each line was prepared using *Agrobacterium*-mediated transformation (Bayer 2003, 44).[80] The application related to canola 'lines' with modifications for:

---

71 Defined as, 'to denote canola with a specific genetic modification derived from a single transformation event', although 'this usage is intended to be inclusive of the introduction of the modification into other canola genetic backgrounds by conventional breeding': Bayer 2003, 15 and 38.

72 Being canola T45, Topas 19/2, MS1, MS8, RF1, RF2 and RF3: Bayer 2003, 15–16.

73 This includes all Australian States and Territories: Bayer 2003, 16.

74 Defined as 'the genetically modified organisms covered by this licence, described at Attachment A' and there described as 'Canola' and '*Brassica napus*' that is modified for the category of '[h]erbicide tolerance' and 'Hybrid Breeding System': Bayer 2003, 138 and 143.

75 'InVigor' is a registered trade mark owned by Bayer CropScience GmbH, Frankfurt am Main for the class of goods and services described as '[a]gricultural, horticultural and forestry products and their reproductive material; seeds; grains; live plants' subject to the condition that 'the word INVIGOR will not be used as the name, or part of the name, of a plant variety': Australian Registered Trade Mark 741414 1997.

76 Notably the term 'GMOs' means, 'the genetically modified organisms covered by this licence, described at Attachment A' and Attachment A provides that the 'GMOs covered by this licence are: (a) InVigor hybrid canola (hybrids of canola containing transformation event MS8 and canola containing transformation event RF3); and (b) the GMOs described in the table below' and the table identified the GMOs as 'Canola containing transformation event' T45, Topas 19/2, MS1, MS8, RF1, RF2 and RF3: Bayer 2003, 138 and 143.

77 Being *pat* – T45 and Topas 19/2; *bar* – MS1, MS8, RF1, RF2 and RF3.

78 Being *barnase* – MS1 and MS8; *barstar* – RF1, RF2 and RF3.

79 Being canola Topas 19/2, MS1, RF1 and RF2.

80 Noting that line Topas 19/2 with a binary transformation vector and lines T45, MS1, MS8, RF1, RF2 and RF3 with co-integration vectors: Bayer 2003, 44–5.

a. Glufosinate ammonium detoxification (*pat* or *bar* genes) – tolerance to the herbicide glufosinate ammonium through detoxifying the effects of the herbicide compound in the plant by catalysing the conversion of the herbicide to a non-toxic compound in the plant (Bayer 2003, 41–2). The T45 and Topas 19/2 lines were constructed from the phosphinothricin acetyl transferase gene derived from *Streptomyces viridochromogenes* (*pat* gene) and lines MS1, MS8, RF1, RF2 and RF3 were constructed with a gene with the same function from *Streptomyces hygroscopicus* (*bar* gene) (Bayer 2003, 41–3). Both the *pat* and *bar* genes were modified for plant-preferred codon usage to ensure optimal expression in *B. napus*, and the N-terminal two codons of the *bar* gene in lines MS8 and RF3 were substituted (Bayer 2003, 42). The *pat* gene construct included the constitutive 35S promoter (P-35S) and 35S mRNA polyadenylation (T-35S) signals from cauliflower mosaic virus (Bayer 2003, 43). The *bar* gene construct included the plant promoter PSsuAra from the S1A ribulose-1,5-bisphosphate carboxylase (Rubisco) small subunit gene from the plant *Arabidopsis thaliana*, and mRNA polyadenylation signals derived from the 3' non-translated region from the T-DNA gene 7 (3'g7) of *Agrobacterium tumefaciens* (Bayer 2003, 42). Additional modifications in lines MS1, RF1 and RF2 included the chloroplast transit peptide coding sequence of the *S1A Rubisco* gene from *A. thaliana* (Bayer 2003, 42–3).
b. Hybrid breeding system (*barnase* or *barstar* genes) – enables hybrid generation with one 'line' being male sterile (*barnase* gene, MS line), and the other containing a 'fertility restorer' (*barstar* gene, RF line) so that a cross between the lines (such as MS1 with RF1) restores fertility. This is achieved by the anther-specific expression of the *barnase* gene in the MS line producing cytotoxic ribonuclease only in the tapetum cell layer of the pollen sac during anther development. This destroys those cells and prevents pollen formation that is neutralized by a ribonuclease inhibitor protein in the RF line binding to the ribonuclease and suppressing the latter's activity (Bayer 2003, 40–41). The MS lines MS1 and MS8 were constructed from a ribonuclease gene (the *barnase* gene) derived from *Bacillus amyloliquefaciens*, an anther-specific promoter PTA29 derived from *Nicotiana tabacum*, and mRNA polyadenylation signals derived from the 3' non-translated region of the nopaline synthase gene (3' nos) from *A. tumefaciens* (Bayer 2003, 40). The RF lines RF1, RF2 and RF3 were constructed from a bacterial ribonuclease inhibitor protein from *B. amyloliquefaciens* (*barstar* gene) and then the same anther-specific promoter PTA29 and 3' nos mRNA polyadenylation signals (Bayer 2003, 40–41).
c. Antibiotic resistance (*nptII* gene) – an artefact from the selection and transformation of plants during the early stages of development in tissue culture (Bayer 2003, 43). The *nptII* gene product neomycin phoshotransferase catalyses the conversion of aminoglycoside antibiotics

> and butirosins to non-toxic compounds in plants (Bayer 2003, 43). The lines Topas 19/2, MS1, RF1 and RF2 were constructed from a *nptII* gene from transposon Tn5 from *Escherichia coli*, a nopaline synthase promoter (P-nos) from *A. tumefaciens* and the mRNA polyadenylation signals derived from the 3' non-translated region of the octapine synthase gene (3' cos) from *A. tumefaciens* (Bayer 2003, 43).

Notably, not disclosed were some of the additional nucleotides associated with the constructs[81] and relic sequences from the *Agrobacterium*-mediated transformation[82] (Bayer 2003, 46–8). Presumably these were characterized and disclosed in the Confidential Commercial Information (Bayer 2003, 44–5). Further, comparison of left and right flanking sequences of the transformation sites in lines T45, Topas 19/2 and RF3, the left flanking sequence in lines MS1 and RF1, and the right flanking sequence in line RF2, with sequence databases using standard algorithms revealed 'no significant homology to known genes' (Bayer 2003, 47–8). Perhaps surprisingly, 'significant homology' was detected in the right flanking sequence of lines MS1 and RF1 and the left flanking sequence of line RF2 to *A. thaliana*. But 'in each case the homology was not to any genes with a known function' and was considered 'not surprising' given that 'the entire genome of *A. thaliana* has recently been sequenced' (Bayer 2003, 47–8).[83]

Aventis' GM canola The earlier licence to Aventis of 30 July 2002 to release GM canola into the environment was to carry out a limited and controlled release (field trials) commencing in 2002 (Aventis 2002, 4). This was, 'to conduct plant breeding (including agronomic assessments) and seed production trials for the development of canola cultivars for the Australian, North American and European cropping systems' (Aventis 2002, 7). In assessing the risk for this licence other earlier releases of GM canola were considered that had been assessed and conducted under the pre-existing voluntary scheme (Aventis 2002, 8).[84] No reports were made of adverse effects on human health and safety or the environment (Aventis 2002, 9).[85] However, the limited and controlled release (field trials) risk assessment and risk management plan undertaken by the Regulator for this application *only* considered

---

81 These nucleotides are associated with the inserted genes and are not characterized in the application: Bayer 2003, 46–8.

82 These nucleotides are not characterized in the application, and includes a partial T-DNA containing a portion of the T-DNA including the *barstar* gene in line RF3 and the *pat* and *nptII* genes in Topas 19/2: Bayer 2003, 47.

83 Notably there was no report of flanking sequences for line MS8: Bayer 2003, 46.

84 These were recorded as approvals PR-63, PR-63X, PR-63X(2), PR-63X(3), PR-63X(4), PR-63X(5) and PR-63X(6).

85 Although a number of instances of non-compliance with conditions were recorded: Interim OGTR 2001, 23–4, where sheep were recorded grazing on canola.

lines MS8 and RF3 (Aventis 2002, 11–16), and concluded that the limited release of these lines:

> … in the canola growing regions of southern Western Australia, south-west New South Wales, Victoria and south-east South Australia will not pose any additional risks to human health and safety or to the environment as a result of the genetic modification of the canola (Aventis 2002, 56).

The Regulator asserts that she is, 'reviewing all licence conditions for licences carried over from the voluntary system' and '[i]f as a result of this review, new information becomes available about risks relevant to the release, the licence issued to Aventis would be amended if necessary' (Aventis 2002, 59).

The main conclusions from the MS8 and RF3 risk assessment were: that the GM canola lines were not likely to prove more toxic or allergenic to humans or other organisms than conventional canola; that the risk of the GM canola establishing as a weed was low and not likely to be greater than that of conventional canola; that there was potential for transfer of the introduced genes into non-GM canola crops although the level of out-crossing would be very low; that there was potential for transfer of the introduced genes to weedy relatives of canola through out-crossing although this was also extremely low; and that the likelihood of transfer of the introduced genes to other organisms was also extremely low (Aventis 2002, 56). To address these risks the management plan called for restricting the use, spread and persistence of the GM canola lines (Aventis 2002, 56–7), and this was reflected in the licence conditions (Aventis 2002, 58–9 and 62–84). Further conditions imposed data collection requirements about the rate of out-crossing and the efficacy of pollen traps 'to obtain information to refine management conditions for future limited and contained releases of [genetically modified] canola in order to ensure that the conditions imposed are adequate to manage the risks of gene flow' (Aventis 2002, 79).

Other data identified in the MS8 and RF3 risk assessment and risk management plan was considered relevant for future applications. This included: the reasons for European regulators refusing field trials;[86] the efficacy of pollen traps in limiting the spread of GM pollen; the efficacy of isolation zones, including the rate of out-crossing from canola under Australian conditions at short distances; the persistence of canola in non-agricultural habitats; the factors determining the persistence of canola in non-agricultural habitats; and, whether such releases were likely to result in changes to agricultural practices that might have environmental

---

86 The Belgian Government refused to approve field tests with GM herbicide tolerant canola expressing concerns about pollen transfer, although no details of the assessment were available, 'but further information is being actively sought and will be considered in assessing an application from Aventis for the commercial release of InVigor canola': Aventis 2002, 10.

impacts (Aventis 2002, 20).[87] In justifying the conditions restricting the use, spread and persistence of the GM canola lines the Regulator applied conditions to a standard of 'necessary' and 'adequate' to manage the identified risks (Aventis 2002, 78–84).

Significantly, however, the earlier licenced limited releases to Aventis on 30 July 2002 related to 'InVigor canola' (Aventis 2002, 4).[88] This was described as, 'two GM lines of canola based on a dominant nuclear male sterility gene, and a restorer of fertility gene … [and containing] a gene conferring tolerance to the herbicide glufosinate ammonium' (Aventis 2002, 4). This was further limited to the planting seasons 1 March 2002 to 28 February 2005 (Aventis 2002, 64–5). The outcome and results of this limited release licence might have been expected to provide useful background for Bayer's general or commercial release application on 25 July 2003.[89] In particular, data collection during the field trials might have been expected to have addressed uncertainties in the available data and provide further confirmation about the presumptive risks identified in the Aventis application (Hayes 2004, 27–30).[90] However, the overlap of the Aventis and Bayer applications meant that any data would be limited and its usefulness as quantitative data limited by the power of any statistical analysis.

The Regulator's decision about Bayer's GM canola In assessing whether to impose conditions to manage the risks posed by Bayer's general or commercial release under the GT Act, the Regulator 'consider[ed] the need to impose conditions to manage any risks to human health and safety or the environment', including a 'consideration of whether any conditions would be effective in managing risks', and a 'consideration of whether any conditions imposed could be effectively implemented and compliance monitored and enforced' (Bayer 2003, 27). The standard the Regulator applied was that, 'the release should only be approved if

---

87 Perhaps surprisingly, *barnase* gene expression was *only* correlated with an antherless phenotype, as there was no evidence of *barnase* gene expression through Northern analysis in MS8, although MS8 and RF3 crosses were reported to be fully fertile and might have provided evidence of *barnase* gene expression through Northern analysis: Aventis 2002, 17.

88 Notably, the GMO is not defined in the licence conditions other than as 'GMO' (Aventis 2002, 62–84), although the 'object of most of the conditions is to limit the potential for spread and persistence of the GM InVigor canola in the environment outside the release site or the Isolation Zone, in order to reduce the potential for risks to human health and safety or the environment': Aventis 2002, 78.

89 'The purpose of this [limited] release is to conduct breeding trials to develop lines suitable for use under Australian conditions and produce seed for potential commercial lines and export. Any future releases in Australia would be subject to separate applications and assessments': Aventis 2002, 4.

90 Noting that Hayes says: '[c]urrent field trials only appear to gather information on crop performance. These trials are an ideal opportunity to gather the types of data needed to improve the science of GMO risk assessment': Hayes 2004, ii.

the risks to human health and safety or the environment are low to non-existent and therefore do not require a range of specific licence conditions for them to be managed' (Bayer 2003, 27). The relevant issues were identified as those required by the GT Act, and those raised in the consultation process and the prepared risk assessment and risk management plan (Bayer 2003, 7, 9 and 27). The Regulator also took into account issues raised during the public consultation process in applying a standard of 'considered carefully and weighed against the body of current scientific information' (Bayer 2003, 27).[91]

As a consequence of the consultations and preparing the risk assessment and risk management plan, the Regulator concluded that 'the proposed release does not pose risks to the health and safety of people or the environment in Australia that require management through specific licencee conditions … [a]ccordingly, the licence … contains only minimal oversight conditions' (Bayer 2003, 13). The 'general conditions' included a restatement of the GT Act's licensing condition (Bayer 2003, 139–40) and an additional requirement that:

> The licence holder must provide the Regulator, on the Regulator's written request, signed statements from persons covered by this licence that the licence holder has informed those people of the conditions of this licence that apply to them (Bayer 2003, 139).

The only other 'specific condition' required a written description of a test methodology for detecting the presence of the licenced GMO and any transferred genetic modified materials, and an annual reporting requirement for:

a. Information about any adverse impacts, unintended effects, or new information relating to risks, to human health and safety or the environment caused by the GMOs or material from the GMOs;

…

d. Other information on the progress of the release of the GMOs, including annual surveys, the details of which will be determined in consultation with the OGTR (Bayer 2003, 141).

Preparing the risk assessment and risk management plan first involved a process of identifying 'potential hazards', and then assessing the risks posed by these hazards as being 'negligible', 'very low', 'low', 'moderate', 'high' or 'very high', by considering 'the likelihood of the hazard occurring', 'the likely consequences (impact) of the hazard, were it to be realized' and 'risk management options to mitigate any significant hazards' (Bayer 2003, 27). In preparing the risk assessment and risk management plan the Regulator identified the following hazards:

91 Notably the Regulator received 256 written submissions and 531 'campaign' letters and emails: Bayer 2003, 150.

a. Toxicity or allergenicity, in particular for humans, vertebrates (including grazing animals, birds and native animals), invertebrates (including insects) and soil biota.
b. Weediness, in particular persistence in the environment, agricultural environments, non-cropped disturbed environments, undisturbed environments and spread in the environment.
c. Gene transfer, in particular to other canola crops, *B. napus* vegetables and forage canola, related *Brassica* species (such as *B. rapa*, *B. juncea*, *B. oleracea*), other *Brassicaceous* weeds (such as *Raphanus raphanistrum*, *Hirschfeldia incana*, *Sinapis arvensis*) and other organisms (such as humans, other animals, microorganisms (including bacteria, viruses and fungi)) (Bayer 2003, 29–36).

To assess the risks posed by these hazards the following were considered:

a. Toxicity or allergenicity: this hazard was characterized as the possible toxicity or allergenicity posed by the GM canola lines T45, Topas 19/2, MS1, MS8, RF1, RF2 and RF3 (but not the crosses MS1 x RF1, MS1 x RF2, MS1 x RF3, MS8 x RF1, MS8 x RF2 and MS8 x RF3); from the four additional expressed proteins (PAT, Barnase, Barstar and NPTII); or, that their might be unforeseen or unintended effects from the genetic modification (pleotropic effects) (Bayer 2003, 53–4). These toxicity and allergenicity risks were then assessed by considering the toxicity and allergenicity of conventional canola, the toxicity and allergenicity of the new proteins expressed, the changes to the levels of naturally occurring toxicants and nutritional factors, the potential for altered metabolism of the herbicide, and the likely levels and routes of exposure to GM canola and the introduced proteins (Bayer 2003, 54, 62 and 67). After considering the risks the Regulator concluded the risks to humans were 'very low' (Bayer 2003, 66), and that there were no risks to other organisms (Bayer 2003, 76).
b. Weediness: this hazard was characterized as 'the potential for the GM canola lines to be harmful to the environment due to possible weediness or increased potential for weediness' (Bayer 2003, 79) and 'the possibility that the genetic modification has, either directly or as a result of "pleotropic" effects, increased the weediness of the canola plants' (Bayer 2003, 79). The latter being GM canola lines T45, Topas 19/2, MS1, MS8, RF1, RF2 and RF3 (but not the crosses MS1 x RF1, MS1 x RF2, MS1 x RF3, MS8 x RF1, MS8 x RF2 and MS8 x RF3) (Bayer 2003, 78). The risks were then assessed by considering the inherent weediness of conventional canola and the weediness of GM canola in agricultural environments, non-cropped disturbed environments and undisturbed environments (Bayer 2003, 79–94). After considering the risks the Regulator concluded that the risks 'that the GM canola lines will be more likely than conventional (non-GM) canola

to spread in the environment, and result in more detrimental environmental impact is negligible' (Bayer 2003, 94).

c. Transfer of introduced genes to increase weediness: this hazard was characterized as 'the hazards that might result from transfer of the genes introduced into the GM canola[92] lines T45, Topas19/2, RF1, RF2, RF3, MS1 and MS8 to other organisms could include the production of herbicide-tolerant weeds, some of which may have the potential to compete with native flora thereby reducing biodiversity' (Bayer 2003, 95) (but not the crosses MS1 x RF1, MS1 x RF2, MS1 x RF3, MS8 x RF1, MS8 x RF2 and MS8 x RF3) (Bayer 2003, 95). The risks were assessed by considering the likelihood of genes transferring into other canola, other plants and other organisms (Bayer 2003, 95). After considering the risks the Regulator concluded that gene transfer to other canola was 'inevitable' (Bayer 2003, 107), although the consequences were 'negligible' and require no management conditions (Bayer 2003, 107). The Regulator considered gene transfer (and introgression) with *B. napus* vegetables and forage rape was 'very low' or 'negligible', with other *Brassica* species was 'high', and with *Brassicaceous* weeds was 'extremely low'. In each case it was concluded the risks were 'very low' or 'negligible' and required no management conditions (Bayer 2003, 122–4).
d. Transfer of introduced genes to other organisms – this hazard was characterized as the hazards that might result from transfer of the genes introduced into the GM canola lines T45, Topas19/2, RF1, RF2, RF3, MS1 and MS8 to other organisms, such as humans, animals, micro-organisms, bacteria, fungi and plant viruses (Bayer 2003, 126–33) (but not the crosses MS1 x RF1, MS1 x RF2, MS1 x RF3, MS8 x RF1, MS8 x RF2 and MS8 x RF3) (Bayer 2003, 127–8). The risks were assessed by considering the likely mechanisms of gene transfer and considered to be 'negligible', although there was no positive evidence of gene transfer from any of the GM lines or their crosses to other organisms, the evidence at best being inferences from the low probability of occurrence and persistence (Bayer 2003, 132–3).
e. Herbicide resistant weeds – this hazard was characterized as the 'potential development of herbicide resistant weeds if the InVigor crop-Liberty herbicide combination is used inappropriately' (Bayer 2003, 134). The risk was not assessed but it was considered that it could be managed by complying with the existing conditions imposed by the Australian Pesticides and Veterinary Medicines Authority (Bayer 2003, 134).

Based on these materials and evaluations the Regulator 'considered' that 'the risks to human health and safety, or to the Australian environment, from the

92 Noting that the risk assessment distinguishes between 'hybridization' and 'introgression', and the potential of plants to hybridize between species: Bayer 2003, 95.

commercial release of any of Bayer's seven GM canola lines are no greater than those posed by non-GM canola, for instance, they are as safe as conventional canola' (Bayer 2003, 10).

Discussion

The advent of GMOs promised improved health care, food security, poverty alleviation, environmental sustainability, and so on (Report of the Subcommittee on Basic Research 2000; Hindmarsh and Lawrence 2001, 11–23). However, despite these promises, public and scientific concerns have been consistently raised about the health and environmental safety of GMOs (and GM products) (Stewart and McLean 2004; Hoffmann and Sung 2005), with the consequence that they have attracted regulatory intervention in many jurisdictions (Nap et al. 2003, 8–13; Hayes 2004). In Australia, the GT Act sets out part of the regulatory scheme addressing 'dealings' with 'GMOs' with a risk assessment methodology set out in the *Risk Analysis Framework* about human health and safety and the environment that is theoretically objective and 'science-based':

> For the Regulator, the objective of the risk assessment is to identify potential for adverse effects that GMOs may pose for human health and the environment and their potential impact. It should be noted that risk assessment is a scientific process that does not take political or other non-scientific aspects of an application to use a GMO into account (OGTR 2002a, 12).[93]

The GT Act's approach to assessing risk assumes that physical and natural processes can be reduced to objectively quantifiable probabilities (or rates) and consequences (risk = frequency x consequence) (Slovic 1999, 690). By applying a regulatory framework to constructing the 'problem' of GMO risks, the Regulator's decision provides a solution that establishes a rational dominance over what otherwise might be (whether in reality or otherwise) an uncontrollable health and environmental problem (Rutherford 1994, 40; Levidow 1995, 184).[94] Put another way, the GT Act seeks to provide certainty to an uncertain 'problem' by appealing to an apolitical and objective scientific approach, without acknowledging the uncertainty of science as a methodology for making interpolations (where a given value will occur between two known values) and extrapolations (where a likely value is outside the range of known values but estimated) about likely and

93 Noting also that the risk assessment is to be founded on a 'science-based approach' and 'objective information': Explanatory Memorandum 2000, 14 and 63.

94 Some authors highlight this contention by comparing and contrasting the 'product' regulation and 'process' regulation in the United States and Europe respectively, the former restricting uncertainties to available knowledge about the product use and its characteristics, the latter encompassing broader debates about the place of technology in society: Jasanoff 1995, 324.

unknowable future events. This approach reflects the modern industrialization of science applied to promoting economic growth and national power based on a scientific tradition that relies on the control and management of health and the environment.[95] The problem with this approach, however, is the faith accorded to 'science' as a foundation on which to establish regulatory decisions[96] and the particular narrow framing of the 'problem' (Jasanoff 2003, 240–41) organized around an assessment of known risks and their management (Black 1998, 625–6; see generally Jasanoff 1999; Lee and Burrell 2002, 518–20[97] that the 'science' seeks to address.[98] However:

> ... risk does not exist 'out there', independent of our minds and cultures, waiting to be measured. Instead, human beings have invented the concept of risk to help them understand and cope with the dangers and uncertainties of life. Although these dangers are real, there is no such thing as 'real risk' or 'objective risk'. The nuclear engineer's probabilistic risk estimate for a nuclear accident or the toxicologist's quantitative estimate of a chemical's carcinogenic risk are both based on theoretical models, whose structure is subjective and assumption-laden, and whose inputs are dependent on judgment (Slovic 1999, 690).

---

95 For an overview of the historical and cultural context: Worster 1985; Foucault 1990; policy articulations of this contention in Australia include the *National Biotechnology Strategy* that provides: '[b]iotechnology holds the promise of improved health and welfare for all Australians through better understanding of disease, improved diagnosis, and treatment with more specific biopharmaceutical products. Biotechnology, including the genetic modification of agricultural and food products, also has the potential to deliver productivity, competitiveness and sustainability benefits to Australia': Commonwealth Parliament 2000, 3.

96 See Knorr-Cetina 1999 examining the differences in knowledge as a result of difference epistemic cultures of high energy physics and molecular biology; Feyerabend 1980 suggesting that scientific standards cannot be separated from their practice and use of these standards presupposes immersion in the practice.

97 Noting that cognitive frameworks will also inform the uncertainties considered relevant (Levidow 1995, 181) and the cultures of science developed in genetics and molecular biology capture the metaphor of building using innovative laboratory based methods rather than manipulating a complex genomic system in the broader environment (Scoones 2002, 4–5): see also Latour 1987; Jasanoff 1990).

98 For example, the harm from a GMO might be constructed as a direct risk from the GMO or an indirect risk from the agricultural uses of the GMO, the choice is a an assumption about risk: Levidow 1995, 181; Black 1998, 625; importantly, but not addressed in this chapter, the scientific knowledge derived from this 'science' only provides a relative 'truth about nature' governed by a particular scientific paradigm (Kuhn 1970, 23–34; for example molecular biologists and biochemists might be expected to emphasis different risks reflecting their different values and assumptions about their disciplines: Newell 2002, 15–16), that is 'a socially constructed interpretation with an already socially constructed natural-technical object of inquiry': Bird 1987, 255 and the references therein.

The principal actors framing the 'problem' are the expert scientists (in universities and industry) granted the status of an objective voice (Black, 1998, 622; see also Fischer 1990; Hindmarsh 2001), and a 'dialogue' between the Regulator and the (industry) applicant through the regulatory process (Black 1998, 625).[99] The broader public is only provided with a very limited opportunity to participate in the regulatory decision-making being recognized primarily in their capacity as consumers, either buying or refusing to buy GMOs and GM products (Black 1998, 625 and 628).[100] In short, the GT Act sets out a regulatory scheme for framing hazards, assessing the risks and the accepting those risks considered by the Regulator to have a low probability and/or with manageable consequences as objectively acceptable masked in the rhetoric of apolitical and objective 'science'.

Perhaps most importantly, most releases of GMOs into the environment will refer to unique and infinitely variable risk situations, and so involve a 'non-statistical' or subjective probability assessment[101] relying on, at best, partial and imperfect information that may be, at best, informed by some form of 'science-based' study (Lawson 2002, 201–202; see also Carman 2004, 82–93). Even where rigorous and comprehensive assessments have been attempted for simply constructed GMOs (such as the 'Farm-Scale Evaluations' study in the UK) (Six Articles 2003; see also Gura 2001; Giles 2003),[102] they have proven to be costly, have limited predictive utility for other GMOs (including closely related lines), and do not address all the possible hazards (however characterized) to changes to the wider environment (such as gene flow to wild relatives) (Wilkinson 2004, 439).[103] This approach therefore considers unimportant, or insignificant, low probability adverse events accepting that there is a level of risk that can be managed.[104] Thus, an adverse event

99 These often form 'epistemic communities' with a common view about the risks and the most appropriate form of regulation: Haas 1990.

100 The broader community are left 'incompetent in matters of their own affliction': Beck 1992, 53–5.

101 Noting further that 'probability' itself is a 'mental and social creation' subject to contentious debate: Smithson 1989, 41; see also Gigerenzer 2002.

102 Notably the Australian Commonwealth Scientific and Industrial Research Organisation has concluded that 'while the UK experiment can inform our future research in this area, its findings cannot be extrapolated directly to Australia and are therefore of quite limited relevance to Australian farming systems. The results cannot be applied to Australian GM crops in general': Lonsdale et al. 2003, 3.

103 Wilkinson also suggests such intensive and expensive studies might become impractical as the diversity and complexity of constructs introduced into GM crops expands: Wilkinson 2004, 439; see also Davies 2004.

104 For example, the Regulator considers risks categorized as 'very low' and 'negligible' as acceptable and requiring limited management: Bayer 2003, 29–36; see also Monsanto Australia Ltd 2003, 26–34.

is acceptable below a certain probability threshold (Okrent 1980).[105] This poses two immediate problems, first, the assumption that low probability can be counted as zero, and second, the threshold of the low level probability (Shrader-Frechette 1985, 134–40), which ignores the consequences of any adverse event (albeit very unlikely) (Shrader-Frechette 1985, 142). Entirely outside this assessment are the unknown, unintended effects that are tacitly accepted or considered manageable (Levidow 1995, 181; see also York 2001, 433).

While there is no doubt that a regulatory measure is necessary in some form to address the GT Act's objective of establishing legitimacy about the safety of GMOs (and GM products), the challenge is to 'make visible the non-scientific elements that are always behind risk-influenced decisions regarding who will be allowed to do what to the environment' (O'Brian 2000, 243). Moreover, to acknowledge the uncertainty inherent in the methodology of 'science' as an approach to understanding nature (see generally Kuhn 1970),[106] including definitive information about how much of an activity poses 'no risk' or 'an insignificant risk' (O'Brian 2000, 59–60; see also Wynne and Mayer 1993). The problem with the current GT Act's approach is that it allows for the Regulator, assisted by the Office of the Gene Technology Regulator, to selectively adopt often highly uncertain and contested knowledge about scientific theories and measurement techniques under the guise of consensus expert knowledge. Further, these can then be changed, minimized, magnified or dramatized within that knowledge and subject to the Regulator's particular preferences, social definitions and construction about the acceptability of possible and unknowable adverse outcomes (Beck 1992, 22–3; Levidow 1995, 181).

The Regulator's authority to define the risks within the framework of the GT Act according to the methodology set out in the *Risk Analysis Framework* is perhaps tempered by the requirement that the Regulator seek advice about the risk assessment and risk management plan[107] and comply with various policy

105 For example, a 10^{-6} or lower probability of a human fatality was considered negligible for commercial nuclear reactor safety in the US: United States Nuclear Regulatory Commission 1975, 38.

106 For example, 'we must recognize how very limited in both scope and precision a paradigm can be at the time of its appearance. Paradigms gain their status because they are more successful than their competitors in solving a few problems that the group of practitioners has come to recognize as acute' (Kuhn 1970, 23); see also Latour 1987.

107 Preparation of the risk assessment and risk management plan – from the States, the Gene Technology Technical Advisory Committee, prescribed Commonwealth agencies, the Environment Minister and any local council the Regulator considers appropriate: GT Act s 50(3); after preparing the risk assessment and risk management plan – to seek written submissions from the public, and again seek the advice of the states, the Gene Technology Technical Advisory Committee, prescribed Commonwealth agencies, the Environment Minister and any local council the Regulator considers appropriate (s 52).

instruments.[108] There is, however, *no* requirement that the Regulator comply with any of these sources of advice. The effect of the GT Act, therefore, is to empower the Regulator to construct and then assess the risks of GMOs (and GM products) through a reliance on the rhetoric of science-based objectivity to promote legitimacy in GMOs (and GM products) and generally to promote commercial transactions in GMOs (and GM products). The question is therefore, whether the Regulator's decision promotes legitimacy or undermines legitimacy.

The assessment in this chapter so far suggests a very limited objective 'science' supporting the Regulator's assessments; marked by a failure to acknowledge value judgements in framing the hazards, assessing the risks, and accepting that the identified risks are objectively acceptable. This, we contend, is likely to undermine the legitimacy of the GT Act. A deeper analysis of the Bayer licence for the general or commercial release of GM canola highlights the sorts of contentions that are likely to undermine that legitimacy. These include four aspects: (a) framing the GMO 'problem'; (b) selecting risk issues; (c) making decisions without acknowledging uncertainty; and (d) framing decisions that avoid recognition of who frames them.

Framing the GMO 'problem' This is where the Regulator frames the GMO 'problem' that requires the risk assessment by:

a. Confining considerations about the GMO to those that are not substantially equivalent to the 'conventional canola' (Bayer 2003, 10; see also Organisation for Economic Co-operation and Development 2004). Applying the principles of substantial equivalence (and familiarity) avoids detailed assessments of GMOs by recognizing only those risks posed by the 'novel' GMO, while at the same time promoting biotechnology as an innovative and competitive technology and downplaying potential environmental hazards (Barrett and Abergel 2000).[109] Perhaps more importantly, however, the substantial equivalence approach avoids some critical assessments. For example, canola is a relatively recently domesticated crop with the potential to outcross with its weedy relatives. This raises concerns about the potential invasiveness of GM canola transgenes into the broader environment (Conner et al. 2003, 25–6 and the references therein).
   Applying the substantial equivalence standard to releasing GM herbicide tolerant canola into the environment then is a question of whether the invasiveness of the herbicide tolerance transgene will be different to

108 The Regulator is also required to 'have regard to' any policy guidelines issued by the Ministerial Council relating to risks and ways to manage risks (GT Act ss 23 and 56(2)(d)) and be consistent with any policy principles issued by the Ministerial Council (ss 21 and 57(1)).

109 Although the merits of 'substantial equivalence' remain hotly contested, compare for examples, Miller 1999 and Millstone et al. 1999; see generally McGarity 2002.

traditional canola, there being a documented history of herbicide tolerance entering weedy populations related to the crop (Conner et al. 2003, 24). The invasiveness of releasing the herbicide tolerance transgene is unlikely to be any different to the impact of releasing a non-GM herbicide tolerant variety, although the consequences of the GM canola might be significantly different (Conner et al. 2003, 26 and the references therein).

Thus the Regulator considered the inherent weediness of conventional and GM canola in various environments and concluded, 'that the GM canola lines will be more likely than conventional (non-GM) canola to spread in the environment, and result in more detrimental environmental impact is negligible' (Bayer 2003, 94), although the crosses MS1 x RF1, MS1 x RF2, MS1 x RF3, MS8 x RF1, MS8 x RF2 and MS8 x RF3 were not considered (Bayer 2003, 78).

This, however, is more broadly an issue about the costs and benefits of a particular agricultural strategy of managing herbicide tolerance. It avoids the question about the particular herbicide tolerance transgene and its particular effects, there being no agreed threshold for where a GMO (or GM product) ceases to be acceptably 'equivalent' (Millstone et al. 1999, 525; see also Rowland 2002, 27). This threshold is also a particular problem in assessing the potential toxicity of GMOs. For example, the Regulator was able to conclude that risks to humans of the toxicity and allergenicity of the expressed proteins (PAT, Barnase, Barstar and nptII) compared to conventional canola was 'very low' (Bayer 2003, 66), even though the only data available was either undisclosed or correlated with mostly unpublished data. Further, there are no benchmarks for compositional and other tangible characteristics in making the substantial equivalence determination (Rowland 2002, 27).[110] By using the standard of substantial equivalence the Regulator leaves open the challenge of not taking relevant matters into consideration and applying a threshold standard that does not reflect a consensus of views about what is, and what is not, a 'novel' or (un)safe organism.

---

110 The recent difference of opinion between the United States Food and Drug Administration (FDA) and the Environment Protection Agency (EPA) over the 'substantial equivalence' of the Cry9C protein illustrates the variable standards that might apply, in this example, the EPA found that the Cry9C protein was resistant to protease breakdown, remained stable at high temperatures, and remained intact following four hours in simulated mammalian gastric juices and on this basis concluded that the applicant had failed to show the GMO was 'substantially equivalent in all essential respects to its unmodified parent', while the FDA had approved the application finding 'substantial equivalence': Bratspies 2003, 616–9; other problems arise in determining who is qualified to make this assessment and whether the standard should be applied to individuals or classes: McGarity 2002, 428; Pryme and Lembcke 2003.

b. Accepting that the only way to gain experience with general or commercial releases is to allow general or commercial releases, which promotes this as the best route to gain familiarity with any likely problem and requires the reporting of '[i]nformation about any adverse impacts, unintended effects, or new information relating to risks' (Bayer 2003, 141). The consequence of this approach is to tacitly accept or consider manageable the unknown unintended effects of GMOs.
c. Failing to address the broader ecological concerns (such as community studies, succession studies, ecosystem analysis, population dynamics or organism-environment relationships) (see generally Rissler and Mellon 1996) about 'ecosystems and their constituent parts' and 'the qualities and characteristics of locations, places and areas', required by the GT Act's definition of the term 'environment' (GT Act s 10),[111] and its incorporation of the concepts of ecologically sustainable development (Lawson 2002, 210).[112] This is particularly relevant as ecological sustainability involves a consideration of the long-term ecological consequences of releasing GMOs,[113] including a 'need to consider, in an integrated way, the wider economic, social and environmental implications of our decisions and actions for Australia, the international community and the biosphere' and with a 'long term view' (Council of Australian Governments 1992, 6). The prepared risk assessment and risk management plan show that this has not happened, with no long-term (such as 50 or 100 years) (Burgmann 1999, 131–2) hazards considered or identified. Further, there was no evaluation of the likely 'tillage and herbicide regimes' effects on weed populations as a consequence of using GMO canola resistance to the herbicide glyphosate. Instead the Regulator merely asserted that, '[t]here is potential for development of herbicide-resistant weeds if the InVigor crop – Liberty herbicide combination is used inappropriately' (Bayer 2003, 134). This was a surprising omission as the widespread adoption of herbicide resistant GMOs will effect weed communities towards naturally resistant species, species with inherent characteristics (such as delayed emergence), and herbicide resistant bio-types, each with potentially significant environmental

111 For an analysis of the term 'environment': McGrath 2003, 35; Trantor 2003, 253–4.

112 Attempts to include these sorts of measures in the GT Act were expressly rejected (for example, an amendment 'to promote ecological sustainability': Commonwealth Parliament 2000b, 21181–2) on the basis that '[w]e do not consider a separate definition [of ecological sustainability] is required, because ecological sustainability is not separate and distinct from the environment': Commonwealth Parliament 2000c, 21204.

113 Described as 'costs' that the GT Act was intended to address: Explanatory Memorandum 2000, 6.

and economic consequences irrespective of the herbicide regime (Owen and Zelaya 2005).

Selecting risk issues This is where the Regulator then selectively addresses risk issues by:

a. Overlooking the absence of quantitative data about the GMOs (and GM products) about which the licence was sought. Instead the Regulator relies on correlations and assertions from a variety of sources to find that the risks are low or negligible, and in particular the views and opinions of experts without acknowledging the epistemic cultures from which those views and opinions originate (see generally Knorr-Cetina 1999). For example, the lack of toxicity for humans of the PAT protein from the *pat* and *bar* genes were correlated from unpublished mice and rat feeding studies over 14 days where purified PAT protein (including a recombinant PAT protein) was administered over a period of time where 'no gross internal findings were observed' and '[n]o significant differences were observed' (Bayer 2003, 56). The use of the terms 'no gross' and 'no significant' reflect an assessment that there were some differences between the rats fed with purified PAT protein and an acceptance by the Regulator that these difference were of no consequence (and particularly of no consequence for humans). This then required no further consideration of the consequences of any adverse event (in effect, probability zero for human health and safety) (Rescher 1983, 36). The problem with this approach is that it considers unimportant, or insignificant, what are assessed in the Regulator's view – based on limited data and assertions from a particular epistemic culture – to be the likelihood of low probability adverse events. This tends to ignore the consequences of any adverse event that may be significantly detrimental (even fatal) for particular individuals (Shrader-Frechette 1985, 142).
b. Failing to identify, acknowledge or address inherent value judgments in the assessment of the risks. For example, the Regulator finds the risk of the GM canola being more invasive or persistent than conventional canola is 'negligible' and decides that this is a risk worth taking (Bayer 2003, 11 and 93–4).[114] While this might be a valid and appropriate value judgment, it is still a judgment that accepts some risks that might eventuate, especially over the long term, where the consequences might be considerable. For example, stochastic modelling of the impacts of feral populations of crops on wild relatives suggests over a long period of time (100 years) the invasiveness and persistence of crop species may not be 'negligible' (Burgmann 1999, 131–

114 Perhaps surprisingly, the line or variety of GM and conventional canola investigated and reported by the Regulator were not disclosed either by the Regulator or the cited authority.

2).[115] Perhaps more importantly, however, the Regulator accepts conclusively that GM canola will not persist in undisturbed natural environment by relying on a published study showing GM canola became extinct in such environments after two years (Bayer 2003, 93; see also Office of the Gene Technology Regulator 2002b, 11). This does not acknowledge that there was considerable debate about the merits of the study, its design and the generality of its conclusions (Metz and Nap 1997). Further, even where quantitative risk assessments are available (probability-based inferences), they rely on statistical models with considerable judgment lying in the choice of model and its underlying assumption (Hayes 2004, 38; see also Harding 1998). What might be considered 'not significant' (or 'negligible') overlooks potentially contested conclusions about the methodology and its assessment (climate change modelling provides a current example, see for example, Murphy et al. 2004, as does the safety testing of GM foods) (Carman 2004, 82–93).

c. Avoiding any assessment of the understanding of knowledge or the values involved in acquiring and producing knowledge (and in particular scientific uncertainty) (Bayer 2003, 147).[116] For example, the consequences of unintended or pleotropic effects were assessed in part according to feeding studies of the MS1 x RF1 cross seeds fed to canaries having 'no differences in food consumption, behaviour and body weight between the GM and non-GM diets' (Bayer 2003, 59). This study did not disclose how this data was derived or the experimental design, both involving value judgments about how to conduct the experiment (such as how to measure behaviour) and then assumptions in the statistical model that revealed 'no difference' (assuming the data was subjected to a statistical analysis) (Bayer 2003, 59).[117] A similar criticism applies to the Regulator's reliance on assessing human toxicity and allergenicity-based on unpublished mice and rat feeding studies Bayer 2003, 58–9), and upon an undisclosed line or variety of canola (Bayer 2003, 61).

d. Avoiding any long term or intergenerational assessment of potential impacts, especially the degree of environmental risks,[118] even though

115 Burgmann showed that a 0.5 per cent and 5 per cent escape rate of a competitively inferior crop on wild populations will fall to 1 per cent of their initial population size with a probability of 20 per cent and 100 per cent respectively: Burgmann 1999, 131–2.

116 By way of example, recognized experts may contest the interpretation of data where the risks are uncertain: Krayer von Krauss et al. 2004; see also Walker 1991.

117 The cited reference merely provides: '[a]n avian dietary test was performed with the seed eating canary bird (*Serinus canaria domestica*), and a feeding study was performed with the domesticated rabbit (*Oryctolagus cuniculus*); these studies showed no differences in food consumption, behaviour and body weight between birds or rabbits fed with the transgenics or counterparts': Canadian Food Inspection Agency 1995, 24.

118 Despite ongoing criticism that there is insufficient monitoring and testing to reliably assess the degree of environmental risks: Ervin et al. 2003.

this is an express requirement of the GT Act (GT Regulations r 10(2))[119] and an identified community concern that was 'scientific' (Explanatory Memorandum 2000, 6; see also Okrent and Pidgeon 2000).[120] For example, in assessing the risk of GM canola entering 'undisturbed natural habitats', the Regulator considers '[c]anola having been bred as a cultivated crop *can only* germinate and establish under optimal growing conditions within a well managed agronomic system' (emphasis added) (Bayer 2003, 93). But then the Regulator reviews the results of a 'long-term ecological study conducted at 12 sites in 8 different habitats over a 10-year period', which concluded that '[o]ur results do not mean that other genetic modifications could not increase weediness or invasiveness of crop plants, but they do indicate that arable crops are *unlikely* to survive for long outside cultivation' (emphasis added) (Crawley et al. 2001, 683). Further, the study only examined an undisclosed line of oilseed rape with a kanamycin resistance and kanamycin resistance plus tolerance to glufosinate herbicide modification in English habitats (see also Crawley et al. 1993). It expressly cautioned that other GM traits would require an assessment of their ecological impacts (Crawley et al. 2001, 683).[121] Perhaps significantly, in this study the oilseed rape did not persist beyond the second year (Crawley et al. 2001, 683; see also Crawley et al. 1993, 620). The question of what happened to conventional and GM canola that does persist was, thus, not addressed by the experiment, although the study did note, '[t]he survival of [non-study site] sea beet on open ground elsewhere in Silwood Park, where potted plants had stood in 1992, sounds the cautionary note that perennial plants can persist for extended periods in extremely odd places' (Crawley et al. 2001, 683).

e. Excluding some information as 'confidential commercial information' (Bayer 2003, 8), and not disclosing data and information about the earlier trials of GM canola (Bayer 2003, 18–19). While this may not be significant, failure to disclose the 'confidential commercial information' diminishes transparency and accountability in the Regulator's decision. Moreover, failure to disclose data and information about the earlier trials of GM canola leaves open the possibility that those 'trials' may not have been addressing

119 Notably there is some reference and consideration of a 'long-term ecological study' of weed invasiveness and persistence over 'a 10-year period': Bayer 2003, 93; although this seems a relatively short period when models often consider 100 years: Burgmann 1999, 132.

120 Notably, this was also a significant community concern in assessing the Bayer GMOs: Bayer 2003, 152–6 ('General environmental concerns').

121 In particular traits 'such as drought tolerance or pest resistance that might be expected to enhance performance under field conditions': Crawley et al. 2001, 683; a similar view has been expressed about the particularities of the Australian environment: Lonsdale et al. 2003, 3.

risk issues, but rather agronomic performance and other practical issues (such as seed multiplication).[122]

f. Accepting some of the data supporting the application that was provided by the applicant (Bayer), and some that was unpublished materials (not peer reviewed) (Bayer 2003, 56 and 62).[123] While the applicant and its paid researchers may be well placed to provide data and information about the GM canola, their contributions are open to undermine the GT Act's scheme. This is because 'it may not be in their best interests to draw the possibility of a risk to the attention of prospective consumers and the community generally', and 'consumers might discount the usefulness of industry provided information on that basis' (Explanatory Memorandum 2000, 10).[124]

Making decisions without acknowledging uncertainty This is where the Regulator makes apparently conclusive decisions without acknowledging the uncertainty by:

a. Accepting that the identified risks are 'negligible' or 'very low' (Bayer 2003, 29–36) after considering 'the likelihood of the hazard occurring', 'the likely consequences (impact) of the hazard, were it to be realized', and 'risk management options to mitigate any significant hazards' (Bayer 2003, 27), without acknowledging that the 'science' cannot provide definitive information about how much of an activity poses 'an insignificant risk' (O'Brian 2000, 59–60), or the likely consequences of an adverse event (albeit a very unlikely event) (Shrader-Frechette 1985, 142).[125] For example, studies of hybridization between canola (*B. napus*) and wild turnip (*B. rapa*) in Denmark found between 9 per cent and 93 per cent of seeds produced were hybrids of the two plants (Jorgensen et al. 1998). In contradistinction, a study in England of wild turnips in disturbed ground near canola fields found hybridization in only 0.4 per cent and 1.5 per cent of seeds (Scott and Wilkinson 1998). The risk of canola out-crossing with a wild relative based on these results is not definitive (probably somewhere between 0.4% and 93%). More importantly, the results provide no indication of how much

122 Significantly, the previous Aventis limited or field trial release of GM canola appears to have been directed to these agronomic performance and practical issues: Aventis 2002, 7 providing, '[t]he purpose of this release is to conduct plant breeding (including agronomic assessments) and seed production trials for the development of canola cultivars for the Australian, North American and European cropping systems'.

123 This concerned the toxicity of PAT protein from DeKalb Genetics Corporation (a Monsanto Company-related entity) and the allergenicity of PAT protein data provided by Bayer.

124 Noting also the allegations of undisclosed and overlooked industry provided data often in the form of 'summary data' sets: Schubert and Freese 2004.

125 Although the potential for future consequences exists as a result of, for example, preserved viable seeds in soil layers transferring the risk of gene flow to the future: Gruber et al. 2005.

out-crossing is a risk that is not worth taking. Perhaps most importantly, however, is that horizontal (or lateral) gene transfer into other organisms in the environment is uncontrolled but predictable (and inevitable) (Panoff and Chuiton 2004, 942),[126] but there is no consideration of the likely consequences of such an eventuation.

b. Accepting that certain genetic modifications to the glufosinate ammonium tolerance structural gene (the transit peptide nucleotides in MS1, RF1 and RF2 and the codon substitution in MS8 and RF3) and relic sequences from the *Agrobacterium*-mediated transformation did not require specific consideration or assessment (Bayer 2003, 46–52). Thus, for example, the genetic construction of MS1 and MS 8 might be considered different, even though they both express the *bar* gene, as the BAR proteins are unlikely to be the same in all respects and therefore require a possibly different comparison. By ignoring these minor genetic modifications and not requiring a separate assessment of each transformation event T45, Topas 19/2, RF1, RF2, RF3, MS1 and MS8 (and their crosses) the Regulator failed to make an assessment that each GMO has satisfied the GT Act's requirements. This leaves uncertainty about the risks of those GMOs. Further, in making the assessments about human health and safety, the Regulator took into account the particular components of the genetic modification construction, but in the assessment of the weediness of the different lines and crosses no such detail was required (Bayer 2003, 54–6 and 79–94).

c. Accepting the available data without waiting for the completion of the Aventis field trials that might have been expected to have addressed uncertainties in the available data, and provided further confirmation about the presumptive risks identified in the Aventis application (Aventis 2002, 64–5; Bayer 2003, 143–4). Further, accepting an application where some of the GMOs have never been subjected to limited or field trial release in Australia (notably T45, Topas 19/2, RF1, RF2, and MS1, and some of the crosses) (Bayer 2003, 143–4) accepts that there was no or incomplete Australian data about their character in the Australian environment and that this is of no consequence.[127] In both instances uncertainty remains about the risks posed by the GMOs.

Framing decisions that avoid recognition of who frames them This is where the Regulator frames her decision in a way that avoids her apparent role in deciding whether there are risks that can then be managed by:

126 Panoff and Chuiton describe a failure to take such horizontal transfers into account as 'a denial of scientific knowledge': Panoff and Chuiton 2004, 942.

127 Noting that Bayer has since been granted a licence for a limited field trial release of other MS and RF lines: Bayer 2004.

a. Deciding that the GM canola is 'as safe as conventional canola' (Bayer 2003, 10) applying the substantial equivalence standard. The Regulator's decision might be interpreted as making no legitimate claims about the health and environmental safety of the products (Millstone et al. 1999). Further, the substantial equivalence standard assumes the genetic modification itself is an inconsequential process that is of no concern to either regulators or consumers (Kysar 2004, 554–62).
b. Issuing the licence in uncertain terms to a trademark 'InVigor hybrid canola', and for 'canola' described as 'containing' the transformation event T45, Topas 19/2, RF1, RF2, RF3, MS1 and MS8 (Bayer 2003, 7 and 143).[128] There is no clear statement about what 'InVigor hybrid canola' constitutes (although presumably this will include at least 'canola containing transformation event[s]' MS8 *and* RF3, but it might also include, for example, an MS1 x RF3 hybrid) and whether the licence also extends to 'other' varieties of *B. napus* (such as other cultivars in addition to AC EXCEL and Drakkar) (Bayer 2003, 39) that contain the inserted construct T45, Topas 19/2, RF1, RF2, RF3, MS1 and MS8.[129]

Conclusions About Decision-Making Rigour

The significance of the assessment in this chapter is the finding that the 'science-based' decision-making advocated by the GT Act in practice relies almost exclusively on qualitative assessments. While the inherent uncertainty posed by predicting likely future risks will always remain, the lack of quantitative data that is knowable is an obvious failing in the Regulator's decision. Significantly, such data could be required as part of the application process, as an essential element of licensing field trials (limited releases into the environment), and as part of the ongoing monitoring of general or commercial releases into the environment. Each of these data sources could significantly reduce uncertainty and enhance the legitimacy of the Regulator's decisions. Importantly, this study also shows the complexity involved in assessing GMOs (and GM products) and perhaps points to the increasing difficulty in requiring 'science' to address each of the components of the genetic construction and the possible effects.

128 For example, (1) 'InVigor hybrid canola' being *only* canola hybrids containing the MS8 and the RF3 transformation events; (2) 'InVigor hybrid canola' being hybrids containing either the MS8 transformation event or the RF3 transformation event, or both the MS8 and the RF3 transformation events; and (3) 'InVigor hybrid canola' being hybrid canola *some* of which are the hybrids containing the MS8 and RF3 transformation events.

129 Although this interpretation is likely to be limited in that Bayer has been granted a limited or field trial release licence for other MS and RF lines with a different (confidential) herbicide tolerance gene (Bayer 2004), it appears to be an accepted practice in the Regulator's standard licensing terms: Independent Panel Reviewing the Gene Technology Act 2006, 95.

Conclusions

The *Competition Principles Agreement* is the standard that should be applied to *all* regulatory measures and the GT Act is no different. The role of the *Competition Principles Agreement* is, therefore, essential in the proper assessment of the operation and implementation of the GT Act. According to the *Competition Principles Agreement*'s assessment criteria, the purpose of the GT Act was to address the problems of asymmetric information, with the GT Act establishing an independent institution that might provide the necessary reassurances about community concerns about the health and safety and environmental effects of GMOs (and GM products). It is, therefore, appropriate to assess the operation and implementation of the GT Act according to this framework, and the imperative that the GT Act was *only* justified as a regulatory measure to address the market failure for an institutional assurance about the quality (human health and safety and the environment) of GMOs and GM products.[130]

Our findings challenge the suitability of 'science' alone as a basis for regulatory decision-making to deliver a credible assurance (openness and transparency) about the safety of GMOs (and GM products). The reliance on standards, such as substantial equivalence, and the exercise of decision-making powers without acknowledging the preferences and values inherent in those judgments leaves decisions open to challenge. This is particularly so where the Regulator is in a position to both construct and then assess the risks, and then decide that those risks are objectively acceptable. The situation is perhaps made worst by the potential then for producers and marketers (including the supply chain handlers) of GMOs who are best placed to know and be aware of the potential and scope of the possible risks of GMOs and their consequences, to escape liability in some circumstances.

The solution, in our view, is to acknowledge the subjective judgments and construct the regulatory scheme in a way that adopts these broader considerations and that does not characterize community concerns about the risks of GMOs as a technical, scientific matter within the expertise of experts and free of political and other non-science concerns. This is vital for a legitimating regulatory scheme because of its role in balancing the imposition of a potentially adverse event against individuals and the broader community that they otherwise might have been able to individually reject. While *more* 'science' will enhance the Regulator's decisions, 'science' alone is not enough to avoid a further loss of legitimacy with regard to the current regulation of commercial and general releases of GMOs (and GM products) into the environment.

The effect predicted by our assessment and the theories about asymmetric information will be that purchasers, unable to tell the difference between satisfactory quality and unsatisfactory quality, will drive down the price paying

---

130 Unfortunately, the recent review of the GT Act did not address this perspective and made no empirical assessment of the decision-making rigour: Independent Panel Reviewing the Gene Technology Act 2006, 49–65.

less for satisfactory quality as they are concerned about paying too much for unsatisfactory quality, with the consequence of ever decreasing market price, market quality and market size. Eventually, the size of the market for GMOs (and GM products) will reduce and possibly extinguish as GMOs with increasingly detrimental health and safety and environmental effects (whether valid or not) are placed onto the market.

References

Akerlof, G. (1970) 'The Market for "Lemons": Quality, Uncertainty and the Market Mechanism', *Quarterly Journal of Economics* 84: 3, 488–500.

Australian Registered Trade Mark 741414 (1997) Bayer CropScience GmbH, Frankfurt am Main, 13 August 1997 (Canberra: IP Australia).

Aventis (2002) (Aventis CropScience Pty Ltd 2002), Small and Large Scale Trialing of InVigor Canola (Brassica napus) for the Australian Cropping System and Seed Production: Risk Assessment and Risk Management Plan, DIR 010/2001 (Canberra: OGTR).

Barrett, K. and Abergel, E. (2000) 'Breeding Familiarity: Environmental Risk Assessment for Genetically Engineered Crops in Canada', *Science and Public Policy* 27: 1, 2–12.

Bauer, M. (ed.) (1995) *Resistance to New Technology* (Cambridge: Cambridge University Press).

Bayer (2003) (Bayer CropScience Pty Ltd 2003) *Commercial Release of Genetically Modified (InVigor hybrid) Canola: Risk Assessment and Risk Management Plan*, DIR 021/2002 (Canberra: OGTR).

Bayer (2004) (Bayer CropScience Pty Ltd 2004) Field Trial – Seed Increase and Field Evaluation of Herbicide Tolerant Genetically Modified Canola Incorporating a Hybrid Breeding System: Risk Assessment and Risk Management Plan, DIR 032/2002 (Canberra: OGTR).

Beck, U. (1992) *Risk Society: Towards a New Modernity* (Thousand Oaks: Sage Publications).

Bird, E. (1987) 'The Social Construction of Nature: Theoretical Approaches to the History of Environmental Problems', *Environmental Review* 11: 4, 255–64.

Black, J. (1998) 'Regulation as Facilitation: Negotiating the Genetic Revolution', *Modern Law Review* 61: 5, 621–60.

Botterill, L. and Mazur, N. (2004) *Risk & Risk Perception: A Literature Review*, RIRDC Publication no. 04/043 (Canberra: Rural Industries Research and Development Corporation).

Bratspies, R. (2003) 'Myths of Voluntary Compliance: Lessons from the Starlink Corn Fiasco', *William and Mary Environmental Law and Policy Review* 27: 3, 593–649.

Burgmann, M. (1999) 'Are Australian Standards for Risk Analysis Good Enough? Conserving Snails and Managing Genetically Modified Plants in Fragmented Landscapes', *Australian Biologist* 12: 2, 125–37.

Canadian Food Inspection Agency (1995) *Determination of Environmental Safety of Plant Genetic Systems Inc (PGS) Novel Hybridization System for Canola (*Brassica napus *L),* Decision Document DD95–04 (Ontario: Canadian Food Inspection Agency).

Carman, J. (2004) 'Is GM Food Safe to Eat' in R. Hindmarsh and G. Lawrence (eds) (2004).

Centre for International Economics (1999) *Guidelines for NCP Legislation Reviews* (Sydney: Centre for International Economics).

Commonwealth (2000) *Australian Biotechnology: A National Strategy* (Canberra: Paragon Printers Australasia).

Commonwealth Parliament (1991) *House of Representatives Hansard*, 12 March 1991, 1761 (Prime Minister) (Canberra: House of Representatives).

Commonwealth Parliament (1995) *House of Representatives Hansard*, 30 June 1995, 2793–801 (Assistant Treasurer) (Canberra: House of Representatives).

Commonwealth Parliament (2000a) *House of Representatives Hansard*, 22 June 2000, 18105–106 (Minister for Health and Aged Care) (Canberra: House of Representatives).

Commonwealth Parliament (2000b) *Senate Hansard*, 7 December 2000, 21181–2 (Senator Natasha Stott Despoja) (Canberra: Senate).

Commonwealth Parliament (2000c) *Senate Hansard*, 7 December 2000, 21204 (Parliamentary Secretary to the Minister for Health and Aged Care) (Canberra: Senate).

Conner, A., Glare, T. and Nap, J-P. (2003) 'The Release of Genetically Modified Crops into the Environment', *The Plant Journal* 33: 1, 19–46.

Cotton Seed Distributors Ltd (2001) Risk Assessment and Risk Management Plan: Agronomic Assessment and Seed Increase in Eastern Australia of Transgenic Cotton Expressing cry1Ac and cry2Ab Genes from Bacillus thuringiensis, DIR 005/2001 (Canberra: OGTR).

Council of Australian Governments (1992) *National Strategy for Ecologically Sustainable Development* (Canberra: Australian Government Printing Service).

Council of Australian Governments (1995) *Communiqué – 11 April 1995* (Canberra: Department of the Prime Minister and Cabinet).

Council of Australian Governments (2000) *Communiqué – 3 November 2000* (Canberra: Department of the Prime Minister and Cabinet).

Council of Australian Governments (2004) *Principles and Guidelines for National Standard Setting and Regulatory Action* (Canberra: Department of the Prime Minister and Cabinet).

Council of Australian Governments (2006) *Communiqué – 10 February 2006* (Canberra: Department of the Prime Minister and Cabinet).

Crawley, M., Hails, R., Rees, M., Kohn, D. and Buxton, J. (1993) 'Ecology of Transgenic Oilseed Rape in Natural Habitats', *Nature* 363: 6430, 620–23.

Crawley, M., Brown, S., Hails, R., Kohn, D. and Rees, M. (2001) 'Transgenic Crops in Natural Habitats', *Nature* 409: 6821, 682–3.

Davies, P. (2004) 'Gene Flow and Genetically Engineered Crops' in R. Hindmarsh and G. Lawrence (eds).

Deighton-Smith, R. (2001) 'National Competition Policy: Key Lessons for Policy-making from its Implementation', *Australian Journal of Public Administration* 60: 3, 29–41.

Department of Agriculture, Fisheries and Forestry (2003) *Liability Issues Associated with GM Crops in Australia* (Canberra: Department of Agriculture, Fisheries and Forestry).

Department of Finance and Administration (2004) List of Australian Government Bodies 2002–2003, *Financial Management Reference Material No 1* (Canberra: Department of Finance and Administration).

Donat, K. (2003) 'Engineering Akerlof Lemons: Information Asymmetry, Externalities, and Market Intervention in the Genetically Modified Food Market', *Minnesota Journal of Global Trade* 12: 2, 417–60.

Ervin, D., Welsh, R., Batie, S. and Carpentier, C-L. (2003) 'Towards an Ecological Systems Approach in Public Research for Environmental Regulation of Transgenic Crops', *Agriculture, Ecosystems and Environment* 99: 1, 1–14.

Explanatory Memorandum (2000) *Gene Technology Bill 2000* (Cth) (Canberra: Australian Government Publishing Service).

Feyerabend, P. (1980) 'Democracy, Elitism, and Scientific Method', *Inquiry* 23: 1, 3–18.

Fischer, F. (1990) *Technocracy and the Politics of Expertise* (Thousand Oaks: Sage Publications).

Foucault, M. (1990) *The Will to Knowledge: The History of Sexuality* vol 1 (Robert Hurley trans, first published 1976) (London: Penguin).

Gene Technology (Recognition of Designated Areas) Principle 2003, *Commonwealth Government Special Gazette No. S340* (5 September 2003) (Canberra: Australian Government Publishing Service).

Gigerenzer, G. (2002) *Calculated Risks: How to Know When Numbers Deceive You* (New York: Simon & Schuster).

Giles, J. (2003) 'Biosafety Trials Darken Outlook for Transgenic Crops in Europe', *Nature* 425: 6960, 751.

Gruber, S., Pekrun, C. and Claupein, W. (2005) 'Life Cycle and Potential Gene Flow of Volunteer Oilseed Rape in Different Tillage Systems', *Weed Research* 45: 2, 83–93.

Gura, T. (2001) 'The Battlefields of Britain', *Nature* 412: 6849, 760–63.

Haas, P. (1990) 'Obtaining International Environmental Protection through Epistemic Consensus', *Millennium: Journal of International Studies* 19: 3, 347–63.

Hadfield, G., Howse, R. and Trebilcock, M. (1998) 'Information-Based Principles for Rethinking Consumer Protection Policy', *Journal of Consumer Policy* 21: 2, 131–69.

Hain, M., Cocklin, C. and Gibbs, D. (2002) 'Regulating Biosciences: The Gene Technology Act 2000', *Environmental and Planning Law Journal* 19: 3, 163–79.

Harding, R. (ed.) (1998) *Environmental Decision Making: The Roles of Scientists, Engineers and the Public* (Sydney: The Federation Press).

Harman, E. (1996) 'The National Competition Policy: A Study of the Policy Process and Network', *Australian Journal of Political Science* 31: 2, 205–24.

Hayes, K. (1997) *A Review of Ecological Risk Assessment Methodologies*, Technical Report no. 13 (Hobart: CSIRO Division of Marine Research).

Hayes, K. (2004) *Robust Methodologies for Ecological Risk Assessment: Best Practice and Current Practice in Ecological Risk Assessment for Genetically Modified Organisms* (Hobart: CSIRO Division of Marine Research).

Hindmarsh, R. (2001) 'Constructing Bio-utopia: Laying Foundations Amidst Dissent' in R. Hindmarsh and G. Lawrence (eds).

Hindmarsh, R. and Lawrence, G. (eds) (2001) *Altered Genes II: The Future?* (Carlton North: Scribe Publications).

Hindmarsh, R. and Lawrence, G. (eds) (2004) *Recoding Nature: Critical Perspectives on Genetic Engineering* (Sydney: University of New South Wales Press).

Hoffmann, D. and Sung, L. (2005) 'Future Public Policy and Ethical Issues Facing the Agricultural and Microbial Genomics Sectors of the Biotechnology Industry', *Biotechnology Law Report* 24: 1, 10–28.

House of Representative Standing Committee on Primary Industries and Regional Services (2000) *Work in Progress: Proceed with Caution – Primary Producer Access to Gene Technology* (Canberra: Senate Printing).

Independent Committee of Inquiry into Competition Policy in Australia (1993) *National Competition Policy* (Canberra: Australian Government Publishing Service).

Independent Panel Reviewing the Gene Technology Act (2006) *Statutory Review of the Gene Technology Act 2000 and the Gene Technology Agreement* (Canberra: Department of Health and Ageing).

Interim Office of the Gene Technology Regulator (2001) *Quarterly Report*, March 2001 (Canberra: Interim Office of the Gene Technology Regulator).

James, S. and Burton, M. (2003) 'Consumer Preference for GM food and other Attributes of the Food System', *Australian Journal of Agricultural and Resource Economics* 47: 4, 501–18.

Jasanoff, S. (1990) *The Fifth Branch: Science Advisers as Policy Makers* (Cambridge: Harvard University Press).

Jasanoff, S. (1995) 'Product, Process or Programme: Three Cultures and the Regulation of Biotechnology' in M. Bauer (ed.) (1995) *Resistance to New Technology* (Cambridge: Cambridge University Press).

Jasanoff, S. (1999) 'The Songlines of Risk', *Environmental Values* 8: 2, 135–52.

Jasanoff, S. (2003) 'Technologies of Humility: Citizen Participation in Governing Science', *Minerva* 41: 3, 223–44.

Jorgensen, R., Andersen, B., Landbo, L. and Mikkelsen, T. (1998) 'Spontaneous Hybridisation between Oilseed Rape (*Brassica napus*) and Weedy Relatives', *Acta Horticulturae* 407, 193–200.

Knorr-Cetina, K. (1999) *Epistemic Cultures: How the Sciences Make Knowledge* (Cambridge: Harvard University Press).

Krayer von Krauss, M., Casman, E. and Small, M. (2004) 'Elicitation of Expert Judgements of Uncertainty in the Risk Assessment of Herbicide-Tolerant Oilseed Crops', *Risk Analysis* 24: 6, 1515–27.

Kuhn, T. (1970) *The Structure of Scientific Revolutions* (2nd edition, Chicago: University of Chicago Press).

Kysar, D. (2004) 'Preferences for Processes: The Process/Product Distinction and the Regulation of Consumer Choice', *Harvard Law Review* 118: 2, 525–642.

Latour, B. (1987) *Science in Action* (Cambridge: Harvard University Press).

Lawson, C. (2002) 'Risk Assessment in the Regulation of Gene Technology under the *Gene Technology Act 2000* (Cth) and the *Gene Technology Regulations 2001* (Cth)', *Environmental and Planning Law Journal* 19: 3, 195–216.

Lonsdale, M., Baker, G., Godfree, B., Hirsch, M., Williams, K. and Yeates, D. (2003) *Findings from the UK Farm Scale Evaluation of Genetically Modified Herbicide Tolerant Crops – An Appraisal of their Implications for Australia* (Canberra: Commonwealth Scientific and Industrial Research Organisation).

Lee, M. and Burrell, R. (2002) 'Liability for the Escape of GM Seeds: Pursuing the "Victim"?', *Modern Law Review* 65: 4, 517–37.

Levidow, L. (1995) 'Whose Ethics for Agricultural Biotech?' in V. Shiva and I. Moser (eds) Biopolitis: A Feminist and Ecological Reader on Biotechnology (London: Zed Books).

Ludlow, K. (2004) 'Cultivating Chaos: State Responses to Releases of Genetically Modified Organisms', *Deakin Law Review* 9: 1, 1–39.

McGarity, T. (2002) 'Seeds of Distrust: Federal Regulation of Genetically Modified Foods', *University of Michigan Journal of Law Reform* 35: 3, 403–510.

McGrath, C. (2003) 'A System under Strain: The Regulation of Gene Technology', *National Environmental Law Review* 2, 32–7.

McHughen, A. (2000) *A Consumer's Guide to GM Food: From Green Genes to Red Herrings* (Oxford: Oxford University Press).

Metz, P. and Nap, J-P. (1997) 'A Transgene-Centred Approach to the Biosafey of Transgenic Plants: Overview of Selection and Reporter Genes', *Acta Botanica Neerlandica* 46: 1, 25–50.

Miller, H. (1999) 'Substantial Equivalence: Its Uses and Abuses', *Nature Biotechnology* 17: 11, 1042–3.

Millstone, E., Brunner, E. and Mayer, S. (1999) 'Beyond "Substantial Equivalence"', *Nature* 401: 6753, 525–6.

Monsanto Australia Ltd (2003) *General Release of Roundup Ready canola* (Brassica napus) *in Australia*, DIR 020/2002 (Canberra: OGTR).
Murphy, J., Sexton, D., Barnett, D., Jones, J., Webb, M., Collins, M. and Stainforth, D. (2004) 'Quantification of Modelling Uncertainties in a Large Ensemble of Climate Change Simulations', *Nature* 430: 7001, 768–72.
Nap, J-P., Metz, P., Escaler, M. and Conner, A. (2003) 'The Release of Genetically Modified Crops into the Environment', *The Plant Journal* 33: 1, 1–18.
National Competition Council (1998) *Compendium of National Competition Policy Agreements* (Canberra: National Competition Council).
National Competition Council (2002) *National Competition Council Legislation Review Compendium* (Canberra: AusInfo).
Newell, P. (2002) *Biotechnology and the Politics of Regulation*, IDS Working Paper 146 (Brighton: IDS).
O'Brian, M. (2000) *Making Better Environmental Decisions: An Alternative to Risk Assessment* (Cambridge: MIT Press).
OGTR (2002a) (Office of the Gene Technology Regulator) *Risk Analysis Framework for Licence Applications to the Office of the Gene Technology Regulator* (Canberra: OGTR).
OGTR (2002b) (Office of the Gene Technology Regulator) *The Biology and Ecology of Canola* (*Brassica napus*) (Canberra: OGTR).
OGTR (2003) (Office of the Gene Technology Regulator) *Handbook on the Regulation of Gene Technology in Australia: A User's Guide to the Gene Technology Act 2000 and Related Legislation* (Canberra: OGTR).
OGTR (2005a) (Office of the Gene Technology Regulator) *Risk Analysis Framework* (Canberra: OGTR).
OGTR (2005b) (Office of the Gene Technology Regulator) *OGTR Service Charter* (Canberra: OGTR).
Office of Regulation Review (1998) *A Guide to Regulation* (Canberra: Office of Regulation Review).
Okrent, D. (1980) 'Comment on Societal Risk', *Science* 208: 4442, 372–5.
Okrent, D. and Pidgeon, N. (2000) 'Introduction: Dilemmas in Intergenerational Versus Intragenerational Equity and Risk Policy', *Risk Analysis* 20: 6, 759–62.
Organisation for Economic Co-operation and Development (2004) 'Biological Resource Management in Agriculture Challenges and Risks of Genetically Engineered Organisms: Scientific Challenges for Risk Assessment', *SourceOECD Science & Information Technology* 11, 328–43.
Owen, M. and Zelaya, I. (2005) 'Herbicide-Resistant Crops and Weed Resistance to Herbicides', *Pest Management Science* 61: 3, 301–11.
Panoff, J-M. and Chuiton, C. (2004) 'Horizontal Gene Transfer: A Universal Phenomenon', *Human and Ecological Risk Assessment* 10: 5, 939–43.
Peel, J. (2004) 'Science and Risk Assessment in International Environmental Law: Learning from the WTO SPS Experience', *American Society of International Law Proceedings* 98, 283–7.

Pildes, R. and Sunstein, C. (1995) 'Reinventing the Regulatory State', *University of Chicago Law Review* 62: 1, 1–72.

Polinsky, M. (1980) 'Strict Liability versus Negligence in a Market Setting', *American Economic Review* 70: 2, 363–7.

Productivity Commission (2003) *Regulation and Its Review 2002–03*, Annual Report Series (Canberra: Productivity Commission).

Productivity Commission (2004) *Regulation and Its Review 2003–04*, Annual Report Series (Canberra: Productivity Commission).

Pryme, I. and Lembcke, R. (2003) '*In Vivo* Studies on Possible Health Consequences of Genetically Modified Food and Feed – With Particular Regard to Ingredients Consisting of Genetically Modified Plant Materials', *Nutrition and Health* 17: 1, 1–8.

Report of the Subcommittee on Basic Research (2000) 'Seeds of Opportunity: An Assessment of the Benefits, Safety, and Oversight of Plant Genomics and Agricultural Biotechnology', *Biotechnology Law Report* 19: 4, 449–536.

Rescher, N. (1983) *Risk: A Philosophical Introduction to the Theory of Risk Evaluation and Management* (New York: University Press of America).

Rissler, J. and Mellon, M. (1996) *The Ecological Risks of Engineered Crops* (Cambridge: MIT Press).

Rogers, N. (2002) 'Seeds, Weeds and Greed: An Analysis of the *Gene Technology Act 2000* (Cth), Its Effect on Property Rights, and the Legal and Policy Dimensions of a Constitutional Challenge', *Macquarie Law Journal* 2, 1–30.

Rowland, I. (2002) 'Genetically Modified Foods, Science, Consumers and the Media', *Proceedings of the Nutrition Society* 61: 1, 25–9.

Rutherford, P. (1994) 'The Administration of Life: Ecological Discourse as "Intellectual Machinery of Government"', *Australian Journal of Communication* 21: 3, 40–55.

Schubert, D. and Freese, W. (2004) 'Safety Testing and Regulation of Genetically Engineered Foods', *Biotechnology & Genetic Engineering Reviews* 21, 299–324.

Scoones, I. (2002) Science, Policy and Regulation: Challenges for Agricultural Biotechnology in Developing Countries, IDS Working Paper 147 (Brighton: IDS).

Scott, S. and Wilkinson, M. (1998) 'Transgene Risk is Low', *Nature* 393: 6683, 320.

Shavell, S. (1980) 'Strict Liability versus Negligence', *Journal of Legal Studies* 9: 1, 1–25.

Shiva, V. and Moser, I. (eds) (1995) *Biopolitics: A Feminist and Ecological Reader on Biotechnology* (London: Zed Books).

Shrader-Frechette, K. (1985) *Risk Analysis and Scientific Method: Methodological and Ethical Problems with Evaluating Societal Hazards* (Boston: Kluwer).

Six Articles (2003) *Philosophical Transactions of the Royal Society* B 358: 1439, 1779–913.

Slovic, P. (1999) 'Trust, Emotion, Sex, Politics, and Science: Surveying the Risk Assessment Battlefield', *Risk Analysis* 19: 4, 689–701.

Smithson, M. (1989) *Ignorance and Uncertainty: Emerging Paradigms* (New York: Springer Verlag).

Stewart, P. and McLean, W. (2004) 'Fear and Hope over the Third Generation of Agricultural Biotechnology: Analysis of Public Response in the Federal Register', *AgBioForum* 7: 3, 133–41.

Trantor, M. (2003) 'A Question of Confidence: An Appraisal of the Operation of the Gene Technology Act 2000', *Environmental and Planning Law Journal* 20: 4, 245–60.

United States Nuclear Regulatory Commission (1975) *Reactor Safety Study: An Assessment of Accident Risks in US Commercial Nuclear Power Plants* (Springfield: National Technical Information Center).

Walker, V. (1991) 'The Siren Songs of Science: Towards a Taxonomy of Scientific Uncertainty for Decisionmakers', *Connecticut Law Review* 23: 3, 567–626.

Wilkinson, M. (2004) 'Abandoning 'Responsive' GM Risk Assessment', *Trends in Biotechnology* 22: 9, 438–9.

Worster, D. (1985) *Nature's Economy: A History of Ecological Ideas* (Cambridge: Cambridge University Press).

Wynne, B. and Mayer, S. (1993) 'How Science Fails the Environment', *New Scientist* 5 June 1993: 138, 33.

York, G. (2001) 'Global Foods, Local Tastes and Biotechnology: The New Legal Architecture of International Agricultural Trade', *Columbia Journal of European Law* 7: 2, 423–72.

Chapter 9
The Universal Declaration on Bioethics and Human Rights: Bioethics, a Civilizing Utopia in the Age of Globalization?

Christian Byk

Summary

By adopting the Universal Declaration on Bioethics and Human Rights in October 2005, the General Conference of UNESCO, the United Nations Organization (UNO) in charge of science and culture, showed the ability of this 'big thing', composed of 191 member states, to bring to a conclusion in barely two years the drawing up of a far-reaching text on a sensitive subject both for citizens and for states. Although it is real and has brought increased esteem to an organization that used to be criticized and that the United States, in a sign of the times, decided to join in 2005, this 'tour de force' should not conceal the limited legal scope of the text adopted.

Although its style is clear but far from lyrical, it is mainly the content of the text and the measures that aim to guarantee its effectiveness that fall short. Indeed the text tackles no contentious issues. That is understandable for human cloning which is the subject of a controversial Declaration adopted by the UNO in 2004. It is less so for biomedical research, which is already the subject of international rules drawn up by the medical authorities (World Medical Association, International Council of Medical Organisations) or organ transplants, as the World Health Organisation (WHO) was able to get the states to agree in 1991 to a series of ethical principles which are to be respected.

Let there be no mistake: this 'substantial weakness' is 'conscious' and, in a way, wanted by the original writers of the text. By taking up the challenge that the 32nd General conference had entrusted to them in 2003, the writers understood that the importance of the text would be less in the apparent illusion of proposing ethical and legal solutions at world level than in the fact of integrating life sciences into global thinking which takes into account cultural diversity and economic and social differences.

The second main cause for concern in the text is the weakness of the procedures that aim to ensure a follow-up of the implementation of the principles set out by the Declaration. Unlike the Universal Declaration on the Human Genome and Human Rights which contains an innovative mechanism for follow-up, the present

Declaration, under pressure from the states, depends on an approach which is essentially based on (the states') good will.

This being so, the first disappointment could be turned into a more positive situation if the various bodies to whom the text is addressed, principally the states but also the scientists of UNESCO itself, took advantage of the Declaration's dynamics and took over the area of international cooperation with their actions as the Declaration encourages them to do.

In this way the Universal Declaration on Bioethics and Human Rights, the first text of its kind with a universal vocation, will not remain unenforced but will add its own stone to the construction of a more balanced global world.

Bioethics and the Founding Values of International Order

International texts are often regarded as contributing little on a legal level by the countries which, before the texts were adopted, already had specific legislation about the subject under consideration. At best, if these countries have defended their interests well, the international text reflects and reinforces the legal solution that they had adopted in their own law. At the worst, and this is what they fear the most in the negotiation process, the solution retained will be an unsound compromise between several diverging legal approaches. These states do not think, or only rather condescendingly, of the fact that this future international instrument also aims to serve as a reference, a guide, to the states which have not yet drawn up legislation. This extension of the legal order to the fallow land of the law of emerging states, thanks to the strength of a dynamic model, is already in itself a positive element in international law.

With the Universal Declaration on Bioethics, a 'reversal of perspective' seems to have been added. The substance of the international text is no longer only a factor in the promotion of internal law; it is also an affirmation that life sciences are attached to universally recognized principles, human rights, and that these founding values of international order constitute, notwithstanding the economic or sociocultural dimension of biomedicine and biotechnology, the heart of the ethical and legal standards which should govern them.

Clearly, this dimension is also found in the scope and proclaimed objectives of the Declaration (see heading 'A'). But it is above all a reading of the stated principles which gives a clear idea of the change. The lively debate which has taken place between countries of the North and countries of the South has given rise, not to a compromise but to a balance between the principles relating to individual rights and the principles concerning collective rights (see heading 'C').

'A' Ambitious Scope and Objectives: Contributing to the Aims of the New International Order

The international dimension of bioethical issues is not new. In a perception of bioethics as an extension of medical ethics, it is reflected in the declarations and position taken by professional organizations, such as the World Medical Association or the Council of International Organizations of Biomedical Science (CIOMS), concerned, since the Second World War, with renewing links with the historical heritage of universal medical ethics adapted to the present world. This dimension can also be found in the policies of harmonizing laws and regulations, mainly in Europe, when the states are concerned about the effects of 'biomedical tourism' which can result from too great a disparity of internal law.

But, with the Declaration adopted by UNESCO, another dimension of the 'internationalness' of bioethics comes to the fore. 'Bioethics' ceases to be simply a 'forum' of preoccupations about the risks resulting from the applications of biomedicine and becomes a 'catalyst of political objectives', the promotion of which had previously been done in a variety of international texts (see heading 'D'). In the process, bioethics asserts itself, outside its original field, that is biomedical science, and embraces a global dimension unlimited by time, protecting biodiversity as well as future generations, the biosphere and cultural groups (see heading 'B').

'B' Bioethics, a New Holistic View of Life

The philosophy of the Declaration clearly breaks with the tradition of breaking ethical questions resulting from the boom in 'new' biomedical technology into sections. Of course, this approach is also pragmatic and 'opportunistic'. The fundamental differences that exist over assisted procreation or techniques of genetic engineering made the task entrusted to the director general of UNESCO of drawing up a Universal Declaration of bioethics including these fields particularly perilous. But the 'thematic' approach was not impossible to carry through, at least for certain issues, as biomedical research or organ transplants had already given rise to the adoption of texts with international scope. The writers of the Declaration, therefore, made the careful choice of giving, not from considered technique and practices, but in a more global way, their vision of bioethics.

Respect for Life is the Leitmotiv of this Vision

This is a respect for all forms of life organised around man and by man himself but it is also a dynamic respect for life open to biological and socio-cultural evolution.

1) A leitmotiv: Respect for life

This will to assert respect for life should not be perceived only as a 'reflex' in the face of the risks connected to the use of new biomedical technologies. Resorting to human rights and rebalancing the powers of science for the benefit of patients and citizens is, of course, an important element for 'preserving the dignity of the person and the universal and effective respect for human rights and fundamental freedom' (3rd point of the preamble). But, the vision of respect for life goes further: involving 'the civilized world' even more, it is a question of taking into account 'the growing influence that the rapid progress of science and technology has on the idea we have of life and life itself' (2nd point).

It is not only what we are but the awareness that we have of it and the social and global organization that follows that are at stake. Consequently, it is a matter of urgency – but it is an existential urgency – for 'the international community to set out universal principles on the basis of which mankind will be able to respond to the growing number of dilemmas and controversies to which science and technology give rise for mankind and the environment' (4th point).

The connection thus made between mankind and 'his' environment is a visible sign of the conviction acquired – by the emergence of problems raised by the extensive 'domestication' of 'our' environment – that the planet is a whole and our activities, however useful and necessary they may be, should treat the branch on which we are sitting with care. More precisely, there is the awareness of a chain of possible consequences the effect of which could have a devastating dimension, even if, unlike the nuclear risk, there is not always a visible and traumatic explosion. Therefore, the Declaration states that is it 'aware that human beings are an integral part of the biosphere and that they have an important role to play by protecting each other and by protecting other forms of life, in particular animals' (11th point). This is nothing less than a call to build another Noah's ark.

The final objectives of the Declaration – the ones which, if carried out, would establish the outcome – certainly go in this direction:

- safeguarding and defending the interests of present and future generations; and
- emphasising the importance of biodiversity and its preservation as a common preoccupation of mankind' (Article 2 VII and VIII).

2) A dynamic combining progress and responsibility

Although respect for life in all its forms should guide mankind's actions with regard to the implementation of science and technologies, this permanent reference of the Declaration is in keeping with 'a dynamic process', 'aware of the ability peculiar to human beings to think about their existence and their environment [to] avoid danger and assume their responsibilities' (1st point). It is not, therefore, a purely 'conservative' approach that aims to set human life and the other forms of life in stone but it is a question of emphasizing the necessary quest for a balance between 'the progress of science and technology, based on the freedom of science and research, and the promotion of the well-being of individuals, families, groups or communities and mankind as a whole' (12th point).

In the same way that man and his environment are one, or at least there is continuity between them, the success of this dynamic does not depend solely on technological and scientific factors, even envisaged in a prospective way (10th point) but also on a sociocultural, even political, dimension. The first words of the preamble remind us of 'the ability of human beings to … sense injustice and … to display a moral sense' and it is said, almost as a conclusion, 'that moral sensitivity and ethical thinking should be an integral part of the process of scientific and technological development'. Bioethics should be aiming to reconcile 'hard' sciences and human sciences, and why not to reconstruct them! Therefore, the 'Declaration deals with ethical issues raised by medicine, life sciences and associated technologies applied to human beings, taking into account their social, legal and environmental dimensions' (Article 1b).

This 'global vision' is an essential element in the debate whose objective is 'to encourage a multidisciplinary and pluralist dialogue on questions of bioethics between all the interested parties and within society as a whole'. Even more, it takes part in the search for solutions insofar as it is acknowledged 'that a person's identity has biological, psychological, social, cultural and spiritual dimensions' (16th point) or that 'health does not depend solely on the progress of scientific and technological research, but also on psychosocial and cultural factors' (13th point).

Through this reasoning, the Declaration not only pronounces 'the progress of science and technology as being the source of great benefits for mankind' (12th point) but it also makes a necessary association between it and 'cultural diversity, source of exchanges, innovation and creativity', as 'mankind's common heritage' (15th point).

3) Bioethics, signalling social transformations?

On reading the 10th point of the preamble, it is easier to understand the political vision that the Declaration sets out. For UNESCO it is a question of 'displaying the universal principles founded on common ethical values in order to guide scientific and technological development as well as social transformations … taking into account the responsibility of the present generation towards future generations'. In this perspective, 'bioethical issues, which must have an international dimension, should be dealt with in their entirety …'

4) A civilizing utopia

The reference, made in points 5 to 7, to the international and also regional texts relating to human rights, bioethics and some other more precise themes (biodiversity, health, cultural diversity or the protection of ethnic minorities) shows not only the desire of the Declaration's writers to integrate it into a large legal corpus connected with human rights but, even more, to make bioethics the dynamic link between the diversity of the goals of these texts and other objectives outside the sphere of the international law of human rights as those encapsulated in the texts elaborated by the World Trade Organization. By carving these texts on the same stone, like the French Republic's motto 'liberty, equality, fraternity', bioethics gives them a common direction aiming to allow 'all human beings, without distinction, to benefit from the same high ethical norms in the field of medicine and life science research' (last point of the preamble). Bioethics, by assuming its vocation to organize the world, promises us mankind reconciled with itself, able to find a balance between freedom of science and well-being of individuals, between scientific progress and sociocultural factors, between men and other forms of life.

This 'civilizing utopia' will not fail to provoke criticism. Is it the easy conscience of the states which have all adopted the Declaration (apart from limited reservations expressed about some points)? Or justification of the system of the United Nations and UNESCO in particular, who are, nevertheless, incapable of finding solutions to situations of conflict or deep differences (as in the area of human cloning or birth control)? To preserve some hope, however, isn't it enough to be glad of an approach which, without ignoring the moral turpitude of mankind, replaces it and the institutions which represent it on the path of values?

Although idealistic in its finality, the approach is nonetheless lucid, realistic and pragmatic with regard to the actions that it assumes and encourages.

5) Arousing an awareness of every person's social responsibilities

The idea of thinking of bioethics in a global way is, indeed, the only approach which makes it possible to assess the real scope of such-and-such a technology, to determine the true stakes and to identify prospects early enough for conscious choices to be made. How can we envisage the reality of physician-assisted procreation without asking questions about its role with regard to all the techniques which ensure regulation of births (including, therefore, contraception and voluntary termination of pregnancy) and without wondering about the place of the child and the family in society? Similarly, the cost of health expenses should lead to an assessment of the technical and social efficiency of what biomedical technologies contribute. Finally, the link between the use of certain technologies and our lifestyles (notably in the areas of food and the environment) should not be neglected both to prevent health and environmental risks which are facilitated by the movement of people and animals, and to envisage the human and environmental consequences of changes in our living conditions.

Neither bioethics nor UNESCO's Declaration constitutes, however, a syncretism of all the objectives proposed by the various international measures mentioned in the preamble. It should just try to deal with the issues relevant to its field, 'taking into account their social, legal and environmental dimensions', as Article 1a emphasizes. That is why three general objectives are particularly highlighted: equitable access to advances in medicine, science and technologies, the safeguarding of the interests of present and future generations and the conservation of biodiversity (Article 2 VI to VIII).

However, although it is realistic as regards the force of the words, the text neither dictates nor enumerates the measures to be implemented but aims to make the various actors aware of their social responsibilities. This involves first of all the states, as the text comes from an intergovernmental organization and the states remain on the international level of major actors of the implementation and credibility of the international commitments, even if they are non-binding. The first target then is to 'guide the states in the formulation of their legislation and their policies' (Article 2I). But the text does not forget the role of the diversity of the actors every day: 'individuals, groups, communities, institutions and societies, public or private' whose decisions or practices may be pertinently guided by the Declaration (Articles 1b and 2 II). The declarative form of the text gives everyone the chance to appropriate its political force. This is the encouragement of multidisciplinary and pluralist dialogue advocated by Article 2V. If the Declaration does not impose any form of action, the dialogue to which it invites the actors in the field of bioethics cannot be purely academic. It is the means to couching objectives and above all principles in something concrete.

'C' Political Balance Between Individual Rights and Collective Rights

'The desire for something concrete', which is manifest in the Declaration, is both a sign of pragmatism and a mark of political will. The pragmatism comes from the idea that to reach a certain degree of credibility, a Universal Declaration on Bioethics, which furthermore does not try to govern any technique in particular, should cover every situation, every move in the field of bioethics. Hence the phrase that is highlighted as the common denominator of the principles proclaimed: 'within the field of application of the present Declaration, those to whom it is addressed should, in the decisions that they make or in the practices that they implement, respect the principles hereinafter'.

'The political will' is what results positively from the confrontation, during negotiations between government experts, between developed countries wishing that the text might exclusively 'frame' the human applications of biomedicine and the developing countries wishing that the declaration might not leave outside its scope issues (health, poverty, illiteracy, access to water, control of natural resources, respect for ethnic communities) which are decisive for the well-being and survival of their populations. All of the principles recognized by the Declaration are divided between a reminder of the fundamental principles of bioethics (see heading 'B') and the insertion of a series of principles relating to the promotion of a collective dimension and the desire, for the benefit of the greatest number and the most underprivileged, to rebalance a state of affairs which accentuates the gap between rich countries and poor (see heading 'D').

1) The fundamental principles of bioethics

The Declaration's text is not particularly imaginative in this respect – but could it be? – It universalizes principles, heirs of the history of bioethics, which are recognized in most national or international texts in this field. At the most, for the implementation of these principles, reference is made to certain particular cultural aspects which make it necessary to adapt them to the persons or situations involved. Based on human dignity and human rights, these principles are: beneficence and non-maleficence, autonomy, protection of vulnerable persons and justice. 'This is the bioethical tetralogy'. However, the lack of reference to the non-patrimoniality of the human body and its parts cannot be considered an oversight.

2) Respect for dignity and human rights (Article 3)

What can be the meaning of the fact that dignity which is a value and human rights which are a tangible illustration of it are the subject of one Article entitled 'human dignity and human rights'? No doubt this is the mark of indivisibility that links dignity and human rights, the latter getting their specific character from this quality which is common and essential to all men and which flourishes in human rights.

It could, however, be objected that putting the two notions on the same level does not take into account the 'transcendent' dimension of human dignity whose aura covers, for example, the embryo or stem cells whereas the scope of human rights is more restricted. Moreover, the particular weakness and vague character of 'the obligation fully to respect human dignity and human rights and fundamental freedoms' set out in Article 3 are regrettable. Does not writing something so obvious weaken the scope of the text and its dynamics? The values and rights announced are not a legal restraint and the states are not 'deserving' because they observe them. The values and rights are a reference, a guide for behaviour and policies.

Article 3b, which asserts the supremacy of the individual, should be understood not as an expression of a selfish legal absolutism – it would certainly have been better to speak of the supremacy of the human being, following the example of the Oviedo Convention – but as a reminder of a risk: the risk of another totalitarianism based on the incorrect use of science and technology. Should not this same logic which in the name of dignity encourages a distrust of the state have also led to a distrust of the free play of the market applied to the human body and its parts and to a hope that solidarity between men is not transformed into a new sort of cannibalism? Could not what has been written for the human genome – 'in its natural state it cannot give rise to financial gain' (Article 4 of the Universal Declaration on the Human Genome and Human Rights) – be transposed for the body and its parts?

It is paradoxical that the states which have been most committed to denouncing the looting of their natural resources by the developed countries should not have deemed it useful to solicit the adoption of a principle condemning the lucrative trading of the human body.

3) Beneficence and non-maleficence (Article 4)

Although these are classic principles of the bioethical tetralogy, the assertion that it is good to maximize the benefits and reduce to a minimum the risks is still no easier to implement here, even as a simple objective. Indeed, although in the past these principles could easily guide the doctor in charge of a patient to fix the choice of a treatment, it is not certain that they can be implemented today with the same apparent ease in all circumstances. Research will not always have direct beneficial individual effects. Some individuals or groups will sometimes see their benefit 'nibbled away' to the advantage of other groups. The needs of public health may lay a great burden on individuals, a burden which is justified to preserve collective interests (as in the case of a pandemic). In this way everything becomes a matter of circumstances and the reference to the double principle now functions rather as a form of the principle of precaution in the field of biomedicine.

4) Autonomy and its corollaries (Articles 5, 6 and 9)

A 'key notion' of bioethics and modern medicine, freed from paternalism, 'autonomy' is not only a 'revenge' of the common law of human rights, which makes all individuals equal subjects in law; it is also the expression of the subject's participation in medical and scientific activity as a citizen or consumer. To express that this is part of a precise social and legal framework, the Declaration explains the two sides of autonomy: on the one hand, faculty and power of decision as regards medical or research interventions and practices which apply to our person and, on the other hand, responsibility towards others for the possible consequences of our decisions. It is evident for jurists and ethicists that some people's absolute autonomy necessarily supposes the end of freedom for all and therefore of the equality of subjects of law.

It was perhaps necessary to recall this evidence which is necessary for establishing any social contract, and which prevails in a state of law, insofar as the intervention of medicine has sometimes managed to make the participation of some actors of new biomedical techniques anonymous, or even to 'reify' it. Thus the medicalization of the donation of sperm, which only allows a glimpse of the donors in the form of frozen sperm and so removes the risk of seeing the intrusion of a third party in the family relationship assimilated to a new type of adultery, or the pooling of donated blood for the manufacture of blood derivatives according to industrial processes, have helped to make donors anonymous. By sometimes forbidding even any questioning of their responsibility, the law has consecrated this new sociology. It is not certain that Article 5 of the Declaration will put an end to these waivers of common law.

'Consent' (Article 6) is the natural corollary of the principle of autonomy and the first two paragraphs of this Article which are applicable, for the first, to medical interventions and for the second, to scientific research, comply with the definition of informed consent which is usually retained in international texts. However, the third paragraph is particularly interesting in that it recognizes that in the case of research carried out on a group of persons or a community, it might be pertinent to request, as well as the consent of each of the members concerned in the group, the authorization of the community's legal representatives. The implementation of this text which confirms the legitimacy of some groups or communities to protect common interests, is, however, subordinate to the existence of legal representatives (the group must enjoy a certain social recognition) and supposes that the group presents common characteristics related to the research undertaken. From a legal point of view, this text should be able to justify judicial action carried out in the name of a group or a community.

'Protection of private life' (Article 9) is the second corollary resulting from the principle of autonomy. The text reasserts the general principle of the use of personal information in compliance with the ends to which the obtaining of it was authorized. It admits exceptions, but does not specify the content, referring instead, to establish the limits, to the respect of international law and in particular the international law of human rights. It is in this perspective that the issue of the use of genetic or biological data collected for research purposes should, if necessary, be resolved to set up a register for the fight against terrorism.

5) Protection of vulnerable persons (Articles 5, 7 and 8)

A person's physical or legal condition is of no consequence in relation to the fact that they, like every other person, have rights. It would be particularly paradoxical, perverse even, if human rights did not benefit the people who, because of their vulnerability, find themselves in some way exposed to more frequent or more serious risk of these rights being affected. It is therefore not in the existence of rights but in the exercising of them that their condition may be distinguished from other people's. To compensate for their inability to exercise their autonomy, it is necessary to plan particular measures to protect their rights and interests.

The need to set up a 'law for the legally incompetent' is not in itself a great discovery for the jurist except that in the biomedical field this law, to be effective and fulfil its objective, presents a certain concrete character. More than in other fields, it takes into account the reality of the situations. Protection is not limited only to people who have legally incompetent status. The reasons justifying the existence of that status do not cover all the situations which could need particular protection when faced with biomedical interventions.

But this protection should not be understood as reducing to nothing the person's autonomy. Since the biomedical decisions that have to be made involve their whole physical and psychological self, and even their private and family life, they should participate, all the more so as their discernment develops and grows or they become more lucid. In any case, apart from a refusal of certain interventions, even expressed in simple terms, prior instructions or the designating of a trustworthy person should be taken into account to define their interest to be protected.

This concrete, pragmatic approach also explains why the text of Article 8 calls for protection of individuals but also for groups because of their particular vulnerability. The text, however, says nothing about the possibility or not of recognizing particular rights for groups as such, since this aspect of the implementation of protection depends on the various national or regional legal systems. In this respect it could be argued that the Declaration reinforces a classic approach to the recognition of rights by emphasizing, as Article 7 shows, concrete issues involving persons – and not groups – who are unable to express their consent.

6) Justice (Articles 10 and 11)

This principle has to be understood as the affirmation of a concrete rule involving the way of treating people in the field of biomedicine. What has to be emphasized here is that this rule finds its source in a legal principle, the principle of equality, whose scope is no longer limited to equality of rights. The alliance between two attributes of man, dignity and capacity as a subject of law, confers on equality a fundamental character whence comes the ethical and political need for fair treatment, without discrimination.

(i) equality, justice and equity This is the dynamic, positive aspect of the principle of justice: all human beings should be treated fairly and equitably. This idea, already contained in the convention on biomedicine and human rights (Article 3: equitable access to health care), is an indication to act in such a way that each person benefits from treatment according to their needs, which implies a certain degree of efficiency in its implementation. This requirement, which appears for the first time in a text of universal scope, will undoubtedly constitute a difficult but crucial point in future relations between industrialized countries and developing countries, severely plagued by health problems.

(ii) non-discrimination and non-stigmatization As well as the burden of disease, some people are 'pointed at', even treated unfairly because of their illness. Many AIDS sufferers still experience social ostracism. Fear, ignorance, the existence of ethnic, cultural or political conflicts are often the justification for making someone who is suffering from a terrible new disease bear the weight of an illness that frightens and is not controlled. Scientific knowledge, as in the field of genetics, and biomedical techniques can also be misused to classify and grade individuals or groups according to physical or biological features; finally they can be used as a pretext for policies of 'ethnic cleansing' and genocide. Consequently, 'no

individual or group should be subjected to discrimination or stigmatization for any reason whatsoever'. Biomedicine should not fuel racism either 'political' or ordinary.

This double aspect of the principle of justice which integrates the taking into account of social and cultural diversity, quite clearly reveals the link between the 'classic' principles of bioethics and principles, which appear to be new, with a collective dimension, introduced in the Declaration.

'D' The Emergence of Values and Collective Rights in the Field of Bioethics

The basic principles of bioethics, to which the Declaration gives a universal dimension, have never eluded the collective approach which is necessary for their implementation. There are indeed no principles of bioethics without the existence of a certain effectiveness of biomedicine, which supposes a health system, a drugs industry, the ability to train professionals and, moreover, the ability to ensure lasting funding for these activities.

However, this collective perception until now had only one goal: satisfying needs, recognized as so many individual rights. With the 'new principles' introduced by the Declaration, the collective aspect is no longer a guarantee of the realization of individual rights; it is the manifestation of a reorientation of values and rights which until now were the basis of bioethics. On the one hand, diversity becomes a reference to be taken systematically into account in defining policies, making decisions and exercising practices in the biomedical field. On the other hand, the pursuit of the realization of individual rights should lead to neither an exaggerated individualism, nor to an anthropocentrism which is dangerous for the respect of life, hence the consecration of the principle of solidarity between people present and to come and the consecration of the principle of responsibility with regard to the environment and the biosphere. Thus human rights are open to new perspectives so as not to be confined to the defence of human selfishness.

1) Diversity

To give the Nation its cohesion and bring forth free citizens from the hierarchical social statuses that organized society under the *Ancien régime*, the *Déclaration des droits de l'homme et du citoyen* in 1789 voluntarily disregarded geographical, cultural and social particularism, creating a Republic which was one and indivisible, made up of citizens who are equal in law, whose merit alone should prevail to gain access to public functions and honours.

(i) The encounter between human rights and life sciences does not aim directly to construct a political society. Its object is to protect the individual and also communities and groups from the risks that the misuse of techno-science can make their integrity and identity run. Consequently, the importance of diversity must not

be overlooked: it is not only a biological factor but also a cultural and historic factor of the development of mankind. In this logic, the recognition of diversity is part of the continuity of the principle of equality with regard to biological and genetic diversity: 'All different, all equal.' It is because there is a fundamental equality of all human beings in dignity and in law (Article 10 of the Declaration) that no individual or group should be the object of discrimination or stigmatization (Article 11). And to prevent all discrimination the cultural dimension of identity cannot be ignored (Article 12).

(ii) However, although bioethics, linked with human rights, fulfils a function of protecting the identity both individual and collective of human beings, it also contributes to the debate on choices, values and policies. In this respect, cultural diversity and pluralism are two essential elements for making the bioethical debate an authentic study of the relations between science, ethics and society – hence the importance of its multidisciplinary character – and giving it a certain social legitimacy, in particular with regard to the role played by ethics committees.

Thus, taking into account the importance of cultural diversity and pluralism gives respect for dignity and the rights of others its fullness. It follows, without any contradiction at all, that pluralism and cultural diversity 'should not be put forward to damage human dignity, human rights and fundamental liberty or the principles mentioned in the present Declaration, nor to limit its scope' (Article 12 *in fine*). To remove all risk of autonomy of bioethics, the Declaration explains that bioethics should not be conceived as a 'global' ethic which would have all cultures living together in a general relativism denying the universal and political scope of the human rights message. Bioethics' international triumph does not open the way to post-humanism relegating human rights to the background in favour of a community spirit organized on a world scale.

2) Solidarity and responsibility

The place of the concept of solidarity is not strictly speaking new in international texts about social rights, whose collective and economic dimension is obvious. It was, however, up till now still rather limited in texts concerning bioethics which essentially put forward an individualistic approach to human rights aiming to allow the patient to regain his autonomy *vis-à-vis* the doctor. The European Convention on Biomedicine and Human Rights (1997) nevertheless includes an Article 3 on equitable access to health care. But it is above all in the context of the work done by UNESCO on the relation between human rights and the human genome that the reference to solidarity has been developed. The Universal Declaration on Human Rights and the Human Genome (1997) includes a whole section devoted to 'solidarity and international cooperation' and the International Declaration on the Protection of Genetic Data (2003) plans provision for the circulation of data and knowledge and the sharing of benefits.

The present Declaration only extends the scope of the principle of solidarity to all bioethical activities – which is already in itself a considerable event. It also gives this solidarity which, because it applies to present people and to future generations, to human life and to the environment, has become multifaceted, a single, moral and political justification: social responsibility. This clearly asserts that science and medicine, because of their consequences on life, cannot follow the example of culture and be objects of absolute freedom.

(i) Solidarity with regard to men, and particularly developing countries As a general principle of ethics as well as a rule of proof of good management of social interests, solidarity is asserted unemphatically, even without enthusiasm because the term 'encouragement' used about it can seem feeble given the urgency of humanitarian situations. But the Declaration is lucid and serves a useful purpose by linking solidarity between human beings and international cooperation (Article 13). It refers to the key notion of social responsibility of which it declines the contours with regard to health, extended to social development (Article 14).

It is a reminder that solidarity is a commitment on the part of everybody, a 'fundamental objective' of governments in relation to their people (the countries of the south, just like the countries of the north, should feel concerned) but also of 'all sectors of society' (Article 14a). It is a call for a general mobilization to promote health and social development because 'the right to enjoy the best state of health that he can attain constitutes one of the human being's fundamental rights, without distinction of race, religion, political opinions or economic or social situation' (Article 14b).

And to illustrate the priorities that the progress of science and technology should promote, the Declaration highlights the situations which, with regard to the possibilities offered by this progress, remain the most distressing: access to quality care and essential drugs, access to water, improvement of living conditions and the environment, elimination of marginalization and exclusion, reduction of poverty and illiteracy (Article 14 b i to v). Reading this painful list of woes, some people will no doubt want to paraphrase this admission of a prime minister and say that 'bioethics cannot take on all the misery of the World'. It is, however, significant that it takes its share and reconciles objective and reality. In this regard, the text of the Declaration opens up an interesting avenue. The reminder of the objectives alternates with some suggestions about the acts of solidarity to carry out. Thus, while asserting the principle of sharing benefits resulting from research and its applications for the benefit of society as a whole and the developing countries within the international community, Article 15 indicates the forms that this sharing could take.

It is a case of reinforcing what exists both on the level of infrastructures for health and research, their personnel and the concrete means, notably in drugs, new products and installations designed to provide lasting and appropriate aid to persons and groups who have participated in the research but also indirectly to the whole of the population for whom quality services are still lacking (Article 15 a i to vii).

The message about the balance to keep is not one-sided. It is also addressed to those who are likely to benefit from this provision and to their governments. Article 15b, by emphasizing that 'the benefits should not constitute inappropriate incentives to participate in research', may also be interpreted as a denunciation of the passiveness of some governments in drawing up public health policies over the long term and in opting for solutions which would have access to care for the greatest number depending on participation in international research projects. 'Research revenue' would be as harmful to the health of populations as "oil revenue" is to their development.

(ii) Responsibility to future generations This is not a case of bequeathing a better world to our descendents. The sad memory of the totalitarianism which, during the twentieth century, sacrificed the present generations to the search, with short-lived success, for the happiness of future generations does not make it possible to think in this way. So taking into account the interest of future generations is seen in a less ambitious way: not guaranteeing them a society of well-being but simply protecting them from the harmful effects of life sciences. The text of Article 16, however, remains careful in defining the contents of this protection, being content to give as an example the notion of 'genetic constitution', saying that it should be included in this protection. This is a reference to the Universal Declaration on the Human Genome and Human Rights adopted by UNESCO in 1997, as this text forbids reproductive cloning and practices contrary to human dignity.

Moreover, to define the notion of future generations and of the needs and interests to safeguard, one could usefully refer to the Declaration adopted in the same year by UNESCO about the responsibilities of the present generations to the futures ones. Among the principles engaging the responsibility of the present generations, the following principles are more particularly in relation with life sciences: freedom of choice, maintenance of the perpetuation of mankind and the preservation of life on earth, protection of the environment, human genome and biodiversity, non-discrimination. As can be seen, the notion of protection of future generations is largely linked to the notion of protection of the environment.

(iii) Responsibility with regard to the environment and the biosphere This idea which appeared in 1972 has kept developing since then in the great international texts relating to the protection of the environment and biodiversity. Article 17 of the Declaration summarizes this evolution. It takes up the idea of a balance to be found between all forms of life: this is the reference to the interaction between human beings and other forms of life. It is an implicit reminder that biological and genetic resources are part of mankind's common heritage and that it is consequently necessary to manage access to them appropriately, that is, according to their usefulness and without discrimination. It emphasizes, finally, that faced with the risks of reckless technical and economic exploitation of these resources,

traditional knowledge and human beings as a whole are likely to play an eminent role in the protection of the environment, the biosphere and biodiversity.

For all that, was it necessary to introduce such an Article in a text which is essentially destined to deal with the ethics of biomedical techniques which have appeared since the 1960s? The answer is certainly negative if the text is perceived as encompassing under the term of bioethics only the questions relating to the growing place of life sciences in the organization of our society. It may be positive if we consider that, centred on the questions that involve medicine and human life, this text cannot ignore the overall perspective in which life sciences have their place, and more particularly the law which is devoted to them. In this logic, this Article should be perceived as a necessary reference to a more general preoccupation, to a legal corpus which is different but complementary. It is a bridge made all the more indispensable that the present Declaration has chosen not to govern each of the biomedical techniques but to present itself as a text of dynamic references destined to inspire the actors who are responsible for the implementation or the regulation of these practices.

A Dynamic of Principles Born of the Contradiction of Interests

Is this fusion – confusion, some will think – between a biomedical approach and a social and environmental, even alternative, approach to bioethics so surprising? By 'inventing' the word bioethics, did not Resselaer von Potter intend to make man aware of his responsibilities in the face of the planet's exhausted resources and the environmental imbalances resulting from human industrial activity? Likewise, didn't the important role played by theologians and moralists in the conceptualization and the implementation of the principles of bioethics offer the guarantee that, from the start, the spirit of solidarity and justice would be an element of essential cohesion of the principles of bioethics?

From a sociocultural point of view, what sense can be given to bioethics, apart from the protection of individuals and the human species against the possible misuses of science, if, instead of maintaining man in the making of history and culture, it contributes with technoscience to legitimizing the idea of a human being reduced to their biology or genome? Lastly, from a geopolitical point of view, was it not necessary, when unable to resolve all the unhappiness of the world, to open for the suffering of the most disadvantaged countries a way of political expression which would be acceptable to everyone and to give them a place to build in the order of things in the world to come?

Only UNESCO could by its mandate accomplish this infinitely delicate task. The mysterious alchemy of international negotiations thus bequeaths to the universal community a Declaration which is 'surprising' because of its apparently fragile balance. It will find voice and strength, like the wheel, only as it advances. Hence, the importance of the provisions affecting the implementation of the principles and the promotion of the Declaration.

Chapter 10

Conclusion: Shuffling the Law and Biology iPod

Barbara Ann Hocking and Joseph Henry Vogel

It is often instructive to return to the place where one begins. In the Foreword to this anthology, Justice Michael Kirby eloquently assessed our endeavours as a cornucopia of ideas about the intersections between law and biology. He elaborates the metaphor by drawing an analogy between the poems he had to memorize as a child and the diverse topics of this anthology. Poems he memorized long ago have returned to him, sometimes unexpectedly, and enriched his perception of disparate events. Oh, how things have changed! In modern education, memorization is taboo and yet we would not refuse the Justice's analogy. A simple updating makes it all the more powerful *and* hopeful. Although children today usually cannot recite even one poem in its entirety, they will, nevertheless, burst into song when triggered by seemingly mundane stimuli. The ubiquitous iPod has expanded the poetic repertoire by at least one order of magnitude. Lyrics *voluntarily* learned will revisit tomorrow's adults and enrich their perception of disparate events as memorized poems once did. Precisely because the number of songs on an iPod is so great, the 'shuffle' function prevents the temptation of choosing favourite songs over and over again. Now for the application of the updated analogy: we find ourselves with an expanded set of ethical situations which is at least one order of magnitude greater than the precedents that pre-date modern biotechnologies. We must upload them onto our mental iPod and recall them at propitious moments as new events arise. The best way to do so is to 'shuffle' our metaphorical songs, giving equal time to ethical situations that may seem to be of peripheral interest to each contributor's expertise.

The power of our mental iPod lies in the social sphere. We recall that the core thesis of 'The Tragedy of the Commons' was that '*the morality of an act is a function of the state of the system at the time it is performed*' (italics in original) (Hardin 1968). Due to the human tendency 'to do the wrong thing', Garrett Hardin believed that 'continuing education' was essential in finding the non-technical solution to ethical dilemmas. All of the contributors have offered insights into the ethical implications of the emerging biotechnologies. Whether our individual and collective insights resonate with the public will depend on the metaphorical iPod of the social sphere. Whereas ours may be case law and biology, the public's is usually art and entertainment. So, it is fitting that we take this conclusion beyond the point where the individual chapters end. We believe that verisimilitude in the arts combined with an astute commentary by academics, can initiate a public conversation about problems that have no technical solution. We ask: what can be uploaded on our mental iPods that will facilitate Hardin's 'mutual coercion, mutually agreed upon?' We will end this anthology with some suggestions:

Novels

Were it to be novels, we could shuffle modern thrillers with established classics. Preoccupation with manipulation of our biological nature is core to a genre of literature that begins with Mary Shelley's *Frankenstein* (1818)[1] and extends to popular works, like Margaret Atwood's *Oryx and Crake* (2003). Indeed, over the past two centuries, scores of novels have presaged a brave new world contingent upon discoveries of our biology and technologies to manipulate it: 'Dr Frankenstein's unnamed monster may well be merely a metaphor for humankind's dangerous flirtation with science (given new meaning through recent breakthroughs in genetic engineering)' (Turcotte 2004, 68). For *Oryx and Crake*, the unintended consequences have found expression in an imagined future '... populated by genetically screened, physically perfected humans' which '... feels like a nightmare'(Adams 2004, 28).

The extent to which genes and tissues are providing commercial opportunities for modern scientists, and the public's concerns about 'mad scientists' seeking patents on human genes and tissues provided fertile ground for prolific writer Dorothy Nelkin, whose books included *The DNA Mystique: The Gene as a Cultural Icon* and *Body Bazaar: The Market for Human Tissue in the Biotechnology Age*. With unbridled optimism, Steve Olson states that: 'The story written in our DNA is one of great promise, not peril'. Indeed, the storyline has all the elements of a bestseller: adventure, conflict, triumph, and sex – lots of sex. The story ranges from the jungles to the deserts to the icy plains and across thousands of human generations. It is the story of us, from our humble origins as 'the third chimpanzee' (the title of Jared Diamond's acclaimed book)[2] to a position of mastery over our future genetic evolution (Olson 2003, 7).

1 Freely available at (www.gutenberg.org/etext/84).

2 J. Diamond (1992) *The Third Chimpanzee: The Evolution and Future of the Human Animal* (New York: Harper Collins, Inc).

Theatre

Were it to be theatre, we could shuffle new plays about stem cell research (for example, Judith Johnson's 'Nobody Lives for Ever')[3] with old classics of immortality (for example, adaptations of Bram Stoker's *Dracula*)[4]. The role of the academic in law and biology will be to evaluate the verisimilitude of such plays and engage the public in conversation. Such a task will not be easy for the reasons expressed by Richard Hindmarsh and Geoffrey Lawrence, stalwart critics to biotechnology: '… because of the problems of that script and its [technical] language, many have difficulty hearing, believing, understanding, or agreeing with it; it appears as a theatre of the absurd' (Hindmarsh and Lawrence 2004, 40).

Movies

Were it to be movies, the memory on our mental iPod would quickly fill to capacity. Hollywood loves scripts borne out of new or imagined biotechnologies. Some are formulaic and a favourite genre is the 'mad scientist' who runs amok in the laboratory, oblivious to any ethical consideration as they pursues discovery and invention. From *The Fly* to *The Nutty Professor* we witness a fascination with renegade scientists. Because movies are a medium that command an audience several orders of magnitude greater than those of novels or theatre, it is fitting in that we devote proportionally more attention to the potential afforded by film.

Consider the H.G. Wells classic *The Island of Dr Moreau* published in 1896 at the dawn of the film industry.[5] Despite the commercial success of the book, the first movie adaptation appeared only in 1933 under the title 'Island of Lost Souls'. The film starred Charles Laughton in a 'smoothly demented form as the doctor on a remote island who surgically transforms animals into men' (Nicholls 1984, 199). Until 1958, it was banned in Britain, apparently for its cruelty to animals (Robertson 1989).The revolution in molecular biology since the discovery of DNA in 1953 quickly made the 1933 adaptation technologically outdated. The next adaptation of *The Island of Dr Moreau* was in 1977 and stars Burt Lancaster and Michael York. The script employs genetic manipulation rather than surgery as the method of madness. In other words, the bioethical dimensions raised in the novel to film adaptation shifted from the cruelty of the 'House of Pain', a.k.a. the laboratory, to the moral implications of the products of that laboratory, viz., the transgenic humans. The third adaptation of *The Island of Dr Moreau*, released in 1996, goes

3 Judith Johnson (2008) 'Nobody Lives Forever', 7 May 2008, available at (www.wellcome.ac.uk/News/Media-office/Press-releases/2008/WTD040128.htm) and last visited on 16 June 2008.

4 Hamilton Dean, Dracula (play), first of at least nine adaptations, staged in London in 1924.

5 Freely available through (www.gutenberg.org/etext/159).

from the ethics of genetic manipulation to the ethics of the concentration of power wrought from the success of genetic manipulation. Dr Moreau, played by Marlon Brando, sets out to engineer a superior species of humans and world domination is the explicit objective.

Whichever version of this film one chooses, it is clear that Wells' story holds appeal due to the human fascination with the possibility of directing our evolution as well as the environment we inhabit. The message and warning of 'science out of control' reflects a legitimate concern about the fundamental uncertainties associated with biotechnology.

Sharing this higher taxon of message and warning through entertainment is Steven Spielberg's 1993 film *Jurassic Park*, based on the novel by Michael Crichton (1990). Its story is also sensationalist. A number of dinosaur species are accessed through the DNA of their blood extracted from mosquitoes, fossilized in amber. Scientists reconstitute the remnant DNA and inject it into enucleated embryos which are gestated in surrogate reptiles. The movie exaggerates the real possibility that the preserved DNA of extinct animals may one day enable us to resurrect vanished species and reintroduce them into the environment.[6] The film has been both highly praised and criticized, indicative of the controversy needed to explore the ethical dimensions of problems for which there is no technical solution. For example, a reviewer from *The Roanoke Times* lambasted the film as an 'Attack on biotechnology' which 'revives the Frankenstein image of amoral scientists unleashing forces they cannot control'. However, other reviewers welcomed the notion that we may be pushing the scientific boundaries beyond the limits which are acceptable to human dignity (Turcotte 2004, 68).

As entertaining as science fiction may be, more useful for the public conversation about the ethical dimensions of biotechnology are those movies which are verisimilar to both the existing technology and human behaviour. To date, we believe the best is *Gattaca*, the 1997 film about human genetic engineering. The enigmatic title is the name of an aeronautics company as well as a nucleotide sequence in our DNA. The success of *Gattaca* for the purpose of debate is evidenced by the director's neologism 'genoism', which means illegal genetic discrimination. The story is elegantly simple: the lead character in a 'not too distant future' is tested at birth for a range of characteristics because his parents opted *not* to engineer the composition of his DNA. On the basis of statistical correlations between genotype and phenotype, his future capabilities are perfunctorily revealed to the parents and educational decisions are made accordingly during his formative years. *Gattaca* was so convincing in its portrayal of a future society where families and individuals were destined by their genes and the quest for perfection pivoted round these genes, that genoism gained much currency. However, the boy as a young man overcomes the stigmatization of his genome. Through a black market in hair,

---

6 See, R. DeSalle and D. Lindley (1997) *The Science of Jurassic Park and The Lost World. Or How to Build a Dinosaur* (BasicBooks, New York).

fingernails, skin flakes and spit swabs, he assumes the identity of a contemporary whose bioengineered future has been literally crippled and traded.

One scientist from the Australian academy finds *Gattaca* sufficiently verisimilar to be 'used to teach students a little about genetic testing and genetically modifying organisms'(Gooding 2004, 31). Interpreted through the lens of economics, the movie is a scathing critique of David Ricardo's 'comparative advantage' when (mis)applied to the gene. Not only is equity lacking but, counter-intuitively, so too is efficiency! The movie ends with the protagonist achieving a goal which would have otherwise been precluded by disclosure of his genetic identity.

The iPod is Not Just a Metaphor

Our metaphorical iPod morphs into a real one when uploaded with works of art that explore some of the various issues touched upon in the 'shuffle' of this anthology. We have mentioned just a small fraction of the novels, plays and films that touch upon the ethics explored in the previous nine chapters. The memory on our metaphorical iPod must be infinitely expandable for the reason cited by Hardin, viz., the necessity of continuing education. In other words, we academics and the public alike must flesh out the ethical dimensions of biotechnology that evolve *pari passu* with scientific knowledge about ourselves and our environment. A nexus of law and biology is necessary for the requisite conversation. However, as this conclusion hopes to impart, it is not sufficient for the new ethical challenges that await us. Informed engagement is, and that will continue to unfold for future generations

References

Atwood, M. (2003) *Oryx and Crake* (Toronto: McClelland and Stewart).

Crichton, M. (1990) *Jurassic Park* (New York: Alfred A. Knopf Inc).

Gooding, J. (2004) 'Hollywood's science test', *The Australian Higher Education*, 31 March 2004.

DeSalle, R. and Lindley, D. (1997) *The Science of Jurassic Park and The Lost World. Or How to Build a Dinosaur* (New York: Basic Books).

Diamond, J. (1992) *The Third Chimpanzee: The Evolution and Future of the Human Animal* (New York: Harper Collins Inc).

Hardin, G. (1968) 'The Tragedy of the Commons', *Science*, 162: 1243–8, available at (www.garretthardinsociety.org/articles/art_tragedy_of_the_commons.html).

Hindmarsh, R. and Lawrence, G. (2004) 'Recoding Nature Deciphering the Script' Chapter 1 in R. Hindmarsh and G. Lawrence (eds) *Recoding Nature: Critical Perspectives on Genetic Engineering*, 23–40 (Sydney: UNSW Press).

Johnson, J. (2008) 'Nobody Lives Forever', 7 May 2008, available at www.wellcome.ac.uk/News/Media-office/Press-releases/2008/WTD040128.htm and last visited on 16 June 2008.

Nelkin, D. and Lindee, S. (2004) *The DNA Mystique: The Gene as a Cultural Icon* (University of Michigan Press).

Nicholls, P. (1984) *Fantastic Cinema An Illustrated Survey* (London: Ebury Press).

Olson, S. (2003) *Mapping Human History (Genes, Race and Our Common Origins*. (Boston, NY: First Mariner Books).

Robertson, J.C. (1989) *The Hidden Cinema: British Film Censorship in Action, 1913–1975*, 55–9 (London: Routledge).

Turcotte, G. (2004) *Border Crossings Words and Images* (Blackheath, NSW: Brandl and Schlesinger).

Index